The Colonial Moment

The Colonial Moment

Discoveries and Settlements in

Modern American

Poetry

Jeffrey W. Westover

NORTHERN ILLINOIS UNIVERSITY PRESS / DEKALB

© 2004 by Northern Illinois University Press

Published by the Northern Illinois University Press, DeKalb, Illinois 60115

Manufactured in the United States using acid-free paper

All Rights Reserved

Design by Julia Fauci

Library of Congress Cataloging-in-Publication Data

Westover, Jeffrey W.

The colonial moment : discoveries and settlements in modern American poetry /

Jeffrey W. Westover.

    p.   cm.

Includes bibliographical references and index.

ISBN 0-87580-325-3 (acid-free paper)

1. American poetry—20th century—History and criticism. 2. Colonies in literature.

3. Nationalism and literature—United States—History—20th century. 4. Postcolonialism

in literature. 5. Imperialism in literature. I. Title.

PS310.C62W47 2004

811'.509358—dc22

2003027082

For my parents, Chet and Connie Westover

Contents

Acknowledgments

• I am grateful to Robert Kern, Guy Rotella, Suzanne Matson, two anony-
mous readers, and the editorial staff at Northern Illinois University Press for
their advice concerning the revision of this book. They patiently waded
through earlier drafts that were far too long, and their recommendations
strengthened my study. Any persisting flaws in it are my own responsibility. I
owe a special debt of gratitude to Guy Rotella for his many years of mentor-
ship, and I am thankful to Mary Lincoln for her advocacy as my editor.
Kalpana Seshadri-Crooks gave me one starting point for this study by intro-
ducing me to Benedict Anderson's *Imagined Communities,* while Andrew Von
Hendy, Stephen Tchudi, Tony Trigilio, James Najarian, and Mary Thomas
Crane provided helpful advice about drafting a book proposal and finding a
publisher. Rosemarie Bodenheimer's encouragement spurred me on as I fin-
ished the book.

I would also like to thank George Hart for commenting on a draft of the
epilogue, Colin Robertson and Sabrina Golmassian for proofreading various
chapters, and the English Department at the University of Nevada, Reno, for
the postdoctoral fellowship (2001–2003) that supported my work on this
study. Thanks as well to the English Department at Howard University for
hiring me as an assistant professor and thereby providing the means to com-
plete the revision.

I am particularly pleased to thank Peter and Kevin Westover, April Mounts,
Lori Nofziger, Michael Faletra, Annie Lugthart, Ray Tice, Dan Shank, Deidre
DeRoia, George Graham, Sandy Marxen, Susana Martins, Diana Cruz, Amy
Waltz, Colin Robertson, and Prateeti Ballal for their affection and moral sup-
port during the drafting, revising, and editing of this work. I am grateful as
well to Sabrina Golmassian for her love and confidence in me as I brought
the project to completion. Finally, I cannot adequately thank my parents,
Chet and Connie Westover, for their sympathy, interest, and encouragement
during the writing of this book. I would never have succeeded without their
generous and unstinting faith in me. My dedication of *The Colonial Moment*
to them is a loving acknowledgment of their share in its publication.

A portion of the chapter on Hughes was published in an earlier version in
Callaloo, while part of an earlier draft of the chapter on Frost appeared in
Texas Studies in Literature and Language. I am thankful to the editors of those
journals for permission to reprint that material in altered form here.

The
Colonial Moment

Introduction

DISCOVERIES AND SETTLEMENTS IN

MODERN AMERICAN POETRY

• This study examines the way five modern American poets portray the colonization of the New World and the history of the United States. It considers such representation in terms of traditional American anxiety about cultural legitimacy, an anxiety that Lawrence Buell attributes to "the United States's status as the first modern ex-colony to win independence" ("Post-American" 90). Among those modernists who did not become expatriates, Hart Crane, Robert Frost, Langston Hughes, Marianne Moore, and William Carlos Williams address the colonization of America and the development of U.S. history in a number of important texts. My grouping reflects the fact that all these poets retained their citizenship and remained in the United States instead of permanently moving to Europe. It acknowledges the canonical status of these writers at the same time that it highlights the diversity of American culture by attending to the perspectives of a woman, a gay man, and an African American. I have excluded relevant work by Wallace Stevens and expatriate poets due to space limitations and to the fact that others have begun to offer postcolonial interpretations of it.[1]

The poems I consider constitute American identity as well as disrupt and undermine it. In doing so, they dramatize not only the process of nation-building but also the ideological reproduction of this process in the form of a familiar narrative, a narrative inherited yet substantially different from the one to which such previous writers as Ralph Waldo Emerson and Walt Whitman contributed. The rapid industrialization and urbanization of the nation at the end of the nineteenth century and during the first two or three decades of the twentieth century distinguishes this period from earlier ones in American history. Such changes led writers to rethink models of the United States as exceptional, as "nature's nation," or an illuminating "city upon a hill" from perspectives of turn-of-the-century immigration, a mass market economy, and the increasingly global reach of U.S. commercial and military influence. The modernists' self-consciousness concerning national matters, I argue, reflects the conflict of their time between the colonial history of their country and its growing status as a world power. Taking as my point of departure the fact that, as James Wilson and others have argued, "the United States has always been simultaneously a republic and an empire" (1), I analyze the conflict between republican and imperial dimensions of U.S. culture in important work by my quintet of writers.[2] While the term *empire* entails policies of social control as well as commercial and regional expansion, *republic* refers to a system of democratic government based on elected political representation and the promotion of freedom and equality.[3]

In *Literary Culture and U.S. Imperialism,* John Carlos Rowe suggests that a colonizing impulse continued beyond the birth of the United States. "Well before the United States emerged as a global player," he writes,

> it developed techniques of colonization in the course of breaking the colonial rule of Great Britain and establishing its own national identity. Such colonial practices emphasized the control of different peoples, their labor, and their means of communal identification. Whether encouraged to assimilate to U.S. culture or racially targeted for exclusion, people and their social behaviors, as much as territory and markets, were the focuses of U.S. colonization. (7)

Rowe's analysis provides the basis for a pragmatic definition of imperialism that moves beyond territorial expansion to include a disciplinary control of populations inside and outside the national borders of the United States. It also underscores the connection between U.S. domination abroad and the phenomenon Rowe calls "internal colonization": "Virtually from the moment the original colonies defined themselves as a nation, there was an imperial project to restrict the meaning of the American by demonizing foreigners, in part by identifying them with the 'savagery' ascribed to Native and African Americans" (7). In what follows, I focus on the poetic representation of such policies, but like Rowe and others, I also emphasize the role of commerce and expanding markets in U.S. imperialism during the first half of the twentieth century.

The title of my study reflects the double resonance of the colonial era in the work of these poets, for it is not merely a dead past to which they return but an inaugural moment in the living tradition of their nation. To name the era of American modernism "postcolonial" (in the sense either of "after" or "beyond" colonization) would be to misname it insofar as colonial anxiety and inspiration continue to engage the imagination of writers during the first three decades of the twentieth century and insofar as the United States consolidates its imperial power on a global scale at this time.[4] In addition, such power distinguishes the United States from countries gaining independence in the same century. Amritjit Singh and Peter Schmidt acknowledge this difference by articulating U.S. postcoloniality in relation to its imperialism: "the U.S.," they point out, "may be understood to be the world's first postcolonial *and* neocolonial country" (5). The poetry I consider puts the emphasis more on the colonial heritage and the neocolonial expansions of the United States than on its postcolonial status. Williams, for example, adopted the mythology of discovery and colonization in the essays of *In the American Grain* and articulated a poetics of the national through his emphasis on local landscapes and people. Frost and Moore became famous public figures later in their careers partly by crafting roles as quintessential Americans through their references to the colonial era, while *The Bridge* embodies Crane's celebration and interrogation of American history partly by focusing on national origins. From an allied but distinctive viewpoint, Hughes represented his and other black Americans' relationship to both the United States and Africa. These poets not only inherited but also remade the mythology of discovery and colonization as a cultural paradigm in their era.

The poems I discuss reflect the nationalist concerns of their authors in both overt and oblique ways. They articulate a national "we" in ways that may be broadly codified as ironic, celebratory, heuristic, optative or utopian, and dialectical. In designating these categories I do not intend too rigid a typology because any given work may fit more than one category at a time.[5] The contradictions between republican norms of equality and imperial impositions of hierarchy in the United States condition the discursive field against which these categories may be understood and inflect each poet's articulation of a national "one from many." So does a widespread anxiety about the poet's relationship to place as both topographic site and literary status.

Moore's poems, for example, offer ironic insights into the ambiguous relations between colonists and Indians on the one hand and African slaves on the other, but the poems also celebrate the achievements of American culture as a whole. As a result, the national "we" that emerges in her work could be classified as both ironic and celebratory. Moore foregrounds her association of place with history and national identity in "Virginia Britannia." While anxiety about place is muted in this poem, the contradictions between the colonists and the Native Americans they vanquished play a central role in it. Moore playfully evokes a sense of anxiety about the cultural validity of her nation's artistic accomplishments in "England," "People's Surroundings," and "The Student," but her light-handed treatment obscures this anxiety.

Williams conveys his preoccupation with national concerns more directly, representing the national community in modes that are primarily heuristic but also celebratory and ironic. His vigorous polemics in "The American Background" (included in his *Selected Essays*) and *American Grain* demonstrate not only his enthusiasm for the trope of discovery (which gives his national "we" a heuristic inflection) but also his anxiety about his relationship to his particular time and place (which makes for an ironical "we"). Although Williams based his poetry on a devotion to the local, the excesses of his rhetoric in "The American Background," *American Grain,* and other texts point to his anxiety about the outcome of his effort in *Paterson* to honor the place that came to function as a synecdoche for his nation.

Like his compatriots, Frost represents American history in terms of the conflicts between Native Americans and the descendants of the colonists who supplanted them, while Crane's personal displacements and the motifs of homelessness and wandering that pervade *The Bridge* reveal his anxiety about his relationship to his country. Frost's national "we" is by turns ironic and celebratory, sometimes markedly patriotic but often double-tongued and questioning in its perspectives. The emphasis on performance in his poetics, as in that of Moore and Hughes, also gives his work an open-ended, speculative quality. While the optative mode may be the principal one for Crane's enunciations of a national "we," since an important section in *The Bridge* dreams of a hybrid New American through the ceremonial union of natives and newcomers, his work also expresses the ironic discrepancies between republican ideals and imperial aspirations. *The Bridge* asks whether such figures as the hoboes and the drunken sailor portrayed in "The River" and "Cutty Sark" have as much importance to America as "the Czars / Of golf" satirized in "Quaker Hill" (*Poems* 92–93). Furthermore, Crane's brief stay on his mother's estate on the Isle of Pines in Cuba while he was composing *The Bridge* reflects his effort to win a place for himself in the world and in his writing from a location that was at once beyond the political boundaries of the republic but within the economic sphere of its empire. Finally, Hughes experiences his relationship to his nation as a dialectical conflict of allegiance and longing—allegiance to fellow black Americans and the principles of American democracy, and longing for recognition by his nation and the communities of the African diaspora that rival it. This poetic typology of national discourse can help illuminate important features of the work covered by my study, but I use it provisionally, to introduce the general features of the poets' discourse. It should be regarded as a pragmatic device rather than a definitive classification, since its categories often overlap.

The ambivalence these poets harbor toward their nation reflects not only their temperaments but also the developing status of the country. They began their careers when the United States was beginning its rise as a world power. The international tendencies of modernism can sometimes obscure this fact. As Martin Sklar writes in *The United States as a Developing Country*, "the events of the period 1890s–1916 were directly formative—a birth time—of basic institutions and social relations of twentieth-century U.S. society as it evolved toward mid-century" (38). One of the changes inaugurated during this era was "the assumption by the U.S. government of new roles and alignments in the international economy and world politics, which proved to exert an enduring impact on the nation's subsequent domestic and foreign relations alike" (40). Such developments provide an important context for understanding the national and colonial themes in the work of these poets. Williams's preoccupation with American history in *American Grain* (1925), for example, reflects a general concern about such matters, a concern evident in the promotion of American culture by such writers as Van Wyck Brooks, Randolph Bourne, Waldo Frank, and Lewis Mumford (known as the "Young Americans").[6] In a similar vein, Pound wrote in "Patria Mia" (1913) that "America has a chance for Renaissance" and "I believe in the immanence of an American Renaissance" (*Selected Prose* 102, 128).

In *The Harlem Renaissance in Black and White,* George Hutchinson views the era's emphasis on nationality as both a cultural and an economic phenomenon (7). Drawing on Sklar's study, he explains that the American economy shifted from "proprietary capitalism" to "corporate capitalism" during the turn of the century. The shift had important implications for American culture in the 1920s. "It was because of national economic development," Hutchinson observes, "that the United States had a surplus of educated young people freed of the necessity to engage directly in production of basic goods, and therefore in a position to function as 'intellectuals' outside traditional social institutions" (8). Such events lay behind the advent of the little magazines in which cultural nationalism came to be articulated. Other important changes of the period included the nationalization of markets, politics, and social identities, the development of mass production and mass distribution, the growth of national "feminist, labor, and civil rights movements," "the emergence of the modern university," and the assertion of U.S. political and economic power in the global arena. "During the two to three decades leading up to the 1920s," Hutchinson writes, "the basic social relations and institutions of the United States were being nationalized as never before" (9).

As a result of such developments, the period was, as C. Barry Chabot remarks, "preoccupied by things American—the nation's past, its social life, its culture, and especially its unfulfilled promise" (17). Perhaps the title of Brooks's famous essay "On Creating a Usable Past" (1918) best encapsulates this preoccupation. Charles C. Alexander identifies Frank's *Our America*, Harold Stearns's *Liberalism in America*, and Louis Untermeyer's *The New Era in American Poetry* as heralds of "a potential awakening in America" (87). The manifesto of *The Seven Arts*, a feisty though short-lived magazine (November 1916–October 1917) edited by James Oppenheim and Waldo Frank, reflects a similar concern. Khalil Gibran, Van Wyck Brooks, and Robert Frost served on the advisory board of the magazine, and their work appears in its issues. According to Arthur Wertheim, the manifesto "was probably first written by Frank as part of a prospectus sent to various authors and interested parties" (178). An excerpt gives a good sense of the group's nationalist fervor: "It is our faith and the faith of many, that we are living in the first days of a renascent period, a time which means for America the coming of that national self-consciousness which is the beginning of greatness. In all such epochs the arts cease to be private matters; they become not only the expression of the national life but a means to its enhancement" (Editorial 52). The probably unintentional echo of Pound's "Renaissance" in "Patria Mia" underscores the depth of the period's concern about the status of U.S. culture.

Wertheim notes that, despite their enthusiasm, the writers for *Seven Arts* distinguished their nationalism from "zealous patriotism." He explains:

> they disliked imperialism and opposed the political nationalism of Europe that had led to World War I. They hoped, instead, that chauvinism could be channeled into cultural rather than military manifestations. Nor was their concept of cultural identity a narrow one, since the staff wanted to broaden the scope of American culture by recognizing the contributions of immigrant groups. (179)

According to Warner Berthoff, the "visionary propagandizing" of cultural nationalism coexisted with "a prophetic reexamination of American behavior in relation to its known historical origins" (89). Berthoff's concept of a "national self-audit" during this period helps account for the prominence of national and colonial themes in the work of the poets I cover, and it reflects their often critical attitude toward these themes.

Walter Benn Michaels's discussion of the Immigration Acts of 1921 and 1924 and of the Indian Citizenship Act of 1924 in *Our America: Nativism, Modernism, and Pluralism* provides a controversial context for my project that can be compared to the cultural nationalism of the Young Americans, for his analysis of the "nativist modernism" informing the work of contemporary novelists reflects a concern with American identity that was often chauvinistic. As Michaels points out, the Johnson Act (the Immigration Act of 1924) prevented "aliens" from becoming "citizens by putting a halt to mass immigration," while "the Citizenship Act [paradoxically] guaranteed that Indians would not become citizens by declaring that they were already citizens. . . . Both acts," he continues, "participated in a recasting of American citizenship, changing it from a status that could be achieved through one's actions (immigrating, becoming 'civilized,' getting 'naturalized') to a status that could better be understood as inherited" (32). According to Michaels, writers of the period express resistance to immigration and Indian citizenship by figuring legitimacy as a matter of birth and blood rather than personal action. In his view, "nativism in the period just after World War I involved not only a reassertion of the distinction between American and un-American but a crucial redefinition of the terms in which it might be made" (2). In fact, Michaels views nativism and modernism as structurally allied, more or less inseparable "efforts to work out the meaning of the commitment to identity—linguistic, national, cultural, racial—that . . . is common to both" (3).

As Benjamin Spencer suggests, however, there are other relevant events of the period, ones that complicate Michaels's equation of modernism with nativism. "With the growth of the Southwest, the granting of statehood to Arizona and New Mexico in 1912, and the presence of a large Indian population in the area," Spencer writes, "renewed attention was drawn to the aboriginal culture and history. . . . [T]his heritage . . . had evolved into a rich complex of arts and rituals; and it was to this high cultural level that Americans and artists were generally attracted" (6). Spencer's comments imply that the modernist vogue of "the primitive" manifests itself in the mystique of the American Indian. Like the legislation cited by Michaels, the statehood of Arizona and New Mexico also played a part in the growing vogue of Amerindian culture during the early decades of the twentieth century.

I draw upon Michaels's characterization of American modernism not only to analyze modern poets' figurations of national identity but also to articulate the tensions that resonate both within and around them. In a critique of Michaels's assessment of Faulkner, for example, Charles Altieri calls attention to the differences and possible discrepancies between a writer's political position and his representation of the political interaction and views of the characters he creates on the page: "the gulf between Faulkner and his characters," writes Altieri, "requires us to postulate within modernist culture more than one attitude toward . . . racial matters so that one can foreground the tensions from which these doublings emerge" (109). To lose sight of such tensions ignores the irony and ambiguity so central to modernist aesthetics and oversimplifies history. In order to avoid this pitfall, I focus on moments of conflict in the texts I consider. In contrast to Michaels's approach, my study examines poetic articulations of national identity in light of both the country's origins as a colony and its contemporary imperialism.

Benedict Anderson and Homi Bhabha offer theoretical perspectives that facilitate such an exploration. Anderson's conception of the nation as "an imagined political community" provides a model for analyzing modernist representations of the history and development of the United States. In his essay "DissemiNation," Bhabha modifies Anderson's model in order to emphasize the fact that the development of national narratives is a continuous and contested process. In this regard, Bhabha's delineation of the "pedagogical" and "performative" aspects of nationhood offer relevant categories for my study. In Altieri's clarifying terms, Bhabha's category of the pedagogical corresponds to "identity claims" that are "imposed," whereas the performative corresponds to those that are "negotiated" (Altieri 112). Bhabha's division of the process of imagining the nation into these two primary modes helps illuminate the way modernist poets adapt and challenge inherited accounts of their nation's birth and development. For example, while the subject matter of Frost's "The Gift Outright" exemplifies the pedagogical dimension of the nation by representing its people as heroic pioneers bent on forging a new community, his famous recitation of the poem at John F. Kennedy's presidential inauguration embodies the performative aspect of the nation as a realizable social entity. Since Bhabha characterizes the pedagogical as a "static" set of past events that accumulate over time and the performative as the action of repeating that tradition in order to reproduce it in the present, his model allows not only for the "accurate" reproduction of the same story but for the disruptive, dissenting enunciation of stories ignored by the monolithic formulations of the pedagogical. As this implies, the performative can both reinforce and rebel against the dominant expression of the nation's history. So while "The Gift Outright" articulates a mainstream view of the nation, and Frost's reading of the poem at the inauguration reinforces that view, modernist poetry also dramatizes the antagonisms between groups within the country. Like Frost's "Gift Outright," Hughes's "Theme for English B" makes clear that the pedagogical and performative often overlap: "Theme" presents a scene of instruction, but it also acts out the conflict between the speaker and the teacher in a way that reveals national identity and history to be simultaneously received and contested. The pedagogical and performative are different phases of the same representational process.

In Bhabha's account, the pedagogical inculcates a monolithic doctrine of national formation and citizenship, one in which both nation and citizen become fixed particulars. The performative, on the other hand, both enacts and troubles these terms instead of teaching a single definition of them as some immutable dogma. In the course of its performance, the nation takes on a particular meaning, but one that can change over time as events and populations shift the boundaries of the national comity. As Judith Butler argues, "a structure gains its status as a structure . . . only through its repeated reinstatement" (13). In each generation, for example, citizenship is performed by individuals and groups in various, sometimes contesting, ways.

In the mode of the pedagogical, on the other hand, *settlement* functions like a perfect verb, for its action is completed and its meaning fully established. When the history of a nation accumulates, it gathers an institutional solidity that it did not possess at birth but which is socially constructed and not necessarily accurate (Bhabha 154). From the top-down perspective of the pedagogical, the nation is an established social order into which individuals are organized. The pedagogical view is idealist and conservative, looking back in time toward a point of origin in which the nation exists prior to and apart from the contemporary citizens who grow up in it. In the United States this point can be called the era of settlement, understood as a singular, ahistorical moment at which an old culture met its sudden eclipse in the establishment of the current one. But in the performative mode, settlement operates as an open-ended process. As performed, the nation is understood not as a singular settlement by one set of people but as a series of negotiations between an array of groups.

Bhabha's notion of an internal split in the nation provides a way of interpreting poets' accounts of the conflicts between various populations in the United States, especially between European Americans and Amerindians on the one hand and between European Americans and African Americans on the other. In contrast to Michaels's emphasis on inheritance and achievement or, in Werner Sollors's terms, on descent and consent in the period's conceptualizations of "legitimate" American citizenship, Bhabha's terminology stresses the discursive construction of these categories as well as the political interests that inform them. One dimension of my study, in other words, may be characterized as a mapping of the self-representations of American poets via national discourse. In this respect, it analyzes the different forms of cultural nationalism embodied in their poems. In addition, however, I explore modern poets' use of national discourse as a means of *driving* their poetic projects. For, although Bhabha's binary of pedagogical and performative is instructive, there is a larger sense in which any poem is a performance. As R. P. Blackmur (paraphrasing Kenneth Burke) writes, "the language of poetry may be regarded as symbolic action" (3). In other words, the poems I explore represent the nation as a unifying force or contested political community and treat the nation's origin as a source of creative inspiration. They symbolically act on received ideas as much as they react to them.

While the cultural nationalism of the "Young Americans" provides a broad context for understanding the poems I consider, Frank's rhetoric in *Our America* furnishes a special rationale for my study. In his introduction, he frequently characterizes the cultural crisis of American society as a form of linguistic deficiency. In an expansive metaphor that recalls *The Bridge* as well as *Paterson*, for instance, he writes that "America is a turmoiled giant who cannot speak" (4). Frank diagnoses this condition but offers an incomplete prescription for its cure:

> We know that if America is dumb, the reason is that consciousness within America has not yet reached that pitch where the voice bursts forth and is clear and is understood. The problem is not to force America to speech. Such forced speech must be what most of ours has been: the parroting of foreign phrases, lip service to the maturity of England and of France—or worse, expression of the one formed and conscious entity in American life, the world of commerce. The problem is rather to lift America into self-knowledge that shall be luminous so that she may shine, vibrant so that she may be articulate. (4–5)

Frank's argument is that the problem of America is one of articulate self-disclosure. Such disclosure, or discovery, can only be achieved through language. Frank's word for this may be interpreted as a pun: "articulation" comes to signify both apt expression and a holistic composing of the self. America will find its adequate self-expression only when it has formed itself fully. Hence articulation as communication derives from articulation as a process of self-fashioning.

American modernists take on Frank's challenge of bringing the nation to "self-knowledge" and of rendering it "articulate," though they do so in self-reflexive and often unromantic ways. Their articulation is twofold, for it entails both the careful fitting together of respective parts (*poiesis* as production, or performance) and the enunciation of meaning and identity (*poiesis* in the form of the poet's speaking voice or completed poem). They view their poetic projects (their "making" of America in the representative domain of language) as unsettled and unsettling, open-ended and ongoing, and yet they also see the poem as the fixed object of their desire, the solid embodiment of their achievement. Although they do so in various ways, their poems offer a collective remedy for the problem identified by Frank. Together, these poets respond to Frank's virtual call for a new poetry just as Whitman's poetry "answered" Emerson's in the previous century. As Michael North points out, others were to share Frank's joint concern with "articulation" and American culture. In a 1920 essay for the *Dial*, North reports, "James Oppenheim nominated poetry as 'Our First National Art,' as long as it used 'only our American speech, the resultant of a new environment, mixture of races and new experience'" (129). Although Frank's words may not have exercised the same influence on his contemporaries as Emerson's did on Whitman, the relationship between Frank and his contemporary poets is broadly analogous to the one between those two predecessors.[7]

Williams, for example, explicitly notes his concern with language in the unpaginated preface to *American Grain*. "In these studies," he writes,

> I have sought to re-name the things seen, now lost in a chaos of borrowed titles, many of them inappropriate, under which the true character lies hid. In letters, in journals, reports of happenings I have recognized new contours suggested by old words so that new names were constituted. . . . It has been my wish to draw from every source one thing, the strange phosphorus of life, nameless under an old mis-appellation.

Like Frank, Williams sees the problem of a valid link to the American past and the development of a culture as a problem of articulation: "We are still struggling to express, as we could not do it with the old language, that which must require a new coinage, the economic, social-esthetic liberation of which we still believe America capable, the Nuevo Mundo! of the discoverers" (qtd. in North 150–51). As an American poet, Williams seeks new words for a New World.

This project, of course, is not new—as my allusion to Whitman hints.[8] For many of the modernists, the issues of cultural nationalism came to be embodied in the figure of Whitman. As Ezra Pound wrote, "Whitman established the national *timbre*" (*Selected Prose* 124). Whitman makes explicit his concern to articulate the experience of his fellow citizens, to elaborate the expressive words of America, in "Song of Myself":

> Through me many long dumb voices,
> Voices of the interminable generations of prisoners and slaves,
> Voices of the diseas'd and despairing and of thieves and dwarfs,
>
> Voices of cycles of preparation and accretion,
> And of the threads that connect the stars, and of wombs and of the father-stuff,
> And of the rights of them the others are down upon,
> Of the deform'd, trivial, flat, foolish, despised,
> Fog in the air, beetles rolling balls of dung.
>
> Through me forbidden voices,
> Voices of sexes and lusts, voices veil'd and I remove the veil,
> Voices indecent by me clarified and transfigur'd.
>
> I do not press my fingers across my mouth. (211)[9]

This outpouring of voices provides the most important literary precedent for the work American modernists would take up as their nation entered a new century.

Frank praises Whitman's example in *Our America*, yet his focus on the pioneer's harsh existence is a curious throwback to a pre-Whitmanian America. One can, nevertheless, read Frank's concern with his nation's inarticulate state as an updating of Whitman's project for a new generation. Whitman himself repeatedly called for such updating:

Poets to come! orators, singers, musicians to come!
Not to-day is to justify me and answer what I am for,
But you, a new brood, native, athletic, continental, greater than before known,
Arouse! for you must justify me. (175)

Recognizing that Whitman "broke" what Pound referred to as "the new wood" of the New World, many American modernists conceived of their moment as "a time for carving" it (Pound, *Personae* 90).

Of the modernists who remained in America, Williams most directly seeks to continue the project in Whitman's terms. For Williams as for Whitman, the poetic effort to articulate experience opposes the many forms of censorship and self-censure. Whitman's declaration "I speak the pass-word primeval, I give the sign of democracy" (211) both brings to birth the representative word of America and stands as an example to follow. Whitman's exuberant nationalism, however, expresses a different cultural gestalt, for his celebration of the youthful independence and vigor of his countrymen belongs to an earlier era. As Pound saw it in 1909, Whitman "is his time and his people," but his example represents "a beginning and not a classically finished work" (*Selected Prose* 145). While the modernists inherited Whitman's legacy, they also sought to "make it new" by altering it in the service of their own cultural moment. In his critique of Whitman's literary descendants, for example, Pound argued that "They take no count of the issue that an honest reflex of 1912 will result in something utterly different from the reflex of 1865" (*Selected Prose* 110).

In his effort to convey a sense of "Our America" to a European audience, Frank harks back to pioneer days, as if to suggest that the legacy of this experience lingers in ways that were not wholly influenced by Whitman. In fact Frank ascribes the contemporary failure of American speech to an inappropriate persistence of an earlier era's silence:

> The stern problem of self-preservation brought intensity to their inner inhibitions. And the inviting immensities of the American field suggested outward movement to their activities. The pioneer became a man, innerly locked, outwardly released. He marched three thousand miles, but he kept so close the secrets of his breast that at the end he had forgotten them. (20)

In his contribution to the 1922 anthology *Civilization in the United States,* Van Wyck Brooks agrees with Frank. "That old hostility of the pioneers to the special career," he writes, "still operates to prevent in the American mind the powerful, concentrated pursuit of any non-utilitarian way of life" (193). In Frank's formulation, the pioneer's labor circumvents his poetic capacity: "His legs moved, but not his tongue" (20). This legacy, Frank argues, gave rise to the need for a viable language. While Whitman's example represents an earlier attempt to rectify this problem, such an effort is by nature perennially incomplete. Whitman's direct addresses to future writers testify to his sense of the open-ended nature of poetry in a democratic state. Despite Whitman's enthusiastic portraits of pioneers, Frank focuses on the limitations of pioneer culture and insists on its residual effects. In Williams's work in particular (but also in such poems as Frost's "The Gift Outright," "Immigrants," and "A Cabin in the Clearing"), one finds an artistic transformation of Frank's view of the pioneer.

In some respects, such treatments of America's settler heritage coincide with Bourne's perspective in "Transnational America," an essay he published in the *Atlantic Monthly* in July 1916:

> Just in so far as our American genius has expressed the pioneer spirit, the adven-turous, forward-looking drive of a colonial empire, is it representative of that whole America of the many races and peoples, and not of any partial or tradi-tional enthusiasm. And only as that pioneer note is sounded can we really speak of American culture. (256)

This idealization of pioneer initiative and independence informs many of the poems I explore, but many poems also reflect the problems of "a colonial em-pire" and the conflicts between "the many races and peoples" of America. In fact the settlements undertaken by the European pioneers—with Native Americans, African Americans, and new immigrant Americans at the begin-ning of the twentieth century—equally inform the work of the poets in this study in a way that is far-reaching yet not always as evident.

In the American context, the act of settling entails supplanting; it is at once a venerated event for the descendants of pioneers, functioning as a cul-tural paradigm for those descendants and a reminder of the moral costs of the displacement of another population. As Bhabha writes,

> The nation fills the void left in the uprooting of communities and kin, and turns that loss into the language of metaphor. Metaphor, as the etymology of the word suggests, transfers the meaning of home and belonging, across the "middle pas-sage," or the central European steppes, across those distances, and cultural differ-ences, that span the imagined community of the nation-people. (139–40)

The displacement of peoples resulting from immigration to America constitutes a loss that needs to be redeemed, and the vocabulary of the national offers a way of doing so symbolically, through the medium of language. This metaphor-ical transfiguration of experience issues in the popular rhetoric of settlement.

Settlement is at once the foundation of the republic and the expropriation of others: "The settler makes history and is conscious of making it," writes Frantz Fanon; "his life is an epoch, an Odyssey. He is the absolute beginning. . . . Over against him torpid creatures, wasted by fevers, obsessed by ancestral customs, form an almost inorganic background for the innovating dynamism of colonial mercantilism" (51). In this respect, the mythology of the pioneer reflects the conflict and injustice that exist at the very heart of the nation.

Settlements, in other words, both founded the nation and inform it, for on the one hand cabins, farms, and forts provided the economic and military base of colonists, while on the other a series of political "agreements" and legal resolutions, fueled by prejudice and self-interest, dispossessed whole peoples. By incorporating these two bodies of meaning, settlement comes to function as a synonym for conquest, negotiation, and the process of nation-making. Poems such as Moore's "Virginia Britannia" and "Enough: *Jamestown, 1607–1957,*" and Hughes's "American Heartbreak," which are meditations on the Jamestown settlement, as well as Frost's "The Gift Outright," clearly embody this double meaning.

The theme of settlement looms large in the imagination of Williams as well. In "The American Background," for example (an essay that Frank and others invited Williams to compose for the book *America and Alfred Stieglitz*), Williams squarely positions his discussion of American culture within a postcolonial context (Mariani, *New World* 350). After setting up an opposition between indigenous and European cultural forces and arguing a need for some fusion of the two, Williams explains that the Eastern seaboard states, which were closely allied with European culture, soon gained political ascendancy over territories further inland, which paralyzed the development of an effective native culture. Admitting that the "borrowed lack of attachment" characterizing colonial rule is not "solely an American difficulty," Williams adduces other instances of colonial conflict in order to show that lingering colonial condescension—both on the part of Europeans abroad and their ideological adherents within the nation—harms postcolonial cultures. The effects of such attitudes, Williams insists, may be

> seen in such things as the steady decay of life in the Shetland Islands, while the Faroes, less favorably situated to the north, too far for exploitation by the London markets, have begun a regeneration under a rediscovered genius of the place. A like impetus is behind the bombing by a young and patriotic Breton of the memorial celebrating the absorption of Brittany by a greater France. The attempt of an unrelated culture upon a realistic genius of place is deeply involved in these events, as in the undying movement to free Ireland.
>
> But in America the struggle was brilliant and acute. It was also on a vaster scale.
>
> Many of us, who should know better, are quick to brand Americans with the term "colonial" if in a moment of irritation some Yankee stands up and wants to wipe out, let us say, French painting. In a loud voice he lets go: We can paint as well—or intend shortly to do so—as them damned frogs. We'll show 'em. . . .
>
> In poverty and danger America borrowed, where it could, a culture—or at least the warmth of it ad interim. But this, valuable for the moment and later also as an attribute of fashion and wealth, fixed itself upon the mind until, the realization of the actual, original necessity being largely forgotten, it even went so far that Americans themselves no longer believed in it.
>
> Meanwhile an unrelated Hopi ceremonial—unrelated, that is, except to the sand, the corn, the birds, the beasts, the periodic drought, and the mountain sights and colors—was living in the farther West. (*Essays* 145–46)

Williams's careful contextualization of the invective he offers in the middle of this passage defends its American speaker against the accusations of provincial ignorance it would otherwise deserve. Rather than merely championing Yankee pluck, Williams adumbrates the sociohistorical context necessary for understanding it. This passage shows Williams's awareness of the global dimensions of colonization and his ability to analyze his own nation's situation within a global field. It offers a significant point of reference for my study because it makes explicit what many other passages from Williams's prose and poetry either imply or elide. Here the poet demonstrates the kind of comparative study of postcolonial texts that Buell has advocated among Americanists ("Melville" 233).

Williams's reference to the "unrelated Hopi ceremonial" at the end of this passage from "The American Background" puns on the term "unrelated" so that it means "supposedly not associated" as well as "not connected by kinship." Although the Hopi ceremonial is an example of a culture different from the colonial, Williams figures the monument of Hopi culture as akin to the surging life of the earth. Williams's pun would seem to support Michaels's theory that whites tried to defend their political and economic power against the new immigrants from eastern Europe by inventing Native American pedigrees for themselves. Sometimes Williams appropriates Native American culture as that which is most truly American in the same way that (according to Michaels) a central character in Willa Cather's novel *The Professor's House,* Tom Outland, does. In Cather's writing (as well as Calvin Coolidge's), Michaels argues,

> identity is a function of inheritance, but what gets inherited is not just a biology, it's a culture. . . . It is what will prove to be this extraordinarily fruitful equivocation about inheritance that makes the American Indian—conceived at the same time as biologically unrelated to and as an ancestor . . . —play so crucial a role in the developing idea of cultural identity. (37–38)

Yet Williams's repetition of "unrelated" signals his midsentence revision of the word, for while the Hopi ceremonial has nothing in common with European-derived culture, it is integrally related to the earth. This relation is an expression of the centrality of the local in Williams's epistemology and poetics and of his use of an Indian heritage to figure his neo-Romantic devotion to his nation and its meaning. In his reading of Hopi culture, then, Williams finds inspiration and support for his own commitment to the material reality of a specific place.

As a great deal of Williams's writing demonstrates, in fact, modernist writers continued to be inspired by the nineteenth-century dream of achieving literary independence from European traditions. "For more than fifty years," writes Spencer, Williams "maintained that American writers have neither understood their New World heritage nor created the distinctive idiom that would at once clarify and express it" (108). Williams's analysis in "The American Background" supports Spencer's claims, for it testifies to the poet's concern with the cultural independence of his country:

> It isn't just to say that the acquisition of borrowed European culture was in itself a bad thing. It was, moreover, inevitable that it should be brought here. As inevitable as the buying of legislatures many years later in order that railroads might with the least possible delay be laid across the country. It is only unfortunate that this sort of thing should be taken to be virtue itself, a makeshift, really, in constant opposition to the work of those good minds which had the hardihood to do without it. The appurtenances of Europe came in with their language and habits, more finished than anything native could have been—that is, barring Indian workmanship and manner, which were of slight value in the East. (*Essays* 144)

In this passage Williams argues that the nation's artists need to conceive of their culture as something entirely new and yet viable. As Michael Bernstein puts it, "Williams was convinced that the *same* poetics could never be adequate to both Europe and the United States" (198). In keeping with his commitment to the local, Williams meditates upon the ingenuity of his predecessors and on the need for an aesthetic appropriate to a truly new world. Buell's argument that the intended audience for some nineteenth-century American texts was not solely American may be extended to modernist poets, for Williams may be directing his remarks in this passage not only to Americans at home but to expatriate American writers like his former fellow schoolmate Pound and to European modernists ("Postcolonial Anxiety" 205–8).[10] Moreover, in *American Grain*, Williams explicitly addresses Frenchmen in "The Founding of Quebec" ("you" [69] and "you French" [74])—and in "Père Sebastian Rasles" (107–29). In "Père Sebastian Rasles," there is even a specific addressee, for in this chapter Williams "records" his conversation with the scholar Valéry Larbaud regarding the Puritans, the French Catholics, and their respective interactions with the Indians and the land.[11]

Williams is not alone in addressing himself to a non-American audience. Frank does the same in *Our America*, as the book's introductory remarks to Jacques Copeau and Gaston Gallimard make clear:

> Seeing these impressions upon your mind, I had a view of the sheer surface of my country. I understood how false it was, its simplicity and arrogance, and how deliberate was this falseness, that falseness should cover it and hide it from itself. The whole vast problem of reaching to the hidden vitals, and of bringing these up—their energy and truth—into the play of articulate life, came to me. And I saw that America was a conception to be created. (3–4)

It is from the American's experience of witnessing two Europeans' "impressions" of his nation that the American comes to some understanding of it. In other words, self-consciousness for the member of the formerly colonized country is arbitrated by the responses of the European: "So it is, my friends, that writing this book for France, I write it for America—writing it for you, I write it for myself" (5). In some sense, the American is performing for the European as much as for himself and his American readers. Frank admits as much when he writes of his friendship with Copeau and Gallimard: "As Frenchmen, they helped me see America" (xi). The upshot of this performance is a new engagement with the substance of his national heritage and identity. According to the rhetoric of the passage, "the articulate life" so desired by the writer remains an impossible ideal, apart from the foreign impetus to think and create provided by his European friends. In addressing his introduction to the two Frenchmen, Frank makes explicit what the nineteenth-century writers left implicit in their declarations of literary independence: the anxiety of European influence.

Like Frank and Williams, Bourne addresses the status of American culture, arguing that "With the exception of the South and that New England which, like the Red Indian, seems to be passing into solemn oblivion, there is no distinctively American culture. It is apparently our lot rather to be a federation of cultures" (256). His outlook is more optimistic than this remark suggests, however, for he sees his nation as surging with possibilities:

> Strangely enough, American genius has flared forth just in those directions which are least understood [*sic*] of the people. If the American note is bigness, action, the objective as contrasted with the reflective life, where is the epic expression of this spirit? Our drama, our fiction, the peculiar field for the expression of action and objectivity, are somehow exactly the fields of the spirit which remain poor and mediocre. . . . We are *inarticulate* of the very values which we profess to idealize. But in the finer forms—music, verse, the essay, philosophy—the American genius puts forth work equal to any of its contemporaries. (256; emphasis added)

Significantly, "verse" appears on Bourne's list of the "finer forms" of art at which Americans succeed. Despite this success, however, he believes Americans remain "inarticulate" in terms of the "values" that are presumed to be most American. In this passage at least, Bourne does not seem to think poetry can articulate the action, objectivity, and grand gestures he attributes to American business and popular life. But since language is the provenance of poets, one might reasonably look to them for the articulation of the most characteristic qualities of a people's heritage and experience.

In their effort to face the implications of the colonial origin of their country, modernist poets sought to articulate a coherent national "we," and they did so in ways that exemplify Bhabha's categories of the pedagogical and the performative. In Frost's "The Gift Outright" and an important scene from Crane's *The Bridge,* for instance, we perceive the pedagogical dimensions of nation-building and nationalism, but in such poems as Williams's "Pastoral" ("When I was younger") and Hughes's "I, Too," "we are confronted with the nation split within itself, articulating the heterogeneity of its population" (Bhabha 148). Bhabha's account of this process echoes the articulation described by Frank in *Our America*. Bhabha emphasizes the heterogeneity of national populations, whereas Frank argues the need for an integrating influence in national life that is at once social and psychological. In "Virginia Britannia," Moore reminds her readers not simply of the diversity of the American population but of the conflict between peoples from which the nation emerged. Her poem shows how the nation's constitution is split from the very moment of its foundation; it thereby gives some voice to the tense articulations existing between groups within the nation. Hughes reflects a similar rift in his poetic meditations on the relationship between his sense of himself as a marginalized American and his African heritage. And in "The Vanishing Red," a poem that provides a compelling counter to the triumphal patriotism of "The Gift Outright," Frost offers a sly parable about the relations between European Americans and the indigenous Americans they sought to replace.

By figuring their exploration and celebration of the origins of the United States as an elaboration of their own poetic projects, modern American poets reflect the antagonism of their time between the tradition of their nation as a former colony and its status as an incipient world power. Although the origins of U.S. imperialism are sometimes traced to such military adventures as the Mexican-American and Spanish-American wars in the nineteenth century or in the pattern of westward expansion that characterized the nation's early history, some historians have argued that imperial enterprise informed the United States from its very beginnings as a colony. In *The Contours of American History*, for example, William Appleman Williams argues that the commercial and political system of mercantilism brought into existence both the English colonies and the nation that united them. In framing his theories of individual freedom and right, John Locke assumed the domestic wealth and political stability brought about by empire. Since the founding fathers based their vision of a new nation on assumptions shared with Locke, the United States was from its birth what Williams calls a "republican empire":

> Both theoretically and practically, Locke's individualism was dependent upon expansion and empire. And only by setting aside the entire question of the relationship between the mother country and the colonies could he define freedom for citizens of the Metropolis as the crucial issue. As a result the tension between the individual and the state centered upon the access to and division of the rewards of empire. Fundamental questions concerning the nature and allocation of responsibility in society were discounted by Locke because he assumed the existence of a stable and profitable empire. (62)

Fanon advances a claim that teases out one of the consequences of Locke's perspective and makes a connection between the institution of property (where *property* signifies both real estate and characteristic quality) and the process of colonial settlement. "The settler," Fanon argues, "owes the fact of his very existence, that is to say, his property, to the colonial system" (36).

Since Locke's theory, which became the prevailing American ideology, is ultimately founded upon the robust economy of an imperialist society, the colonial origin of the nation prefigured the imperial career that followed. As Richard Van Alstyne puts it (adopting a phrase from George Washington), the United States was a "rising empire" from its birth (1).

If we articulate this insight with the cultural nationalism of the modernist period and its poetic representations of the nation's colonial origins, then the contradictory cultural relations of the period come more clearly into view. As North points out, for example, writers of the Harlem Renaissance shared the desire to contribute to a national art with their white counterparts, but white writers failed to form a sympathetic alliance with them. "Instead of growing . . . into a truly multicultural modernism," North writes, "the Americanist avant-garde demonstrated instead a persistent inability to understand how race fit into its conception of modern America, or how the language of African America fit into its conception of 'plain American'" (128). The various representations of the colonized "other" in the form of the Amerindian as well as the African American both underscore and challenge traditional views of American history, bequeathing a heritage of conflict to their successors. In other words, the poetic quest of American modernists for an independent and clarifying "word" on behalf of their nation reflects both the effort to create a new union between artists of various racial and ethnic backgrounds (functioning as one example of Bourne's "beloved community") and the imperialism that flourished in the period of dollar diplomacy and police actions in the Western Hemisphere—in Cuba, the Dominican Republic, Haiti, Nicaragua, and Panama, for instance.

By reviewing the deployment of the "myth" of the voyage to and the settlement of America in a range of different contexts, I show how this myth both organizes the culture's experience of itself and often disfigures the representation of minority experience. At the same time I intend my study to show, along with North's *The Dialect of Modernism* and Hutchinson's *The Harlem Renaissance in Black and White,* that in their shared commitment to national culture, black and white writers alike undertook poetic quests for words that would give authentic voice to the varied experience of their nation. Although white writers failed to appreciate their efforts and dilemmas, black poets also considered the role of the nation in their verse. The widespread representation of colonization—of the nation's founding moment—reflects a general concern of modern American poets. In accordance with the imagist project of charging words with the realities they signify, the poets whose work I consider express their efforts to make the nation more articulate and aware of its dimly comprehended life.

Chapter *I*

MARIANNE MOORE'S GEOGRAPHY OF ORIGINS

• Like Randolph Bourne, Marianne Moore seasoned her pride in her country with moral protest against racism. As David Kadlec shows, for example, in "England" she challenges "the essentialism that underlies nativist visions of a distinctive American race" (28). Kadlec's study of the relationships between contemporary developments in genetics and Moore's aesthetics admirably complicates Walter Benn Michaels's account of nativist modernism in *Our America*, for it articulates her rejection of xenophobia and racism. In "England" and even more dramatically in "Virginia Britannia," Moore presents a picture of America that calls into question epic statements of the nation's history in the form of totalizing "master narratives." Reconstituting her country in the form of a linguistic collage, her fragmented portrayal of colonial history in "Virginia Britannia" disrupts the process whereby national narratives become "natural" and standard. In "England," Moore achieves a similar effect through studious negation ("no proof-readers, no silkworms, no digressions"; "grassless, linkless, languageless country"; "no conclusions may be drawn") to describe American culture, even as she defends its value in the imposing context of older ones. The modesty of her claims in "England" reflects her strategic acumen, for the limitations she imposes on her account of the nation permit a precision and accuracy that are lacking in grander but less carefully expressed claims: "To have misapprehended the matter," she reasons, "is to have confessed that one has not looked far enough" (*Complete Poems* 46–47).[1] Moore's method in "England" and "Virginia Britannia" is characteristic, for throughout her work she refuses to read national history in monolithic terms, presenting it instead as a composite of competing narratives that reveal the conflict between America's competing traditions of republican democracy and imperial subordination. Her interpretation of national origins perhaps finds its greatest expression in "Virginia Britannia," but before I turn to a consideration of this poem, I briefly discuss Moore's response to the nativism that Michaels regards as central to modernism.

• As Kadlec points out, "In poems like 1921's 'The Labors of Hercules,' . . . Moore spoke out directly against such patrician proponents of Nordic supremacy as [Prescott] Hall, [Robert] Ward, and Madison Grant, likening the barrenness of elite restrictionists to the emptiness of the truisms that they exploited" (38). Kadlec explains that Hall and Ward were "leaders of the elite and influential Boston-based Immigration Restriction League" and Grant a "New York society lawyer" who in 1916 published *The Passing of the Great Race*, a text to which Michaels refers in *Our America* (38). In their readings of Moore's poem, both Kadlec and Elizabeth Phillips focus on the image of the mule as a symbol of hybridity. Moore's goal is

> To popularize the mule, its neat exterior
> expressing the principle of accommodation reduced to a minimum:
> ....
> to prove to the high priests of caste
> that snobbishness is a stupidity,
> the best side out, of age-old toadyism
> kissing the feet of the man above,
> kicking the face of the man below;
> to teach the patron-saints-to-atheists
> that we are sick of the earth,
> sick of the pig-sty, wild geese and wild men;
> to convince snake-charming controversialists
> that one keeps on knowing
> "that the Negro is not brutal,
> that the Jew is not greedy,
> that the Oriental is not immoral,
> that the German is not a Hun." (53)

Moore's odd locution "one keeps on knowing" reinforces the stubborn resistance evoked by the figure of the mule, for the ongoing "knowing" reflects the speaker's prophetic insistence on the truth in the face of popular prejudice and represents the acts of knowing and writing as continuous processes: as she writes in "The Student," "Science / is never finished" (101). Moore defends the values of freethinking and uncensored speech, reminding her readers that racist attitudes blind those who possess them.

Kadlec and Phillips point out that, as a cross between a horse and a donkey, the mule is a perfect image for the miscegenation that troubled nativists so deeply. As Phillips explains:

> The impassioned poem is pertinent to a decade characterized by political corruption, lawlessness, and bigotry. The disintegration of Woodrow Wilson's presidency, the "return to normalcy," and the disillusionment with the vision of "a world safe for democracy" after the "war against the Huns" fed the distrust of the alien and foreign. "Pure" America was in danger of becoming as hybrid as the mule, so Congress, in 1921, adopted policies of rigid restriction on immigration. Hatred of nonconformism and liberalism took new and ominous forms, including the sinister

revival of the Ku Klux Klan. Blacks, Jews, Chinese, Catholics, and recent immi-
grants were alike victims of the Klan as its membership spread throughout the
country. Marianne Moore's was one unaccommodating protest against the resur-
gence of nativist know-nothingism. (160–61)

In line with Phillips's suggestion, Moore's phrase "one keeps on knowing" de-
nounces the "know-nothing" rhetoric of nineteenth-century nativism, particu-
larly when considered against the universal higher education espoused by "The
Student." The "know-nothing" policy of denying bias in order to maintain privi-
lege violates the science and democracy that "The Student" persuasively defends.[2]
   "The Labors of Hercules" counters nativism by attacking the main premise
behind it, that some people are naturally inferior. Moore implicitly opposes
this claim by promoting her first Herculean task of popularizing the mule. In
advocating this approach, she defends not only the stalwart individualism
but also the emerging hybridity of American culture in the 1910s and 1920s.
The "wild men" whom Moore castigates in "Hercules" are not savage others
but already established citizens—"high priests of caste" (53). As Moore wrote
in a *Dial* editorial in 1926, "We are often reminded that the civilized world is
uncivilized" (*Prose* 167). In "Hercules," and to some extent in "Virginia Bri-
tannia" as well, the aggressive defenders of the republic become the savages
they accuse their enemies of being. By showing that they become the very
threat they fear, Moore metamorphoses the concept of the savage, revealing
it to be an unjustified projection of white Anglo-Saxon anxiety.
   By resisting nativism in this way, Moore fashions a kind of cultural nation-
alism that allows for the critique of her country's colonial origins. "Virginia
Britannia" celebrates and criticizes the nation on an even larger scale than
"Hercules," while her later poem "Enough: *Jamestown, 1607–1957*" revisits
the subject matter and perspective of "Virginia." Both poems directly address
the colonial and latter-day "settlements" with Indians and others that preoc-
cupied her era. In addition, "Virginia" figures the poet as explorer in a way
that parallels Williams's *In the American Grain*, Stevens's "The Comedian as
the Letter C," and Crane's *The Bridge*, all of which figure poetic imagination
as a colonial quest. Finally, later in her career Moore performs, or "signifies
on," American citizenship through her playful "masquerade" as George
Washington by making her tricorn hat and cape her public symbol, and this
performance complements similar ones in her poems. "Moore's customary
wearing of the hat associated" her, writes David Ross Anderson, "with the
political ideology that the tricorn symbolizes—a republican tradition em-
bodying beliefs in civic virtue, vigilance against tyranny, pluralism, and self-
restraint" (31). As she wrote in a 1965 article for *Women's Wear Daily*, "Dress
is an adjunct and should conform with behavior" (*Prose* 597).

• In her meditation upon the colonial ruins she describes in "Virginia Britan-
nia," Moore reflects upon the origins of the United States and on the conflicts
involved in them. As Cristanne Miller remarks, the poem represents Moore's

"fullest response to U.S. history" ("Black Maternal Hero" 802). Eulalia Piñero Gil adds that, as "a historian of her time," Moore "constructed a fragmentary heteroglossia of voices hardly portrayed by books of history more concerned with the discussion of great events" (52). Over the course of the poem, Moore patiently works out a vision of her nation by observing it within the rich context of nature. I view Moore's poem as "performing" (to use Bhabha's term) and questioning the meanings of her nation rather than representing its birth in triumphal form. In "Virginia Britannia," Moore grapples with her nation's history by interpreting a founding place and the historical documents describing it. As Charles Berger argues, Moore "uses 'Virginia Britannia' as a way of thinking about how American identity might be defined in collective, national terms without degenerating into rabid and hateful nationalism" (283).

In his discussion of "The Old Dominion," a suite of poems in which "Virginia Britannia" first appeared, John Slatin shows how the poem corresponds to the cultural nationalism of the Young Americans and to Williams's consciousness of himself as an American artist:

> In the poems of "The Old Dominion" we see Moore writing as one who is, like James, fully conscious of belonging in ways that have little to do with formal declarations of citizenship. Like James, she is conscious of embodying within herself and in her work the peculiar relationship which has obtained between America and its inhabitants since the first Europeans set foot on the continent. She writes as one who knowingly and openly participates in a tradition and a history, and she consciously takes her identity from that participation. (209)

Charles Molesworth similarly recognizes a connection between cultural nationalism and Moore (his quotation, by the way, is drawn from an earlier version of Moore's poem, which several commentators favor over the final one): "In part, Moore is answering the writers of the 1920's, such as Waldo Frank, who felt America could create a cultural renaissance simply by an act of will. The despair of history is offset by the glory of nature, but nature's glory is conditioned by history's 'lack of intellect and delicacy'" (288). Both Slatin and Molesworth demonstrate that Moore's poem provides the articulation called for by Frank, for it gives voice to the cultures and conflicts of American experience. Nevertheless, Moore's ironic characterizations of John Smith, of the "crowning" of Powhatan, and of human endeavor in general, seem to be more critical of history and less awed by representative men than some critics have suggested.

Although the following claim by Slatin would on the face of it appear to be true, for example, it perhaps applies better to the first published version of the poem, which he is writing about, than to the version Moore preferred: "The landscape of Colonial Virginia is not a natural one: it is a human artifact, a carefully constructed . . . and preserved historical record" (211). Slatin's claim is only partially persuasive because it ignores Moore's repeated observations of cases in which nature has *overwhelmed* the original settlement by ero-sion, natural growth, or burial. Although the site has been preserved, this preservation is by no means definitive or complete, as recent excavations of the site demonstrate (Association for the Preservation of Virginia Antiqui-ties). "Virginia Britannia" is also interested in the ways the settlement (like Stevens's "jar in Tennessee") "imposes" on its landscape.[3] Moore's later poem about Jamestown, "Enough," suggests a similar view. In line with her beliefs about the fallenness of humanity, Moore represents "the Old Domin-ion" as a weak and impermanent settlement on the changing surface of the earth. This reading becomes more compelling in light of the poet's sympa-thetic but ironic references to Amerindian culture and colonization. For Moore, the artificial landscape of the Jamestown ruins is embedded in a "transhuman" and ungovernable nature. In "Virginia Britannia," nature threatens as well as nurtures.

Although the poem evokes a complex national landscape, it does not con-form to the oversimplifying pattern Bhabha finds in many forms of national discourse: "The recurrent metaphor of landscape as the inscape of national identity emphasizes the quality of light, the question of social visibility, the power of the eye to naturalize the rhetoric of national affiliation and its forms of collective expression" (143). Instead of naturalizing the political discourse of the nation, Moore opposes nature to nation by conceiving human culture as a part of a larger, more powerful, and insufficiently understood ecosystem. In Moore's poem, nature serves as the matrix for everything, including hu-man constructs such as the "nation." In the latter portion of "Virginia Britan-nia," Moore's statements about Amerindian, English, and African cultures amount to a small-scale comparative anthropology, reflecting the fact that "The origin of the nation's visual *presence* is the effect of a narrative struggle" (Bhabha 143). The distance between nation and nature brings into focus some of the discrepancies at work within the nation's "traditional" (or peda-gogical) image of itself. Although Moore's poem only rarely dramatizes the strictly human world of politics in which such a struggle occurs, it does show that the stability of the nation—including citizens' conception of and rela-tion to their country—is subject to important, nonhuman forces. For Moore, the world of human struggle is circumscribed by the superior forces of nature: the nation is a human artifact, a political construction not as stable and pow-erful as it gives itself out to be. Bhabha's "narrative struggle" is necessarily re-stricted to the world of human affairs, and Moore shows just how fragile and divided this world can be. Moore's closely observed accounts of the relations between English colonists and aboriginal Americans bring into focus the con-tradictions impelling this discursive conflict.

"Virginia Britannia," then, "re-imagines" the colonial origins of the United States by judging them against the diversity and continuity of nature. For Moore, it is the organic cycle of birth and death with its ongoing promise of renewal that "grounds" true glory, not a heroic but uncritical nationalism. As a result, the view of the nation's population that emerges in her poem is more complex and varied than the one presented by the English colonists and the myth of origin it embodies. Through her investigation of a particular historical place (Jamestown) and text (William Strachey's *Travaile into Virginia Britannia*), Moore reflects upon the cultural differences between English colonists and the Amerindians they met, making judgments about the relations between them and the consequences of these contacts. By representing and reflecting upon such encounters, Moore critiques as well as celebrates the myth of national formation in "Virginia Britannia" and "Enough: *Jamestown, 1607–1957.*" In fact, her celebration is itself a profound critique.

Indeed, throughout "Virginia Britannia," Moore's reverence for the power of nature and her sense of its grandeur provide a context for making human judgments that is appropriate to the New World. In describing the linguistic synthesis that informs "Virginia Britannia," for example, Bonnie Costello writes that Moore "draws attention thematically to the cacophonous variety of language (its blend of Indian, English, French, and Negro idioms) as a key to the crazy quilt of the landscape" (251). This feature of the poem shows one way in which Moore enunciates what Frank called the "mystic Word" of America (10). As she told Donald Hall in an interview in 1961, "I should be in some philological operation or enterprise, am really much interested in dialect and intonations" (*Reader* 254).

Unlike others, I read Moore's treatment of nature in the final version of "Virginia Britannia" to be a way of positioning herself as a critical reader of history. The perspective on nature that she develops in the poem, though neither Edenic nor fully transcendent, provides a nonhuman domain that the poet draws on as a source for critiquing the world of human culture and history. Despite Moore's Christianity (which Molesworth characterizes as liberal and tolerant though not unorthodox), her treatment of nature approximates Robinson Jeffers's anti-anthropomorphic conceptions of nature. Moore's representation of her speaker as an observer, together with her vocabulary of scientific description, suggests that nature is in some ways wholly "other." The perspective that emerges in "Virginia Britannia," however, also sees nature less as pitted against humanity (as in the medieval and Enlightenment views) than as including humanity, even though human beings fail to recognize their appropriate place within it. Moore's conception of the relation between nature and culture is holistic; in her view, the world of human beings is a circle within the larger circle of all nature, as in a logical set. Ultimately, Moore draws on her descriptions of the organic aspects of the landscape in order to triangulate her perspective on human history and make accurate judgments about it.

Moore's strategy of combining images of human culture with images of nature shows her interest in the various dramas of human interaction with the environment and with other human communities. The fact that the poem takes a historic site as its subject also shows that Moore is interested in the varying relationships that human beings have forged with their environments over time. However, Moore also takes pains to show how human and natural history are at odds. Nature overgrows the material remains of the first Virginia settlers, hiding away their history in a newly forming stratum. It is chiefly through the conflict between natural process and human culture that Moore levels her criticism against prejudicial attitudes toward so-called savage peoples and against a human hubris that conceives itself as being beyond and better than the sum of nature itself. This is one of the several ways, Moore shows, in which history is a layered and compound phenomenon charged with conflicting forces. Another such layering consists in the way American history encompasses the social practices of extremely different cultures. Although Moore focuses on the initial English settlers and the Amerindians they met, she also refers to the black Africans who were brought to the New World first as indentured servants and then as slaves, and she raises challenging issues about the colonists' relationships with both groups, suggesting that those relationships are fundamental to the culture that developed from them.

In the first stanza, Moore shows the interplay of human and natural worlds. Reeling off references to organic objects in sparse, scientific rhetoric after the manner of Darwin, at the beginning of her poem she craftily combines the imagery of animals and invaders, of plants and pavements:

> Pale sand edges England's Old
> Dominion. The air is soft, warm, hot
> above the cedar-dotted emerald shore
>   known to the red-bird, the red-coated musketeer,
>   the trumpet-flower, the cavalier,
>   the parson, and the wild parishioner. A deer-
> track in a church-floor
>   brick, and a fine pavement tomb with engraved top, remain. (107)

In this passage Moore intertwines the human and nonhuman through a strategic deployment of adjectives. She modifies both bird and musketeer by the same color (red), for example, and she refers to a trumpet-flower and cavalier in the same line. This interweaving continues throughout the passage, juxtaposing "parson" and "wild parishioner" with the "deer- / track" embedded in a "church-floor / brick." In the distinctive landscape of Moore's poem, as Melissa Monroe has observed, carefully worked artifacts sit side by side with the wildest creatures of nature (Monroe 72–73).

In a humorous yet significant twist, moreover, the atmosphere of Moore's New World landscape is relatively inviting ("The air is soft, warm, hot / above the cedar-dotted emerald shore"), while the ancestral parishioner from England who has settled in it is "wild." (This characterization of the parishioner, moreover, gently echoes Moore's acerbic denunciation of the racist "wild man" in "Hercules" and her more positive but ironic description of America as "the wild man's land" in "England.") Moore's mixing and matching of the vocabularies of nature and culture prepare her reader for the interrogations of race and of savagery and civility that she undertakes later in the poem. The preserved deer track in the brick of the church floor constitutes an intriguing historical artifact, for it embodies the inseparability of nature and culture. The track is the trace of nature implicated in its supposed opposite, human culture. Moore's description thus undoes the familiar opposition between the two.

The point of this gesture is not only to show that one member of the pair, nature, is "implicated" in the other, culture, but also to demonstrate the falsehood of the premise that human culture is the superior member of the pair. Moore's method ultimately indicates that, if anything, nature provides the necessary matrix for culture, the very stuff out of which it is made, which means that culture depends upon nature and is therefore in some ways subordinate to it. The overshadowing presence of nature looms above the ground of human culture:

> The now tremendous vine-encompassed hackberry
> starred with the ivy-flower,
> shades the tall tower;
> And a great sinner lyeth here under the sycamore. (107)

For the poet, it is the passage of time that reveals the true character of the relationship between nature and culture. In the organic terms developed in the poem, it is only from the vantage point of "now" that the hackberry tree presiding over Jamestown is recognized as "tremendous" and as standing higher even than the "tall tower" built by the colonizers. As Laurence Stapleton indicates, "the starred tree *shades*" the tower, which is "a different thing from being merely higher than the tower" (102). The tree shelters and protects the tower, but it also outstrips and overshadows it.

Stapleton and Molesworth point out that Moore drew her evocative images of nature and culture from a visit she made to Jamestown. Moore refers to the "deer-track" embedded in the "church-floor," and Stapleton notes that there were also prints of a dog's paw and a woman's shoe preserved in other bricks (102). More important, Moore's possibly ironic report of the Puritan rhetoric that so grandly closes the first stanza ("And a great sinner lyeth here") points to the fact that the roots of the sycamore actually grew "out of the tomb of an early minister, Dr. James Blair, and his wife Sarah" (Stapleton 101). Although the image is hardly explicit, the intertwining figures of sycamore roots and sinner's corpse provide another image of the interpenetration of the human and natural worlds in Moore's poem.

In her very first verse, Moore introduces the phrase "Old Dominion," which she repeats two more times in the course of the poem and which she selected as the title of the suite of four poems in which "Virginia Britannia" first appeared (Slatin 208–9). Although "Old Dominion" is actually the nickname for the state of Virginia, Moore's repeated identification of Jamestown by this title successfully foregrounds the "otherness" of history, for "Dominion" remembers the historical fact of England's rule over the early American colonies, while "Old" updates and annuls (or perhaps "sublates") that history. The language of the first two lines makes clear that the speaker belongs to the present and is engaged in an act of historical meditation. The enjambment between "Old" and "Dominion" jars the reader, as if to emphasize by visual and rhythmic means the obsolescence of British rule. In fact, what the speaker describes both is and is not a colony. Once upon a time it was, under the governance of England, but now it is one of those sites whereby the poet's nation commemorates its birth.

In identifying her locale with the terms "Britannia" and "Old Dominion," Moore situates her poem in a place that is somehow a part of the past. By retaining and repeating the antiquated names, Moore insists on the "historicity" of the place. One effect of this is to render her account of the settlement simultaneously familiar and alien, for the landscape of the poem is at once a willed embodiment of the past and, as a memorial evocation of that past, solidly situated in the present. Naming the place "England's Old Dominion" both makes it that place and, because of the antiquating adjective, distinguishes the physically present place that the poet toured from a reconstructed landscape of the past that can exist only in the mind. The dual character of the poem's introductory naming, then, brings into play a dialectic between past event and present memory that operates throughout the poem. It is by means of this dialectic that the poem comes to function as a geography of origins, but it does so without the politics of priority that such geographies sometimes promote—and without any merely wishful erasure of colonial facts.

The second stanza features language that describes the route of Moore's course through this landscape, the journey she must take to map a geography representing it. In the following passage, a butterfly's winding approach to the cemetery furnishes a clue to the indirection that defines the poet's assay of the past:

> A fritillary zigzags
> toward the chancel-shaded resting place
> of this unusual man and sinner who
>   waits for a joyful resurrection. (107)

As though following in the track of the butterfly's volatile course, the poet herself "zigzags" through her verses to a vision of her nation's history. The fragility of the fritillary—its wavering vulnerability in the face of even the mildest of breezes—provides a fine metaphor for the papery fragility of history itself, the history that Moore undertakes to exhume throughout her poem. In following the path of the butterfly, the poet sets out on a quest to determine the origins of her nation. Like Williams in *American Grain*, Stevens in "The Comedian as the Letter C," and Crane in *The Bridge*, Moore models a personal search for poetic origin and maturity on the details of a national archetype.

Nevertheless, just as Moore engages nature and culture in a dialectic that spans her poem, so does she combine an apparently aleatory "narrative" with a fairly strict syllabic verse. The poem's desultory pace and unpredictable transitions give it an air of the random, but the narrative is in fact organized according to the symmetries of more or less uniform stanzas. The tension between the poem's form and narrative mode reflects a dialectic interaction between chance and pattern in the text, dramatizing one way that "The origin of the nation's visual *presence* is the effect of a narrative struggle" (Bhabha 143). The precarious synthesis that emerges at the end probably functions less as a resolution to the tension between poetic and narrative form than as the culmination of an effort to remain open to experience and interpretation. Like her fellow poets Frost, Stevens, and Williams, Moore conceives of meaning as the contingent result of an ongoing process. In this context, any representation, including that of the nation, must be performed and re-performed in order to exist.

In a pungent juxtaposition within the second stanza of "Virginia," Moore reflects upon the differences between English and Amerindians and upon the ramifications of such differences. Following up her picture "of this unusual man and sinner who / waits for a joyful resurrection," Moore outlandishly introduces an exotic Indian place-name:

> We-re-wo-
> co-mo-co's fur crown could be no
> odder than we were, with ostrich, Latin motto,
> and small gold horse-shoe:
> arms for an able sting-ray-hampered pioneer—
> painted as a Turk, it seems—continuously
> exciting Captain Smith
> who, patient with
> his inferiors, was a pugnacious equal, and to
>
> Powhatan as unflattering
> as grateful. Rare Indian, crowned by
> Christopher Newport! (107)

In a single verse, Moore combines her picture of the dead colonist awaiting resurrection with the disjointed first three vowels of the indigenous place-name Werewocomoco. This combination reflects the poet's awareness of the cross-fertilization of the cultures she describes. In the spectacular vocabulary of the passage, Moore uses the richly alliterative Indian word as the name of a place rather than a man, associating with the man himself the town over which he presided.

In the sentence she begins with this tongue-twisting word, Moore includes herself in the communal pronoun "we" when she judges that John Smith's coat of arms was no less outlandish than an Indian fur crown because it was just as much a product of culture as was the Indian symbol of power. By including herself in this "we," the poet acknowledges her own participation in the nationalism she examines. In her notes to the poem, Moore points out that the horseshoe was borne in the beak of the ostrich, that this signified "invincible digestion," and that the emblem in turn "reiterated the motto, *Vincere est vivere.*" The ostrich motif also appears in Moore's "He Digesteth Harde Yron" as an emblem of patient, miraculous stamina, but paired with the motto of conquest ("To win is to live," or possibly, "to prevail is to survive") and in its context as a coat of arms, the image functions as a symbol of imperial conquest.

Moore compares Powhatan to Smith ("no / odder than we were") through a "we" that is implicitly national in character. The line reflects her speaker's participation in the kind of national communion described by Benedict Anderson. It also reflects the poet's sense of justice regarding the conflict between native inhabitants and colonial invaders, providing a clear exception to the pattern of appropriation of Indian heritage by white characters that Michaels finds in American writing of the 1910s and 1920s. Moore acknowledges the history of violence of whites against Indians through her use of the first-person plural pronoun. Its appearance in the sentence personally interjects the speaker into the cultural conflict between English and Indians. Squarely positioning her speaker in this way, Moore takes a stand on behalf of the Indians, challenging the ideology of racial prejudice by showing that the differences between "savage" Indian and civilized Englishmen are neither natural nor essential. In fact, in the earliest published version of the poem (1935), Moore refers to the modern-day descendants of the colonists as "bothered-with-wages / new savages" instead of as the benign "townspeople" of the final version ("Virginia Britannia" 70). As in "Hercules," Moore indicates that the colonists, who prided themselves on their civilized ways, were in fact themselves the savages they despised.[4]

Moore continues her attack against racism by identifying "Indian" with "infidel" when she describes Powhatan as "painted as a Turk" and Smith as "an able sting-ray-hampered pioneer," though she does so without exonerating either man. This shows her evenhanded assessment of the cultural conflict involved in colonization. She observes her characters with sympathy but without sentimentality, for, while the descriptions of Powhatan and Smith appear to reinforce the dichotomy underlying such racism by conflating two pagan "others," the speaker's judgment that the Indian in his accoutrements "could be no / odder than we were" insists that the very concepts of oddity and conventionality are produced by culture. In short, the speaker acknowledges the relativity of cultural practices, and in doing so she presents them on terms more equal than those envisioned by Captain Smith and his contemporaries, despite the "pugnacious" equality that Smith insisted on claiming for himself with Powhatan.[5] This very pugnacity, Moore implies, proved constitutive of the nation that arose in his wake. It is such founding hostility between colonists and Amerindians that Moore subtly yet tenaciously confronts in her poem.

Moore's zigzag syntax also fuses and confuses the persons and qualities of Smith and Powhatan. In the middle of the sentence beginning "We-re-wo-/ co-mo-co's fur crown . . . ," Moore scrambles adjectives and actors so that identification becomes temporarily impossible. The dash that ends a crucial line of the stanza both combines and divides the phrases "arms for an able sting-ray-hampered pioneer—" and "painted as a Turk." Indiscriminately mixing subjects and modifiers, this syntax momentarily mixes up the reader. The tortuous twist of Moore's stanzaic and syntactic structures underscores the heterogeneity of the world born of the colonial encounter between Smith and Powhatan. Moore practically flaunts the polymorphous qualities of her diction in her play on "We-re-wo /co-mo-co's" and "we were," so that Indian and colonist somehow become one another in a puzzling way. In her linguistic transformation of native into colonist and colonist into native, Moore appears to suggest that the demographic heterogeneity she defends in "The Labors of Hercules" is allied to the cultural hybridity that so profoundly marks American life. If "we were" not quite We-re-wo-co-mo-co, his cultural beliefs and practices were at least "no / odder than we were" to the point that the defining features of "the other" and the self become indistinguishable.[6] The fact that Moore uses the terms designating a place ("We-re-wo-co-mo-co") and a people ("Powhatan") for the man who presides over them underscores the exemplary quality of the relations between Smith and Powhatan. Colonist and native metonymically embody the respective peoples they represent.

At the same time that Moore suggests the connections between Indians and colonists, however, her use of the adjective "rare" to modify the "Indian" Powhatan acknowledges the hostility of the relations between these peoples. The word makes one wonder why Moore finds this particular Indian "rare" and what it is she means by this ambiguous word. In what sense, for example, does she consider the Indian leader—whose name was actually Wahunseneka (Sale 297)—uncommon? Does the crowning somehow evince the man's excellent or extraordinary qualities for her? The word "crown" appears to register both the poet's admiration for Powhatan and her sense of irony regarding his "coronation." The irony may have arisen from Moore's reading of the account describing Powhatan's so-called crowning. As Kirkpatrick Sale reports, the ceremony turns out to be "almost a parody of the kind of misunderstandings that were to beset the initial decades of contact among the two vastly different cultures as they vied for dominance in the New World" (297). He explains that "In the fall of 1608 . . . Captain Christopher Newport undertook . . . the coronation of Wahunseneka, chief of the Powhatans," in order to "make him a vassal of the English king and an ally of the Virginia Colony" (296). In John Smith's account of the coronation, which Sale characterizes as a "near-comic scene," Moore's keen eye for irony would have found much to delight her: "A fowle trouble there was to make him kneel to receave his crowne, he neither knowing the majestie, nor meaning of a Crowne, nor bending of the knee, indured so many perswasions, examples, and instructions, as tired them all. At last by leaning hard on his shoulders, he a little stooped, and Newport put the Crowne on his head" (qtd. in Sale 297). According to Gesa Mackenthun, this scene "is one of the finest demonstrations of the ridiculousness of the Europeans' attempts to convince themselves of their territorial rights by performing elaborate rites. It is also known that at least some of the colonizers involved had a clear sense of the ridiculousness of such symbolic acts" (*Metaphors* 202).

Despite the obvious miscommunication it registers between the two groups, the account suggests that Powhatan recognized the ceremony as precisely the subjugating exaltation the English intended it to be. Moore's apostrophe to Powhatan as "rare" reflects her admiration of the man's leadership and of his presumably exceptional ability to discern the political and moral implications of the colonists' actions. Perhaps "rare" also suggests that the veneer of respect accorded to Powhatan by the English singles him out from the myriad Indians who, throughout U.S. history, have been summarily slaughtered or shoved aside. In this respect, "rare" also evokes the phrase "endangered species." Moore's laconic pause and reference to the travesty of Powhatan's crowning indicates her complex sense of the manipulations and exchanges that constituted "settlement."

Moore invokes the name "Old Dominion" a second time in her poem when she turns to a description of the "all-green box-sculptured grounds" of the Jamestown settlement. In the next two sentences, moreover, the word "English" appears twice:

> An almost English green surrounds
>   them. Care has formed among unEnglish insect sounds,
> the white wall-rose. As
>   thick as Daniel Boone's grape-vine, the stem has wide-spaced great
>   blunt alternating ostrich-skin warts that were thorns.
>   Care has formed walls of yew
>   since Indians knew
> the Fort Old Field and narrow tongue of land that Jamestown was.
>
>   (107–8)

Once more, Moore simultaneously posits and negates the presence of the past. Moore's rendering of curious detail regarding the landscape shows how indebted and yet different Jamestown is with respect to the Old World. Of the "box-sculptured grounds" of the settlement, for example, she writes that "An *almost* English green surrounds / them," thereby both likening the look of the grounds of the New World settlement to the carefully cultivated gardens of its parent state and distinguishing them from one another. The perfect iambs of this line stress both that similarity and difference, for the beats fall on the first syllables of "almost" and "English," and on the monosyllable "green." The repetition of the word "English" in its altered, negating form ("unEnglish") also stresses the colony's difference from its mother country at the same time that its very distinction is made with reference to the familiar English context.

In this stanza as in the previous ones, Moore again grafts the natural world and human culture, often continuing to pair the two spheres within single lines. In the sentence "Care has formed among unEnglish insect sounds, / the white wall-rose," Moore divides the direct object of the sentence from the verb that governs it by inserting the modifying phrase "among unEnglish insect sounds." This syntactical arrangement juxtaposes cultural "human care" with natural "insect sounds" in the same line, while it also permits the direct object to be deferred to the next line. The surprise of the enjambment draws the reader up short, as though one had literally stumbled into the structure supporting "the white wall-rose." The point I wish to repeat is that the wall-rose, which is an effect of "Care," represents culture in the form of human cultivation, in contrast to the play of "insect sounds" that nature makes. In addition, although Moore uses a verb in the active voice, the abstract noun that governs the verb renders the actor anonymous. As an act of deliberation, "Care" implies intent, yet Moore's syntax elides the human source of that intent. The riddling obliqueness with which she relates the origin of the wall-rose makes it impossible to determine who nurtured the rose or who built the wall it grows on. Perhaps Moore's purpose in constructing her sentence this way is mimetic; the uncertainty of the language is like the inscrutability of historical records or the difficulty of deciphering weather-beaten sites.

In her repetition of the curiously impersonal phrase "Care has formed," Moore notes the effect of human culture on the landscape she describes: "Care has formed walls of yew / since Indians knew / The Fort Old Field and narrow tongue of land that Jamestown was" (108). The walls of yew provide evidence of human culture in the form of a ruined artifact. The walls intervene between the speaker's historical moment and that of both the original English colonists and the aboriginal inhabitants before them. The rhymed words "yew" and "knew" are rendered even more emphatic by the brevity of the couplet in which they appear, and the three lines together contrast the fort walls of the colonists with the knowledge of the Indians. The precarious balance of the antithesis between colonial fort and Indian onlookers dissolves with the jarring enjambment between "since Indians knew" and "the Fort Old Field." The clipped clause "since Indians knew" comes as a fleeting parenthetical aside, an effect that reinforces the meaning of the last two lines of the paragraph, in which the Indians vanish into the past tense of the verbs "knew" and "was."

In systematically registering the confusions of natural and human history, the poet emphasizes the process of deciphering and analysis involved in the recuperation of history. By foregrounding the constructed character of history, Moore allows for a revisionist interpretation of American origins.[7] Her judicious comparisons of the material culture of English and Indians likewise challenge a merely celebratory view of colonization. Moore's allusion to William Wordsworth's famous immortality ode at the end of her poem reflects her vision of human history as a part of natural history and her attempt

to revise historical interpretations of national origins by means of the per-
spective entailed in this vision. The violent arrogance, or hubris, that Moore
decries in the last stanza is consistent with a perspective she has carefully
elaborated throughout the poem. It is a subdued kind of environmental con-
sciousness, a perspective that recognizes the limits of human achievement by
measuring it against the organic processes of nature.[8]

Aping the voice of a tour guide, Moore invites her readers to "Observe
the terse Virginian, / the mettlesome gray one that drives the / owl from
tree to tree" (108). In doing so she applies the term "Virginian," which
one would expect to have a human referent, to a mockingbird (Monroe
73). Because Moore does not make this referent plain until five lines later,
however, the reader must first play a modest guessing game about the
"species" of Virginian that Moore has in mind. This game provides one
more example of the poem's unions of the man-made and the natural, a
pattern that exposes anthropocentrism as fallacious and potentially de-
structive. Bernard Engel emphasizes this point in his reading of the pas-
sage, for "neither Indian nor settler represent the true spirit of the land."
He argues that Moore's mockingbird

> is a creature of mettle who can adopt the guise of any native bird or with
> insouciance dominate an English garden pedestal. The suggestion seems
> to be that the bird is the true life of Virginia, that in a guarded defiance
> he frequents man's habitations, watching with a self-assurance born of
> his knowledge that he is the permanent heir of the land. (93).

In Engel's view, nonhuman nature overpowers and outlasts the human. But
Moore's arch epithet for the bird ("the mettlesome grey one") also recalls her
use of "mettlesomeness" in the poem "England," where it refers to the behav-
ior of Americans. The shared diction suggests that Moore's characterization of
the mockingbird is part of a broader strategy of national representation on
her part. Her tongue-in-cheek personification in "Virginia" echoes the cul-
tural nationalism of "England" and "The Student."

The very act of naming, embodied in the designation "Virginian," is a
defining act of human culture, the quintessentially poetic gesture. Moreover,
"Virginian" derives from "Virginia," a name given in honor of Queen Eliza-
beth. Naming is a process Moore explicitly refers to later in the poem, where
it is fraught with political significance. Referring to both a colony and a state,
the name "Virginia" reflects the politics of colonization and nationhood, and
the political resonance of Moore's phrase "the terse Virginian" reappears in
the section of the poem that focuses on naming. By playfully mixing the hu-
man and nonhuman worlds in this way, Moore provides a powerful critical
context for assessing the history of the Jamestown colony.

Moore's intertwining of nature and human culture grows more precise and
yet more convoluted in the following description of Jamestown's grounds:

Narrow herring-bone-laid bricks,
a dusty pink beside the dwarf box-
bordered pansies, share the ivy-arbor shade
   with cemetery lace settees, one at each side,
   and with the bird: box-bordered tide-
   water gigantic jet black pansies—splendor; pride—
not for a decade
   dressed, but for a day, in over-powering velvet; and
   gray-blue-Andalusian-cock-feather pale ones,
      ink-lined on the edge, fur-
      eyed, with ochre
on the cheek. (108)

Here, brick paths "share the ivy-arbor shade" not only with other colonial artifacts such as the "cemetery lace settees" but also with the bird described in the previous stanza and with the pansies that, like the settees, border the paths. At this point in the poem the dichotomy between culture and nature is as pronounced as ever, and yet the two categories are every bit as intertwined, for the path the poet treads is made of bricks laid in a pattern named after the skeletal structure of a fish, and the pansies that border the walk are themselves bordered by box shrubs strategically planted and pruned by the colonists. Here is a stanza in which the man-made and the natural are constantly changing—or to put it more precisely still, sharing—places.

Be that as it may, it is the power of the cultural that is given pride of place in this stanza. A proliferation of boxes gives the impression of a planned and tended garden rather than a wilderness, an impression that is reinforced by the echo of Moore's report in her third stanza: "The Old Dominion has / all-green box-sculptured grounds." The twice-repeated phrase "Care has formed" similarly contributes to this effect. The geometrical grid that human beings produce through horticulture, a grid Moore's "box-like" stanzas imitate,[9] reshapes nature's curves and spheres. The "almost English green," or "town square" on which the settlement was laid out tenuously persists against the inroads of a natural order that works against it. The boxtrees bordering the pansies correspond to the abstract boxes or grids used to plan a village, a city, or even a common. In fact the very etymology of *box* reflects the relationship between man-made boxes, be they material (in the form of a house or a park) or imagined (as in the blueprints for a house or park). The boxtree or shrub belongs to the genus *Buxus,* which is a Latin version of the Greek *pyxos,* a word that itself refers to both shrub and human structure. Moore's repetition of "box-bordered" in the fifth stanza of her poem plays on such associations, inviting the reader to think of the grounds as the product of carefully imposed and deployed "boxes." As Pamela White Hadas observes, *Pensées* as well as pansies mark the landscape of Moore's Jamestown (35).

Although I have argued that Moore's language confuses the boundaries between nature and culture at every point in the poem, thereby unsettling the hierarchy implied in the dichotomy between them, the general tendency of the diction in this section would seem to imply the ascendancy of the cultural. In addition to being "box-bordered," Moore indicates that the pansies along the brick path are of the "dwarf" variety. In view of the repeated use of this adjective as a verb in the final stanza, Moore's application of the word to pansies is significant. Here, nature is a shrunken dwarf, circumscribed at every turn by human ingenuity. While it is true that natural resources provide the necessary material for such ingenuity to be manifested, the poem's language at this point suggests that human ingenuity exercises an unabridged dominion over nature. (Perhaps it is a view of human power as possessing complete dominion over nature that Moore means to revise through her repetitions of "Old Dominion." Like the "new dispensation" of the gospel celebrated by the Puritan pilgrims who landed later and further north than the Jamestown colonists, Moore's vision of the actual relationship between humanity and nature antiquates the familiar view of human dominance, rendering it obsolete and hence "Old.")

The repeated epithet "box-bordered" in reference to both sets of pansies, dwarf and "gigantic," appears to reinforce the hegemony of the human. So does Moore's lavish description of the "gigantic" pansies. Like the grass that lasts only for a day, the pansies are not characterized by longevity. However, these pansies are "dressed" in the fine English stuff of an "over-powering velvet." In the figurative terms of this description, the sensuous velvet of the flowers' finery is a product of human industry. The tactile surface of this textile may foreshadow the allusion to "stark luxuries" later in the poem. In any case, the pansies continue to be described in the anthropomorphic terms of their sartorial and cosmetic splendor. If the "gigantic jet black pansies" don a fast-fading velvet that makes them like English colonists, their "gray-blue-Andalusian-cock-feather pale" counterparts seem, despite the Old World provenance of the feather that modifies them, to be painted like Indian warriors. They are "ink-lined" and wear "ochre on the cheek." As Monroe points out, their "fur-eyed" faces suggest the "black looks" and painted features of an angry Indian as much as they connote pollinated anther and stigma (74). Rather than insist on this reading as definitive in any way, I would suggest that the mutually exclusive terms of the reading (Old World or New World, Spaniard or Native American) constitute a conflict whose tension Moore dramatizes in the poem in much the same way as she emphasizes the conflicts between culture and nature.

Furthermore, although I suggested that the language of these passages intimated the dominion of human culture over natural process, I did so with the expectation of reversing myself on this point, because I am arguing that the poem as a whole engages culture and nature in a continuing interplay. The tension between the two terms is once more engaged by Moore's description of the "pride" of the "gigantic jet black pansies," for she writes of them that they were "not for a decade / dressed, but for a day, in over-powering velvet." The language of this wonderful description pulls in opposite directions. On the one hand, the phrase "but for a day" represents the flower as a fragile thing, inferior in its power to human machinations or natural forces ("How with this rage shall beauty hold a plea / Whose action is no stronger than a flower?"). On the other hand, the biblical resonances of "but for a day" apply as readily to human beings as they do to flowers and grass. The same tension that is at work in the anthropomorphic figure is also evident in the compound adjective that modifies "velvet," for "over-powering" has both negative and positive connotations, at once implying intensity or excess ("*over*-powering") and its alternative—superior, conquering strength ("over-*powering*").

In the next stanza, Moore's "'advancin' back- / wards in a circle'" denies the view of history as progress; the image suggests a cyclical model instead. It perhaps recognizes with more objectivity than a linear model of progress both the gain and the loss in human affairs as they unfold over time. The "advancin'" of the black idiom is ironic, since it entails a backward movement that works against the very idea of progress. And yet the end result, which the canny wit of the oppressed can view with a humorous irony, is that one arrives at one's point of origin, repeating the movements and mistakes of earlier generations.

Moore's "at first slow, saddle-horse quick cavalcade" is a pageant of the past, like the train of generations descending from Adam and Eve in Whitman's "Passage to India." The list of marchers in the pageant includes horses and mules, but it also features symbols expressing destructive superstition and prisons that are paradoxically sweet. The "witch-cross door and 'strong sweet prison'" (109) are just as much part of the march of civilization through the course of human history as the less ambiguous figures of the jumpers, mounts, and mules that precede them in the catalogue. Such cultural items, moreover, belie the idea of the inevitability of progress.

The criticism of colonial and American history implied by Moore's reference to "witch-cross door and 'strong sweet prison'" corresponds to the cowbirdlike "taking" of the Potomac and to the "establishment" of the Negro in America that Moore mentions a few lines later. References to both are made in the sentence that describes the pageant, and the syntax presents the two activities as parallel to the circular sequence of history, the backward advance of human beings through time. "Advancin' backwards in a circle" laughs at the notion of linear progress just as it affirms the traditional conception of history as a spinning wheel of birth and death. Since the cowbird is "a small North American blackbird *(Molothrus ater)* that lays its eggs in the nests of other birds" ("Cowbird"), it would appear that Moore intends the cowbird's advance as a trope for colonization. According to this reading, "taking the Potomac / cowbirdlike," as the sneaking and emphatic enjambment suggests, refers to the English displacement of Indian inhabitants. "Taking" the Potomac also corresponds to the crucial later phrase in Moore's poem that defines and denounces imperialism: "no imperialist, / . . . in *taking* what we / pleased—in colonizing as the / saying is—has been a synonym for mercy"

(110; emphasis added). Mixing natural and human history in politically and philosophically significant ways, Moore prefigures her explicit allusion to the colonial theft of land and livelihood from the Indians with this reference to the behavior of an "imperialist" bird. In these lines, the confident "we" of Moore's national communion turns into a national "confessional," for the poet, prophetlike, insists on the sin of her nation, challenging its citizens to confess and repent. As Berger puts it, "the collective 'we' is revealed as implicating 'us' in this taking" (284). In the reference to the cowbird, however, natural behavior is seen as no better than human behavior, so Moore's wry reference to the cowbird's taking also suggests that she seeks a human morality that can curb destructive, but natural, dispositions.

In the same ironic spirit as the black idiom she quotes, Moore refers to the enslavement of Africans. Again, she describes this action in terms that parallel the colonial displacement enacted by the "cowbirdlike" Englishmen; the dispossession of Indians and the disfranchisement of blacks are equally "part of what has come about" during the circular "advance" of American history. Because of their enslavement, Moore identifies "the Negro" as the "inadvertent ally and best enemy of / tyranny." In one version of the poem, Moore had written that "the Negro" was "opportunely brought, to strength- / en protest against / tyranny" (*The Pangolin* 6). Since this line undercuts its purpose of praising black people by perceiving slavery (through post-Emancipation hindsight) as something providentially "opportune," her decision to revise the sentence to the more benign "inadvertent ally" makes sense and also makes the line more palatable to posterity. In making this revision, Moore distances her poem from the mystifying politics and adulterated religious sentiment criticized in Phillis Wheatley's "On Being Brought from Africa to America." In a more positive vein, however, the revision more firmly acknowledges the contribution of blacks in the ongoing enterprise of American democracy.

After her pageant of history, Moore resumes her observation of the flowers in Jamestown square. It is as if the historical meditation were an interpolation in some larger project of natural history. But however out of place this episode may seem, since it is embedded in the stanza, it should be viewed as belonging to the same sweep of natural history in which the various flowers, trees, and animals of the poem participate. In effect, this embedding of references to colonization, Amerindians, Puritan culture, and black folk wisdom in the natural history of the world places human history in a cosmic context, thereby providing a less limited perspective from which to judge it. "Virginia Britannia" presents both natural and human affairs in sharp detail, preserving the integrity of each even as it judges the latter through the lens of the former.

Moore uses the name "Old Dominion" for the third and final time in her poem when she applies it to a list of flowers. She uses items in a botanical catalogue as metaphors for the disparate origins of American citizens. Like the flowers she names from diverse places, the people of America hail from many homes. The plants in her list came to America as a result of human deliberation; they grew from seeds and cuttings transplanted to a new world, and many of the North American plants we are familiar with today are the descendants of such sprigs. Like the U.S. population, these plants comprise a far-reaching diaspora.

Many of Moore's "Old Dominion / flowers" (including the fuchsia, camellia, and magnolia) are actually named after European botanists even if they are not native to the Old World, and most of the flowers she identifies are original to the Old World. The "fruiting pomegranate," for example, comes from "a widely cultivated Old World tree (*Punica granatum* of the family Punicaceae)" ("Pomegranate"); gardenias are "natives of the Cape of Good Hope and of Tropical Asia and Africa" ("Gardenias"); camellias are Asian; the crape myrtle originated in tropical Asia and Australia ("Angiosperms"); and the very name of the African violet indicates its Old World origin. In addition, the African violet recalls the reference a few lines earlier to the Negro's "establishment" on the Chickahominy. According to the terms of the flower metaphor, the "savage other" in the form of the African black actually turns out to be a common domestic presence.

A surprising relationship exists between Moore's catalogue of flowers and her cartography of colonization. Although the poet presents her picture of the "Rare unscent- / ed provident- / ly hot, too sweet, inconsistent flower-bed," in the scientific discourse of natural history, she clearly evokes the "inconsistency" of her flower bed as a metaphor of the hybridity of post-Conquest American culture. As Costello writes, Moore's America is above all

> a place of mixed soils, of an "inconsistent flowerbed.". . . Virginia Britannia, for all its colonizing arrogance, its raw, tactless, pugnacious, dashingly undiffident slogans ("Don't tread on me"), and for all its European pretensions "filled with anesthetic scent as inconsiderate as the gardenia's," is a "magnificent" totality. Moore always celebrates the whole of life, even as she picks and chooses among its parts. (251)

Nevertheless, while Moore's language celebrates what it represents, it marks the ironies and tallies the moral costs of colonial enterprise. Moore's flower bed, together with her references to the box and the other trees on the grounds of the settlement, hints at colonial alterations in the ecosystem. Sale summarizes one sequence of such changes:

> The destruction of old-growth forests meant the elimination of certain intricate econiches and their microbial and faunal patterns, the emigration of bird and animal populations, and the invasion of pioneer species that prevented the natural succession from ever producing again the great trees or the carpets of native wildflowers. Local and regional climatic changes followed, with new conditions of wind, temperature, humidity, and soil moisture, and even seasons that proved inhospitable to many kinds of plants and animals but to which the vast numbers of new European species—cattle, pigs, horses, rats, dandelions, and so on—adapted rapidly, without predators or pathogens to hinder them. (292)

In Sale's view, such changes were caused by "nothing less than" the European colonizers' "war between man and nature" (289). This "transformation of eastern North America," he argues, "may well have been the swiftest and most dramatic environmental change ever wrought by human agency on the face of the earth up to that time—'the largest area in history to be so greatly changed so quickly,' in the opinion of Richard Lilliard in his study of American woodlands" (290). While Moore's language does not damn the Europeans for the changes in the natural world, it does reflect these changes, and it does so in an often ironic, questioning register.

In earlier versions of the poem, in fact, in the final stanza Moore provided a catalogue not of flowers but of trees. Whereas she identifies only three trees (the live oak, the cypress, and the English hackberry) in the revised stanza, she also refers elsewhere to the white pine and the cedar. In the earlier version, these trees

> lose identity
> and are one tree, as
> sunset flames increasingly
> against their leaf-chis-
> elled blackening ridge of green. *(The Pangolin 9)*

In the transformation from many trees to one (which she preserves in different form in the revised version), Moore's lines perhaps record something of the wholesale assault against the environment that was embodied by English colonial mercantilism. "All in all," Sale writes,

> The presence of just a few hundred thousands of the European branch of the human species, within just a century after landing, did more to alter the environment of North America, in some places and for many populations quite irretrievably, than the many millions of the American branch had done in fifteen centuries or more. It took a special kind of mind to see that impact as beneficial, as "progress," indeed as "civilization." But the European (and the American successor) possessed just such a mind: those English who clear-cut their way through ancient primordial forests actually spoke of "making land." (291–92)

For her part, even as she "moves from a horticultural form of domineering to a human, historical sort" (Molesworth 289), Moore also moves back again to a vision of nature's overgrowing force—one decidedly beyond the horticultural—in which human agency has no hand. She gains a critical ground by doing so, establishing a quasi-transcendental moral criterion as a basis for judging human actions. In her transfiguration of the many trees she describes into the single compound tree that disappears in the approaching twilight at the end of the poem, Moore perhaps also commemorates the loss of such trees to colonization and "progress."

In lines that function similarly to those in the latter half of the second stanza, in which she rigorously compared the trappings and insignia of the Indian Powhatan and the Englishman Smith, Moore compares two feminine specimens of each culture:

> Odd Pamunkey
> princess, birdclaw-ear-ringed; with a pet raccoon
>   from the Mattaponi (what a bear!). Feminine
>   odd Indian young lady! Odd thin-
>   gauze-and-taffeta-dressed English one! (109)

Moore employs her familiar compound adjectives in her descriptions of the Indian and English young ladies. The alliteration and rhythmic innovation of these descriptions present vivid spectacles, wonderfully conveying the attractions of each woman's accoutrements. The poet expresses her playful admiration for the "Odd Pamunkey / princess" Pocahontas through the repeated /p/ sounds and nasals of the whole sentence in which the epithet appears and in the exotic detail of the bird-claw earring. In a parallel manner, "taffeta-dressed" handsomely captures the swish of the English girl's skirt. The effective juxtaposition of "Feminine / odd Indian young lady!" with "Odd thin- / gauze-and-taffeta-dressed English one!" pair the two women in a neat, almost ceremonial image. The twin tableaux powerfully express the interaction between the cultures that the poem as a whole investigates. The thrice-repeated "odd" in reference to both women echoes Moore's earlier pronouncement that "We-re-wo- / co-mo-co's fur crown could be no / odder than we were" in the second stanza. The triadic incantation of the adjective, together with the extravagant epithets, not only demonstrates the incommensurability of the two cultures by showing the relativity of cultural practices, however. By exposing the "oddity" of any cultural practice from the perspective of a different one, Moore's diction also attributes an equality to English and Native American cultures by removing the grounds for establishing a hierarchical arrangement of them.

In addition to indicating the equality of cultures, the language of the stanza traces the development of a cultural hybridity. This genealogy perhaps begins with the props associated with each of the girls described, for the Pamunkey's pet raccoon vies for attention with the terrapin meat and French chaise longue of the English girl. The sprawling syntax of the last complete sentence of the stanza conveys a vista of an expanding colonial domain:

> Terrapin
> meat and crested spoon
>   feed the mistress of French plum-and-turquoise-piped chaise-longue;
>   of brass-knobbed slat front door, and everywhere open
>   shaded house on Indian-
>   named Virginian
>   streams in counties named for English lords. (109–10)

The sentence shows off the European wares that signify the girl's social rank while at the same time it weaves together the European and Native American elements of an emerging culture. The hybridity of this new culture is material, geographic, and linguistic, for it encompasses everything from the turtle meat and chaise longue to the streams and regions inhabited by Indians and the Indian and English names for them. In fact, Moore's rhyming of "Indian-" and "Virginian" emphasizes the developing linguistic hybridity of the new culture.

In addition, her meter and syntax stress the cultural union of English and Indian in a newly forming world, while they also intimate the eventual conquest of the Indians by the English. The parallel syntax of "Indian- / named Virginian / streams in counties named for English lords" presents the act of geographical naming on the part of the Indians and English in balanced, even-handed terms. The stresses of the lines reinforce the parallel by falling on the first syllables of both "Indian" and "English," on "named," and on the entities variously named ("streams" and "counties").

These entities are not of the same kind, however, and this fact is significant. The streams identified by Indian names are natural phenomena closely associated with the life and culture of the Indians as sources of food, and geographical markers whereby the Indians oriented themselves (vis-à-vis enemy territories or villages of related tribespeople, for example), whereas the counties with English names are regions whose boundaries represent a polity based on property. "What the Indians owned," writes William Cronon "was not the land but the things that were on the land for use during the various seasons of the year. . . . In nothing is this more clear than in the names they attached to the landscape, the bulk of which related not to possession but to use." In contrast, "the English most frequently created arbitrary place-names which either recalled localities in their homeland or gave a place the name of its owner'" (65–66). As Eric Cheyfitz points out, both systems of naming are in some sense arbitrary since they are equally abstract, and both reflect the cultural perspectives of their namers but do so in significantly different ways. Amerindians lived in a "kin-ordered society," and such "societies possess relatively 'open and shifting boundaries' . . . in the juridical, political, and economic realms." In fact, the "more flexible boundaries of kin-ordered societies are grounded in a relation to the land (as place) that is opposed to that contained in the term 'property,' which is grounded in a notion not of shifting and open boundaries, but of fixed and closed ones" (54).[10]

Cheyfitz also explains how John Locke's "exemplary" account of property and political economy relates to colonial boundaries:

> For Locke, who summarizes the history of Western thought on the subject, the very mark of property is the enclosure: the defining, or bounding, of a place that signals the *perceived* settling, or cultivation, of the place. . . . [It] is this figure of enclosure that marks the frontier between the savage and the civilized; for in Locke's words, "the wild Indian . . . knows no enclosure and is still a tenant in common" (5.26). (55)

Although both streams and counties have cultural valences for each group, the English counties map the landscape as a legal entity, or property, that differentiates them from the conception of streams and regions familiar to the Indians. This legal process is a manner of conceiving the world that was used by the English to implement not only the establishment of farms and homesteads but also their military and political domination of the Indians. As the very name of the colony itself testifies, the act of naming and the act of possession (or "taking title to") were in some ways conceptually coterminous for the English. Those "English counties" would appear on English maps and become one of the mother country's means of governing the new colony. The naming Moore recounts here clearly has political as well as cognitive dimensions, for, as James Delle points out, "every map is created as an instrument of control" (Leone and Silberman 106). "Those who have the ability to construct the forms of space," writes Delle, "have the power over the forms human interaction will take" (Leone and Silberman 18). The honorific title of "Virginia" was Raleigh's way of paying homage to his "virginal" sovereign. So it is in a legal as well as a linguistic sense that those Virginian counties are "named for English lords."[11]

Moore's reference to the streams as "Virginian," however, does two things, only one of which is to signal the political and commercial conquest of the new land by the English. It also recalls the early appearance of the term when Moore applied it to the mockingbird. If on the one hand the word itself extends the political reach of an English queen to a land far from her domestic shores, on the other hand it is applied for a second time to a nonhuman referent. Moore counters her readers' expectations by making her Virginian a mockingbird in that earlier case, and in doing so she sets a precedent within her poem. The net effect of this precedent, I have been arguing, is to break down the boundaries between the natural and the cultural in order to reveal the limitations of human achievement. In this second instance, Moore applies the term "Virginian" to an inanimate natural phenomenon. While this attribution repeats the English effort to control and possess the stream as a natural resource through the legal processes of naming and claiming, the disjunction between name and thing Moore opened up earlier with her catachrestic identification of the mockingbird as "Virginian" arises here as well. Moore's deployment of the word in these two cases is more than a quirk, for it participates in the poem's overarching effort to read the nation's political history from the perspective of natural process and renewal. Moore engages examples of the natural and the cultural in an ongoing dialectic throughout her poem in order to achieve a new synthesis in the meaning of both terms. While many critics have noticed Moore's evocation of the Romantic sublime in the poem's closing allusion to Wordsworth's immortality ode and many have found fault with the manner of this allusion, the New World paradigm of a Native American worldview provides just as relevant a model for the poem as that of English Romanticism. With its view of the interconnected and organic nature of reality, the Amerindian model provides a criterion for making moral judgments about human behavior in the same way Moore's poem does. The cosmos is a web of life in which human beings participate with other beings instead of in opposition to them. While Moore may draw her vocabulary from contemporary biology, the sensibility that governs her use of these words has much in common with an Amerindian weltanschauung.

In a different vein, Moore's allusion to the image of the rattlesnake imprinted on "our once dashingly / undiffident first flag" effects another of those unions of nature and culture I have been describing. Moore's use of the first-person plural pronoun in this phrase again reveals her unspoken sense of participation in the life of the nation as a citizen. This quiet gesture repeats the poet's ready identification with the English colonizers in the second stanza. The poet's immediate identification with the history and icons of her country, dramatized in her later years by her tricorn hat, demonstrates the important role of nationalism in her conception of herself as a poet. To some degree, the poem accepts the grade-school mythology of the nation's origins that is inculcated in every citizen, native and naturalized alike. When she writes that "Priorities were cradled in this region not / noted for humility," Moore celebrates the colony as the cradle of modern democracy, sharing in her nation's sense of itself as a champion of freedom and independence. Her description of the country's first flag as "once dashingly undiffident" innocently admires the rude heroism of its hissing motto. The poet delights in the audacity of the emblem, plainly savoring its upstart pluck.

On a second look at this phrase, however, the admiration becomes decidedly less innocent, for the description is quickly revised by an abruptly judgmental tag identifying the rattlesnake as the "tactless symbol of a new republic." The poet seasons her patriotism with an ironic humor that characterizes the phrase "once dashingly undiffident" as a nostalgic glance backward. The terse tag acknowledges the expression to be the work of tyro statesmen defending a youthful nation. In this passage, as in earlier ones, the flora, fauna, and historical artifacts of Jamestown integrate "the work of human hands" with creatures existing quite apart from such work, for the site boasts "high-singing frogs, cottonmouth snakes and cotton-fields." Like the flag that weds crafty animal with "rattling" caption, the "unique / Lawrence pottery with loping wolf design" also takes an animal for its emblem. Nature and culture intermingle virtually everywhere on the grounds of Jamestown and in Moore's documentation of it. Even the "one-brick- / thick serpentine wall built by / Jefferson" courses across the town's topography in a slithering animal's meandering pattern.

The first complete sentence of the tenth stanza provides a clear declaration of the poem's theme. It makes its statement by way of a simile invoking the natural world that Moore has been at such pains to detail throughout:

> Like strangler figs choking
> a banyan, not an explorer, no imperialist,
>   not one of us, in taking what we
>   pleased—in colonizing as the
>   saying is—has been a synonym for mercy.
> The redskin with the deer-
>   fur crown, famous for his cruelty, is not all brawn
>   and animality. (110)

The serpentine lineation and syntax of this passage present each half of the simile in parallel terms, but the passage presents its brazen declaration in a series of negations. The reference to the banyan is especially precise, since this Indian fig tree sprouts its roots from the top down: its branches put down roots near the parent trunk to grow new trunks nearby. (In killing the parent tree, as the metaphor suggests, the colonizer's dispossession of others ultimately wounds himself as well.) Although the rhetorical effect of such negative statements is modest, the logical sweep of the declaration is universal ("no imperialist . . ."). The fact that Moore is making an absolute claim does not by any means get lost in her syntax, but the universal scope of her historical revision is indefinably muted by both that syntax and the calculated use of litotes throughout the passage. By couching her judgment in the language of negation, Moore renders her predication with a fine precision that is less limiting than a positive thesis would be, for in simply denying that imperialists are merciful, she has escaped any definitive claim about what an imperialist is or might become. Moore's cagey reliance on this kind of logical and rhetorical strategy preserves a horizon of hope in the landscape of her poem. In other words, the destructive impact of past actions need not foreclose the possibility of an improved future. As in "The Labors of Hercules," one of the poet's chief efforts in "Virginia Britannia" is to correct the mistakes generated by prejudice, to alter the legacy of her nation for posterity—without claiming for herself a perfectly righteous position.

The apparent non sequitur that follows Moore's grand moral statement, and which provides a gradual transition to the next stanza, offers a list of the commodities made available by a capitalist economy:

> The outdoor tea-table,
>   the mandolin-shaped big
>   and little fig,
> the silkworm-mulberry, the French mull dress with the Madeira-
>   vine-accompanied edge are,
>   when compared with what the colonists
> found here in tidewater Virginia, stark
>   luxuries. (110)

Perhaps this list is intended as an antithesis to the picture of the savage "red-skin" Moore identifies as "famous for his cruelty" in the preceding line. At any rate, the fact that the goods identified are both finished products ("tea-table," "French mull dress") and the raw materials provided by nature (the variously shaped figs and "the silkworm-mulberry") continues the parallel between nature and culture that appears throughout "Virginia Britannia."

Moore ticks off her inventory of luxury items against a historical background of stress and privation and a theological background of Puritanism. Against the setting of the New World wilderness, the items Moore identifies are shockingly anomalous. As she wrote in "Enough: *Jamestown, 1607–1957*,"

> No select
> artlessly perfect French effect
>
> mattered at first. (Don't speak in rhyme
> of maddened men in starving-time.) (186)

In a situation where survival became both an economic and a social priority, the culture of the tea table and the diversion of rhyming couplets had no place, while the social status signified by elegant haute couture would have been rendered absurd. Nevertheless, as Karen Ordahl Kupperman points out, for the English the "really important category was status" (2), and Moore's catalogue of such luxury items reflects this fact.

On the other hand, the luxury embodied and signified by the delicate and presumably expensive commodities represented a chief evil to the Puritan sensibility of the later colonists who made their historic beachhead further north. From the Puritan point of view, luxury is for the idle, and the refusal to work is a moral failure. Moreover, in its archaic sense as "lustful," luxury is equally anathema to the Puritan. The sensuous allure associated with "the soft fine sheer . . . silk fabric" ("Mull") of "the French mull dress" neatly embodies both meanings. From a Puritan perspective, the "Madeira- / vine-accompanied edge" of that dress only adds insult to injury by ornamenting fine clothing with a lacy border expressing an ungoverned fancy, while the syntactic proximity of "mull," "Madeira," and "vine" conjure, in a more ghostly way, the mulled wine named Madeira.

In addition, the arboreal imagery of the closing stanza figures the generation of a hybrid culture in the New World as a "grafting" of an English sprig onto native trees. As the sun of the poem sets, it becomes impossible to differentiate the native live oak and cypress from "the now aged English hackberry," for the advancing darkness of the evening assimilates all figures to itself so that they are "part of the ground" (111). That ground is a thorough hybrid of English colonists and indigenous Americans.

It is also formed of mull, or a "friable forest humus that forms a layer of mixed organic matter and mineral soil and merges gradually into the mineral soil underneath." The "mull dress" of this ground is present even as it disintegrates—a resonant, at first translucent, film whose opacity gradually increases as it falls to formless dust before the withering breath of the living. This film is the specter of Jamestown's past inhabitants, both Indian and English. In a turn of phrase that becomes elegiac, the English and Indian forebears Moore has described in her poem are "become with lost identity, / part of the ground." Those ancestral Europeans and Amerindians are now part of the ground as "mull," or crumbly loam, returned to the ground as matter to be recycled. (Moore's use of this trope echoes Whitman's in "The Compost" and many sections of "Song of Myself"). In the course of its ritual remembering, Moore's poem resurrects dead progenitors in order to reckon with the conflicts and benefits they bequeathed. In this sense, Moore's poem emerges as a dramatic struggle between past and present. The object of the poem is not merely to celebrate the origin of the nation, but to analyze and judge it from the perspective of the present. The speaker is a patriot, but she is a searching, prophetic patriot who makes great demands on her nation.

The fusion of the natural and "artificial" in "Virginia Britannia" reaches its climax in the last stanza. Moore imagines the boughs of one tree as an intricate filigree and the imposing stature of another as an etching:

> The live oak's darkening filigree
>   of undulating boughs, the etched
> solidity of a cypress indivisible
>   from the now agèd English hackberry. . . . (111)

Such imagery appears as the culmination of the interplay between nature and culture that shapes and unifies "Virginia Britannia." The spare and haunting beauty of the trees, for example, is "leaf-chiseled." In the poem's final movement, however, nature rises higher than "the town's assertiveness." Despite the intermingling of human culture and natural processes throughout "Virginia Britannia," Moore takes pains to celebrate the dominion of nature in this final stanza. While I have been pointing out the interpenetrations of culture and nature in the poem, I have also tried to show that Moore's poem represents culture as dependent upon nature. This dependency is based on a more expansive view of nature than is normally held, and the point of the interchange between nature and culture is to redefine both terms in a way that acknowledges their connections. The hybridity of peoples in the nation that would become the United States corresponds to the hybridity of nature and culture revealed in the poem's transfiguring synthesis of the two. In the concluding lines Moore asks her reader to recognize that, in its sweep and power, natural history encompasses human history. In the silent ground of nature, all human striving is subsumed, and the miniature grandeur of the "dwarf box- / bordered pansies" (108) that gave way before the encroaching pavements of human culture in the fifth stanza are transfigured into expansive "clouds" that "dwarf" both the town they tower over and the "arrogance" of its assertiveness.

The political ramifications of the poem's synthesis of nature and culture derive from the two corresponding dialectics, one between past event and present memory, and the other between English conquerors and the Indians and Africans they dominated. If Moore celebrates the dominion of the New World's nature over the concomitant culture of the nation established there, she does so in order to establish a criterion by which to judge the past and assess its meaning from the perspective of the present. In her effort to plumb the past, Moore pays scrupulous attention to the particular qualities of the landscape it bequeaths. This landscape is both the physical site of Jamestown and the figurative topography of the nation and its history—a landscape fraught with both conflict and possibility. Molesworth and Monroe both point out Moore's oblique reference to the national motto of *"E Pluribus Unum"* in her deriving of one tree from many (Molesworth 287), and Monroe further observes that "the word *indivisible* recalls the 'Pledge of Allegiance,'" in which the United States is described as "one nation . . . indivisible. The many diverse elements of the American scene, original and imported, will, it is hoped, unite in an integrated whole" (76). It is such integrity—in aesthetics and morals alike—that Moore aims at in "Virginia Britannia." After the manner of a prophet, she presents her picture of the nation's origins as an example and a warning to her contemporaries. Moore's excavation of the past allows her to enunciate a view of the world and her nation's place within it, providing the occasion for her to work out her thoughts about the past and to hone her poetic skills, and thereby give voice to the inarticulate experience of her nation described by Frank in *Our America.*

• Whereas "Virginia Britannia" commemorates the poet's personal visit to Jamestown, "Enough: *Jamestown, 1607–1957"* celebrates the 350th anniversary of its founding. Moore undertakes to retell the story of the foundation of her country and provides a variation on themes she previously addressed. The poem was written in response to a commission by the *Virginia Quarterly Review* (Hall 161). While this might suggest that Moore's treatment of the topic was merely fortuitous, the fact that she was asked to write on the occasion of the Jamestown anniversary indicates her stature as a public figure. Moore's celebrity by the time she came to write "Enough" insured a familiarity with her penchant for colonial costume, a penchant on which the commission may even have been partly based.

In the context of her renown, Moore's return to the theme of her nation's origin, her habit of wearing the colonial hat and cape, and her conscious decision to retain both "Virginia Britannia" and "Enough" in her *Complete Poems* ("Omissions are not accidents") together indicate the central role played by her nation's history in her sense of herself as a poet. If the earlier "Virginia Britannia" is longer, more ambitious, and more accomplished than "Enough," both poems nonetheless function as part of Moore's "tale of the tribe," her own versions of her nation's epic career. Both early and late, Moore was exploring her national and poetic origins, reviving by revising

them. Though not as long as Pound's *Cantos*, Williams's *Paterson*, or Whit-
man's *Leaves of Grass*, Moore's repeated treatment of the American theme
shows that she, like them, was also devoted to a lifelong poetic project in
honor of her country's culture.

As in "Virginia Britannia," an implicit assumption of "Enough" is a shared
national experience on the part of her audience. Given its context in the Mc-
Carthyite 1950s, Moore pulls off a fine balance of patriotism and sly,
prophetic wit in her poem. However anticommunist it may be, the perspec-
tive of Moore's narrator is a communal one, and she appeals to the sympa-
thetic power of her audience to identify with the experiences of the colonists
and the famous Englishmen she names. In addition, however, she also ac-
knowledges the humiliation imposed upon the Indians by the English when
she refers to "Poor Powhatan" as an "embittered man."

In contrast to the "doomed communism" of their origins, the Jamestown
colonists excelled when granted loans and their own land: "Three acres each,
initiative, / six bushels paid back, they could live" (185). This self-reliance is
of course a thoroughly American virtue. Instead of merely falling in line with
the conventional paean to a state, however, Moore's sometimes quirky cou-
plets question the credibility of grade-school myths about the founding of
the nation. Her rhyming couplets generate an expectation of a traditional
treatment of her topic, but the actual substance of the lines often critically
scrutinizes this topic. The "pests and pestilence" and the vast numbers of
dead that confronted later visitors to the colony are not presented simply as
heroic challenges to be overcome by the invincible will of proud pioneers.
Nor does she gloss over the English injustices against the Indians. She
points out the desperation of the early settlement when she alludes to the
cannibalism that occurred there. Given the European penchant to project
such cannibalism onto indigenous Americans and Africans (the word *canni-
bal* is itself thought to be a corruption of *Carib*), Moore's reference to a real
instance of European cannibalism suggests that such projection reflects the
fear that Europeans were themselves capable of such behavior. It also helps
correct the historical inaccuracy of early European descriptions of
Amerindian social practices.

In an odd assortment of factors contributing to the progress of the colony,
Moore conveys the economic and political conflicts at work in the early days
of the colony:

> Marriage, tobacco, and slavery,
> initiated liberty
>
> when the Deliverance brought seed
> of that now controversial weed—
>
> a blameless plant-Red-Ridinghood.
> Blameless, but who knows what is good? (186)

Moore's identification of "Marriage, tobacco, and slavery" as the institutions out of which liberty evolved vividly recasts traditional views about the genesis of American democracy; her rhyming of "slavery" and "liberty" is stark and telling. The paratactic grouping of the three nouns suggests they are parallel, showing both that these factors jointly contributed to the survival of Jamestown and that oppressive social practices coexisted with early American "liberty."

The inclusion of marriage in this triad of forces recalls Moore's poem "Marriage" and her arch treatment of that institution in it. The circumspect misgivings expressed by the speaker about marriage and her humorous representations of it offer a set of provocative glosses on the term as it appears in "Enough." In "Marriage," the speaker's tentative identification of marriage as an "enterprise" fits in well with the meaning of the other two terms of the line from "Enough," for tobacco and slavery were certainly enterprises central to the economy of Jamestown and subsequent colonies.

By alluding to the hardships of the original colonists—the "maddened men in starving-time" and their "unnatural" cannibalism—and by arranging such references so that they immediately precede her identification of the socioeconomic practices that supported Jamestown, Moore reveals that the evils of slavery and the social inequalities of marriage in the seventeenth century provided the colonial remedy to its needs. She shows that the political and economic organization of the colony were constituted by antidemocratic forces, and she implicitly argues that the anniversary of Jamestown's foundation provides an appropriate occasion for considering the shortcomings as well as the achievements of American democracy.

Moore's ironic triad of "Marriage, tobacco, and slavery" strikes one as entirely inimical to the principle of "liberty," not only because marriage may seem out of place in that triad but also because the poem has already represented the political character of marriage in its allusion to the alliance between Pocahontas and John Rolfe. The poem's second reference to marriage revisits the political and cultural complications surrounding that alliance. Moore recounts Powhatan's capitulation in response to the kidnapping of his daughter, showing that the military conflict between the English and Amerindians provides an important context for understanding the union between Pocahontas and Rolfe. Moore combats the romantic legend surrounding their union by drawing attention to the acculturation of Pocahontas through education—a process she calls an "insidious recourse." The cultural indoctrination of the chieftain's daughter has predictable enough results: the English "teaching" and "enhancing" of Pocahontas, the poet tartly observes, "flowered of course / in marriage" (185). In this way, "Enough" engages the two meanings of *settlement* outlined in my introduction, as the founding of a colony and as the coming to terms with an alien group; the poem overtly commemorates the establishment of Jamestown by remembering two sets of negotiations that implemented it.

In the first settlement, "Poor Powhatan / was forced to make peace" but remained "embittered" by the conflict with the English, while in the second, his daughter Pocahontas marries John Rolfe. As Cristanne Miller points out:

both contracts have to do with imperialistic altering of power relations. Although Moore implies that Pocahontas, unlike her father, finds at least minimal satisfaction— her new life is "not too tame"—the word "tame" suggests the more ominous "tamed" so strongly that it is hard not to regret her change as much as that of her "poor" royal father. (*Authority* 150)

Moore's irony is compounded later in the poem when she describes the earliest English settlement as "the site that did not flower" (Miller, *Authority* 151). The successful and failed flowerings of "Enough" recall the floral imagery that also permeates "Virginia Britannia." When Moore emphasizes the vulnerability of the colonists' "feeble tower," she echoes her view that cosmic processes "dwarf" human "arrogance" and "assertiveness," physically overcoming and spiritually humbling them. If the tone of "Enough" is perhaps more celebratory than that of "Virginia," its floral vocabulary serves as a caution against the excessive pride of an unexamined patriotism. In her careful coordination of her floral diction with her uncomplimentary narrative of "Marriage, tobacco, and slavery," Moore creates a public poem that conscientiously works against the dangers of blind nationalism. In its more modest way, "Enough," like "Virginia," also counters human history with natural history. The earlier poem on Jamestown resonates within the text of the later one.

Moreover, the poem reflects the skeptical temper of modernism when it asks, "who knows what is good?" Moore's comic characterization of tobacco as "that now controversial weed" gives way to a more ambiguous and interrogatory gloss when she refers to tobacco as "a blameless plant-Red-Ridinghood." "Blameless" reinforces the sense of innocence evoked by the reference to the child heroine, but the hesitant repetition of that adjective in the subsequent line of the couplet turns the assertion of innocence into a question, reminding the reader of the predatory wolf in the Red Ridinghood tale and hinting at tobacco's latent dangers. In asking "who knows what is good?" Moore openly wonders about the simple moral certitude and political stability that came to surround the history of the colony and its memorialized site.

The couplet that follows Moore's searching question expands the irony of the poem by referring to the cargo of fool's gold that the colonists sent back to England. The couplet characterizes the Jamestown venture as an episode of human folly: "The victims of a search for gold / cast yellow soil into the hold." Even though the speaker dismisses communism earlier in the poem, here she criticizes the European greed for gold as self-destructive. The same social and political beliefs that gave rise to "Marriage, tobacco, and slavery" also made the quest for gold a high priority among the colonists.

The financial motivations behind the Jamestown enterprise—which was the capital venture of an English joint-stock company—provide an intelligible rationale for the cultivation of a cash crop like tobacco instead of staple food crops. In their effort to realize profit from the labor-intensive production of tobacco, planters introduced slave labor. And like the enhancement that the suitably reeducated Pocahontas offered John Rolfe, legally recognized marriages to white women advanced the material and political interests of colonial patriarchs. Moore's simple list ("Marriage, tobacco, and slavery") evokes a network of undemocratic social relations that underwrote the foundation of the United States. The marital, agricultural, and economic practices of the colonists all reflect the social conflict and inequity of their time, and Moore's reference to these practices bears on her contemporary moment by identifying such inequities as the legacy of the colonists. Moore closes her poem with an expression of conditional optimism that does not forget the ironies of her republic's colonial origins:

> It was enough; it is enough
> if present faith mend partial proof. (187)

The last line indicates Moore's perspective that America's democratic project remains incomplete and needs to be not only defended but also better fulfilled. The nation's settlements are, in other words, continuous rather than definitive. Although the poem ends on a hopeful note, its view of the sufficiency of the nation as an ongoing enterprise is not unmitigated. The proof she finds is only partial—in both senses of the word. The delicate interplay of faith and proof is what makes history vital for Moore in this poem. The judgment that the unlikely beginnings at Jamestown were "enough" shows that those beginnings were satisfactory but not superior. The moral and democratic excellence Moore seeks for her nation is a hopeful but realistic goal; it recognizes the shortcomings and conflicts of the past and their bearing upon the present. Moore's note to this poem explains the occasion of "Enough":

> On May 13, 1957—the 350th anniversary of the landing at Jamestown of the first permanent English settlers in North America—three United States Air Force super sabre jets flew non-stop from London to Virginia. They were the Discovery, the Godspeed, and the Susan Constant—christened respectively by Lady Churchill, by Mrs. Whitney (wife of the Ambassador John Hay Whitney), and by Mrs. W. S. Morrison (wife of the speaker of the House of Commons). (292)

Like Frost's "The Gift Outright" and "Immigrants," "Enough" is a reenactment of the nation's initial pilgrimage from England to America. It commemorates the nation's origins by reliving the quest to colonize it.

Through her suggestive juxtaposition of "Marriage, tobacco, and slavery," her rhyming of "slavery" with "liberty," and her moral questioning throughout the poem, Moore satirizes the politically sanitized versions of American liberty that have proliferated since the foundation of the United States. Instead of simply praising the efforts of the forefathers as one might expect in a commissioned poem, she makes the celebration of the Jamestown anniversary an occasion for serious historical meditation. In recounting the events associated with the colony's foundation and survival, Moore raises engaging intellectual and moral questions about the nature of American democracy.

- Whereas "Virginia Britannia" and "Enough" focus on New World settings, "England" begins in the nation's traditional motherland and travels effortlessly from one cultural capital to the next in order to defend the viability of modern American culture, albeit in an understated and modest manner. The poem opens with an affectionate description of the "Old Dominion" that paradoxically diminishes the object of its homage. The substance of this characterization is as casual as its lineation, which distributes its significant nouns in its title and its first two lines:

ENGLAND

with its baby rivers and little towns, each with its abbey or its cathedral,
with voices—one voice perhaps, echoing through the transept—the
criterion of suitability and convenience . . . (46)

England may be the motherland, but Moore belittles it in the breezy prepositional phrase she uses to modify it in the opening lines of the poem, designating it as a land of "*baby* rivers and *little* towns." While her sketch of the nation moves beyond such "diminutions," the initial impression is one of patronizing condescension toward a culture whose decorum ("the criterion of suitability and convenience") does not prevent it from being dwarfed by the geographic majesty of the United States, with its continental sprawl and abundant natural resources. Although the undercurrent of rebellion—of taking away with one hand what is offered as a tribute with the other—should not be overemphasized, since the tone of the poem is modest, generous, and complimentary throughout, the ambiguity of the lines prepares the way for the poet's later remonstrations with her silent interlocutor regarding the cultural possibilities of her no longer nascent nation.

Moore's review in "England" of great cultural centers includes not only Western sites such as Greece and Italy, England and France, but China and Egypt as well. Indeed, in the "emotional / shorthand" of the poem, these centers, together with the reference to "the Hebrew language," stand for the cultural accomplishments of Eastern civilization. Despite Moore's tentative concession that America is a place of privation (without social structures, carefully kept lawns and gardens, or a literary language), her rhetorical questions in subsequent stanzas imply not simply that "appearances are deceiving" but that the beauty and finish—the skill and the wisdom that characterize the cultural riches of the various civilizations she identifies—could come to fruition in her own country. Instead of being the poor younger cousin to older, greater nations, America might be the land best suited to benefit from "all that noted superiority" adumbrated in the poem. As a nation of many peoples with many origins in other lands, it could reasonably be expected that America, like the Old World, could play host to the hieratic knowledge and disparate whimsy Moore designates in her references to "The sublimated wisdom of China, Egyptian discernment, / the cataclysmic torrent of emotion / compressed in the verbs of the Hebrew language" and to "the books" of Izaak Walton. The restless journeys of immigrants from so many lands is a specific demonstration of Moore's closing claim that creative play or insight "has never been confined to one locality." The civilizations she names throughout the poem may all contribute to her own nation's culture, so that America turns out to be far less "linksless" than it had originally seemed.[12]

Moore's reference to America as "the wild man's land, grassless, linksless, languageless country" conjures a stereotypical picture of native "savages" and disheveled pioneers with no time for or interest in the refinements of high culture. Yet "wild man's land" also evokes Whitman's poetic pose as "one of the roughs." The phrase sounds out his "barbaric yawp" once more, in a "lady's" modest voice perhaps, but insistently and for a new century. "Grassless" counters the Whitmanian note of "wild man's land," since Whitman explicitly identified his *Leaves of Grass* as a metonymy for his poetic legacy. It may also refer to the environmental degradation caused by reckless commerce and heavy industry. Finally, "linksless" presents America as a completely new place and acknowledges America's separation from European culture and history. The word suggests both America's cultural promise and its predicament. The poet's nation is at once profoundly independent of previous cultures and, by virtue of that very independence, in danger of not producing art. It needs some cultural orientation, some generative sense of tradition from which it may bring such art into being. The nation is both free from stifling inhibitions and yet without a proper heritage. Here "wild man" is positive in the way that Williams's "savages" are Romantic heroes, whereas (as we have seen) the wild man of "Hercules" earns the poet's censure for failing to restrain himself and permitting a bestial prejudice to govern his behavior.

In a way that is congruent with the tone and situation of "Virginia Britannia" and "The Labors of Hercules," two early poems by Moore also enunciate American themes in a critical manner. These poems, which both appear in *Observations* and in the *Selected Poems* of 1935 but not in *The Complete Poems,* represent American scenes in a biblical context. "Is Your Town Nineveh?" includes a glimpse of "the Statue of Liberty" in a setting that mixes the story of the reluctant prophet Jonah with a modern attempt to achieve personal freedom. "The Bricks Are Fallen Down, We Will Build with Hewn Stones. The Sycamores Are Cut Down, We Will Change to Cedars" combines the prophet Isaiah's invective against a misguided Israel with the democratic rhetoric of America ("inalienable energy"). While the language of the second poem (with its plural pronoun "we") is communal and public, that of the first (with its more intimate "You" and "I") suggests a private setting. In "Nineveh," the speaker may even be involved in a complex debate with herself, whereas in "The Bricks Are Fallen" the speaker clearly addresses herself to a separate, unsympathetic audience. These poems as well as the others discussed here show that issues of nationality appear both early and late in Moore's career.

Such poems also correspond to the sartorial performances Moore made famous in the latter stage of her career. If (as in Williams's formulation "no ideas but in things") word may embody world, then conversely, Moore's colonially capped and caped body wittily signifies her nation's republican discourse. Moore's habit of donning her George Washington habit later in life exemplifies another aspect of her performance of her country's meaning, reinforcing in a different but complementary way the mingled celebration and critique of her practice as a writer. According to Molesworth,

> Moore was sought after in the 1960's, it would appear, for her eccentricity and even her incongruous dignity. . . . The new mix of celebrities from politics, entertainment, sports, and culture originated in large measure from the demands and mechanics of the visual media, especially television. Moore's sense of the importance of the visual, as a measure of accuracy, sincerity, even moral probity, was now to be located—if not totally misappropriated—in an altogether different context. Her sense of the visual had, of course, been extended to her own person, through her interest in fashion. So the "trademark" tricorn hat and cape, fastened at her neck with a silver dollar, was sometimes read as a "parody" of the founding fathers, George Washington in particular. Moore had an impish sense of humor and a satirical streak. However, she bought her first tricorne [*sic*] while still in college at Bryn Mawr, so it is unlikely that she first conceived her image as a parody of the father of her country. What does seem more likely is that her self-image had several elements in it: self-protectiveness, a genuine love for formal fashion, a sense of play, [and] a desire to have a public role. (431–32)

Moore's wearing of her hat and cape comport with her representations of American citizenship and civil virtue in "England," "The Student," "The Hero," "Virginia Britannia," and "Enough," as well as such later poems as "Like a Bulwark." Like the discourse of such poems, Moore's colonial hat communicated her commitment to American culture and the political ideals on which it is based. "The importance of its hat to a form," writes Wallace Stevens in "The Pastor Caballero," "becomes / More definite," for "The flare / In the sweeping brim becomes the origin / Of a human evocation," and a hat's "actual form bears outwardly this grace, / An image of the mind, an inward mate" (*Collected Poetry and Prose* 327–28). Moore evoked her nation's history not only in such public poems as "Enough," but also by sporting her tricorn. As she once observed in response to a questionnaire, "There is an integrity of performance," and this integrity extends from the texts of her poems to the text of her attire (*Prose* 593). A metaphor in "Idiosyncrasy and Technique" also suggests the relevance of Moore's playful fashion statement to her work as a writer: "An author . . . is a *fashioner* of words, [for he] stamps them with his own personality and *wears the raiment* he has made, in his own way" (*Prose* 515; emphasis added).

In "Like a Bulwark," Moore brings her linguistic raiment into line with her famous costume, for in it one can see the imaginative adaptation of patriotic symbols for poetic ends. Her reference to "Old Glory" in the final line of "Like a Bulwark" brings to mind the poet's colonial clothes. The bulwark of the title is both a fortifying rampart of defense and the curving upper wall that forms the powerful prow of a ship. As both wall and part of a ship, the bulwark of the poem not only protects but also forges ahead into newly imagined worlds. As the visible upper wall of a ship, it vividly embodies the vanguard of both poetry and patriotism. As wall, the bulwark delineates the boundary that defines the space of the nation. In these respects, the poem directly resonates with the efforts of Williams, Stevens, and others to create an authentic New World aesthetic.

Moore's poem is shaped by the threat of external forces upon the bulwark, a figure one might read as steadfast self, heroic poet, or dutiful soldier. In this regard, "Like a Bulwark" dramatizes the brave and faithful building of a staunch American character, echoing the heroic patience Moore praises in "The Hero." The poetics behind this and other lyrics by Moore is one of stalwart endurance in the face of a harsh adversity, an endurance figured in terms of patriotic pietàs. In the paradox of the poem's central metaphor, the imposing forces that press against the structure of the bulwark are the very forces that constitute its strength. The gravity that tugs the wall's parts downward ensures the "integrity" of the structure as a whole. The identifying banner of the successful self is the signature of the nation to which she belongs. Moore's use of the flag's traditional name invokes the democratic zeal for independence of the country's "founding fathers," the "spirit of '76" celebrated in the famous painting of that name. The phrase "Old Glory" also invests the military imagery with a religious significance that accords well with the stoic existentialism of the individual's battle "against fate," even as it echoes Moore's allusion in "Virginia Britannia" to the new republic's "undiffident first flag." The final line of "Like a Bulwark," "As though flying Old Glory full mast," praises the sailor's steadfast resistance to adversity by compounding Moore's wordplay on "lead-saluted," a phrase that suggests both the homage of a twenty-one-gun salute and the wartime danger of a hail of bullets. The poem expresses a straightforward patriotism, and the central image of the ship brings to mind Moore's brother's long service in the navy. "Like a Bulwark" stands as a fine example of Moore's concern with her nation's culture and morality from a somewhat later period in her career.

As critics have recognized, national matters figure in Moore's poetry throughout her career. The recurrence of this theme indicates its importance to her identity as a writer, and to the poetics she worked out for herself over the course of that career. In Costello's words:

> Moore's America is everywhere and nowhere because it is, like all her landscapes . . . a metaphor of the mind, and of the ultimate poem. The great American poem, for Moore, would be one in which a rich variety of experience would be imagined into a classic unity, a neatness of finish that would leave no stray particular. (252)

Moore's explorations of her nation's life and meaning in her poems and in her costumed, public person constitute her version of the poetic quest for Frank's "mystic Word" of America (10). While it is unique it nonetheless corresponds to the sense of the poem as a quest that Williams, Frost, Crane, and Hughes also shared. Like Moore's, their sense of their nation's origins and its poetics repeatedly merged in important ways in their work as writers.

Chapter 2

NATION AND ENUNCIATION IN THE WORK

OF WILLIAM CARLOS WILLIAMS

• William Carlos Williams registers his sense of both his poetry and his nation in performative terms. For him the poem is an imaginative act as much as it is a textual product. Because "words are the keys that unlock the mind," poems are actions as well as things. As the record of Williams's attempt to defend the view that modern American poetry must invent for itself a new mode of expression, "The Poem as a Field of Action" reveals his tendency to represent poetry as a conflict as well as a quest: "as loose, disassociated (linguistically), yawping speakers of a new language," he writes, Americans "are privileged . . . to sense and so to seek to discover the possible thing which is disturbing the metrical table of values—as unknown elements would disturb Mendelyeev's table of the periodicity of atomic weights and so lead to discoveries" (*Essays* 286). Williams underscores the performative quality of his poetics by emphasizing the spoken word as the source of poetic composition: "it is . . . in the mouths of the living," he writes, "that the language is changing and giving new means of expanded possibilities in literary expression" (*Essays* 291). Like Emerson, Williams believed that "Art is the path of the creator to his work" (Emerson 466).

I argue that Williams characterizes the poem as a vehicle of discovery in order to interpret the history and contemporary state of his nation. Since the process he espouses is improvisatory, the results of his interpretations of the United States are neither predictable nor monolithic. By troping his poems as sites of struggle, however, Williams points the way toward a reading of his work as both a record of national concerns and a representation of ongoing contests over how the nation's history should be written and interpreted. As James Knapp puts it, Williams believed "poems should not be smooth and synthesizing historical generalizations, but archaeological records, the accretion of materials which continue to preserve their mutual differences" (109–10). In "Asphodel, That Greeny Flower," moreover, Williams writes that

       It is difficult
to get the news from poems
       yet men die miserably every day
             for lack
of what is found there.

He suggests not only that something different from "the news" exists in poems, but also that poems offer a figurative form of news that competes with the headlines and rhetoric of the press and radio (*Collected Poems* 2: 318).[1] Williams presents his poetry not only as an alternative to "the news," but also as a rival to familiar but inadequate accounts of the nation and its history.

• "Apology," a lyric that appears in *Al Que Quiere!* (which Williams originally wanted to subtitle "The Pleasures of Democracy"), provides an early example of Williams's concern with the intersection of speech and community. A glimpse of the speaker's fellow citizens prompts him to write a poem:

Why do I write today?

The beauty of
the terrible faces
of our nonentities
stirs me to it:

colored women
day workers—
old and experienced—
returning home at dusk
in cast off clothing
faces like
old Florentine oak.

Also

the set pieces
of your faces stir me—
leading citizens—
but not
in the same way. (*CP* 1: 70)

The poet responds to the "terrible faces" of the working women and to the countenances of the city's leading citizens. Williams declines to say what particular emotions either the colored women or the leading citizens "stir" in him, although it is clear that he feels a sympathy for the hard work and humanity of the women and finds in their faces a peculiar beauty to admire. The leading citizens, on the other hand, seem to stir a combination of indignation and anger at their settled complacency and pride, but since the speaker does not explicitly say so, the feelings they inspire may be more mixed. The last line is the punch line to Williams's joking swipe at his bourgeois leading citizens and a sly assertion that the particularities of "difference" (whether based on class, race, gender, or language itself) generally elude system and speech.

It is clear, at any rate, that the reason for the writing lies in the poet's perception of "the terrible faces / of our nonentities." The experience of such laborers, of women, of "colored" people generally, too often goes untold, and the speaker of the poem wants to record it and honor it. He seeks to show that these people are not at all "nonentities" in the life of the nation and its history. Giving the word a satiric spin, Williams patiently registers the fact of their existence, pulling the word inside out to reveal that they actually are entities, or individuals whose worth belies the social order that nullifies them. Their weary faces are "terrible," for they evoke in the speaker a sense of awe and dread—awe because of the beauty and endurance these women show in dealing with their trying circumstances, and dread because of the injustice "our" nation systematically imposes upon them. Their labor contributes to the commonwealth, and their experience makes them beautiful. Williams's poem tells a story about people who remain "nonentities" from the point of view of "leading citizens"; it calls attention to aspects of the lives of his countrywomen that "the news" fails to register.

In its transformation of "nonentities" into the opposite, "Apology" enacts something instead of merely "saying" something, bringing a record of cherished people into being by virtue of its linguistic performance. The poem's communal "our" aligns the speaker with the dispossessed and overlooked citizenry of his town and, by extension, with his nation. The ambiguous syntax of "The terrible faces / of our nonentities" may signify, moreover, not only a communal reference to the black women as politically and socially insignificant, but also the psychic nihilism perceived by the speaker in the faces of *all* his townspeople, including the town's "leading citizens." Although the poet's effort to speak for others in "Apology" risks being presumptuous, it also reflects Williams's honest attempt to present a fuller, more democratic picture of the world than the one presented in the news. Through its wordplay on "nonentities," the poem embodies Williams's sense of the relational nature of identity and national affiliation, for the social unimportance of the "colored women" arbitrates, or structures, the speaker's experience of personal and communal identity. In this way, "Apology" prefers the republican over the imperial heritage of the United States.

"Apology" offers a rationale for the poet's work of enunciation. It is Williams's brief defense of his poetry, for in it he wants to bring the meaning of his fellow citizens' lives into the definite shape of clear and resonant syllables. The narrator's miniature soliloquy in Williams's *A Voyage to Pagany*, it turns out, applies to all Americans: "What is the place of my birth? The place of my birth is the place where the word begins" (116). The claim suggests that Williams conceives his task as poet and citizen to be a continuous working out of the appropriate word within a constantly unfolding field of words. For Williams, articulation as communication is grounded in articulation as a composing of the self. His pregnant question and answer suggest that language is as central to social reality as it is to epistemology, an insight that figures "being" as a process, or to put it another way, as a present participle rather than a gerund. If in other contexts Williams expresses doubts about the scope and sufficiency of his singular word, he also demonstrates such moments of enthusiasm and confidence in enunciating it on behalf of his fellow citizens. While he recognizes the discrepancy between word and referent, he continues to strive for a poetic idiom that accurately represents his nation's many cultures.

In "The Postcolonial and the Postmodern," Homi Bhabha provides a helpful way of considering Williams's emphasis on articulation. In this essay Bhabha opposes epistemology to enunciation in order to "provide a process by which objectified others may be turned into subjects of their history and experience" (178). If "culture as epistemology focuses on function and intention," Bhabha argues, "then culture as enunciation focuses on signification and institutionalization" (177). Bhabha's sense of culture as both context and process corresponds to Williams's view, in "The American Background," of culture as action rather than artifact. "The burning need of a culture," Williams writes,

> is not a choice to be made or not made, voluntarily. . . . It has to be where it arises, or everything related to the life there ceases. It isn't a thing: it's an act. If it stands still, it is dead. It is the realization of the qualities of a place in relation to the life which occupies it; embracing everything involved, climate, geographic position, relative size, history, other cultures—as well as the character of its sands, flowers, minerals and the condition of knowledge within its borders. It is the act of lifting these things into an ordered and utilized whole which is culture. It isn't something left over afterward. That is the record only. The act is the thing. (*Essays* 157)

For Williams, a truly imaginative response to the world reconfigures it. "Williams's poems at their best," David Ferry writes, "are the sort of acts which he describes" (143). Such acts remake both his and his readers' sense of the world, and when the nation is the subject of his poems, Williams reshapes and often challenges received notions about it.

• In one section of "Asphodel," Williams adopts a persona like that of his eponymous giant, Paterson. The speaker of "Asphodel" is an individual man but also a composite figure who (like the speaker of "Song of Myself") "contain[s] multitudes." By claiming a concern with Columbus's voyage to the New World and by addressing the national and global concerns posed by the atomic bomb, the trial of the Rosenbergs, and the drilling for oil (which he figures as a wound to his own body), Williams adopts a mythic persona in order not only to express the way the public concerns of his time affect him personally, but also to insist that "the news" embodied in poems satisfies a profound cultural need that his nation must acknowledge. He conceives of the poet as both patient and agent, as someone who is formed by his culture and who acts as an influence upon it. Williams argues that poems provide something that is of cultural moment to the "imagined community" of the nation (*CP* 2: 318), a social unit that, according to Benedict Anderson, was historically shaped by the development of the newspaper. In Anderson's view, the newspaper has promoted the modern citizen's sense of national community: "the newspaper reader, observing exact replicas of his own paper being consumed by his subway, barbershop, or residential neighbours, is continually reassured that the imagined world is visibly rooted in everyday life" (35–36). Through reading about otherwise remote events and people in newspapers, individuals begin to see themselves and their neighbors as citizens who belong to a society far larger than any they can directly experience. In effect, the act of reading the newspaper makes the reader a citizen, or at least reinforces his or her sense of being one, for the political and social events reported in it give the reader a feeling of participation in the civic life of an otherwise abstract social unit. The "very conception of the newspaper," Anderson writes, "implies the refraction of even 'world events' into a specific imagined world of vernacular readers" (63).

If the newspaper—or any of the other forms of modern news media—instills a sense of the national on the part of its audience, Williams conceives of his poetry as a medium that rivals the cultural work of the newspaper by satisfying needs that the news cannot. Williams articulates the competition between his writing and that of history and journalism by explicitly referring throughout his work to events of national and historical importance. In *American Grain*, for example, he meditates on various episodes from American history in order to sort out a viable tradition from others that in his view threaten the health of his country's culture, while in a series of early poems (a group that includes "Apology") addressed to his "townspeople," he considers issues relating to an immediate community that may be interpreted as a synecdoche for the nation as a whole. Other poems addressing national matters that will be discussed in this chapter include "Poem" ("Daniel Boone, the father of Kentucky"), "Dedication for a Plot of Ground," "Pastoral" ("When I Was Younger"), "The Forgotten City," "It Is a Living Coral," "Elsie," "Navajo," "Graph," "The Testament of Perpetual Change," and *Paterson*. By conceiving of his work as an alternative to the news, Williams invites his readers to consider the account of his nation and its history that emerges in his writing. By representing his work as a rival source of information about his country, Williams indicates that a discrepancy exists among received notions of the nation's history and the varied experience of its many local communities.

• Williams demonstrates one of the ways his poems offer contested or unexpected representations of national history in "Poem" ("Daniel Boone . . ."). In this piece, he offers a list of heroes for his readers to contemplate. The text makes an appropriate companion piece to *American Grain* because of its opening reference to "Daniel Boone," the subject of one of the book's chapters:

Daniel Boone, the father of Kentucky. Col. W. Crawford, the martyr to Indian re-
venge. Simon Gerty, the White Savage. Molly Finney, the beautiful Canadian
Captive. Majors Samuel and John McCullough, patriots and frontiersmen. Lewis
Wetzel, the Indian killer. Simon Kenton, the intrepid pioneer. Gen. George R.
Clark, that heroic conqueror. Capt. Brady, the great Indian fighter. Davy Crock-
ett, the hero of the Alamo. Gen. Sam Houston, the liberator of the Lone Star
State. Kit Carson, the celebrated plainsmen and explorer. Gen. Custer, the hero
of Little Big Horn. Buffalo Bill, the tireless rider, hunter and scout. Wild Bill, the
lightning marksman. California Joe, the scout. Texas Jack, the government scout
and hunter. Captain Jack, the poet scout. Gen. Crook, the conqueror of the
Apaches. (*CP* 1: 259)

In "Poem" Williams dares his reader to accept his simple list of names and ep-
ithets as a poem—a typical gesture that does more than reconfigure the cate-
gories of prose and poetry. The title is just as provocative, for it asks readers to
interpret the litany, formatted like a memorial plaque covered with the
names of dead veterans, in elegiac terms. In no formal respect is the text dis-
tinguishable from prose. But as Williams argued in *Spring and All,* prose and
poetry are to be distinguished by their relation to emotion rather than by
their visible form: "prose has to do with the fact of an emotion; poetry has to
do with the dynamization of emotion into a separate form" (*CP* 1: 219).
Williams invites his readers to experience his poem in a new context, to as-
sess it according to the imaginative field in which it was composed rather
than as a mere assemblage of names. "Poem" literalizes Walt Whitman's
claim in the Preface to the 1855 edition of *Leaves of Grass* that "the United
States themselves are essentially the greatest poem" (5).

In its references to Daniel Boone, General George R. Clark, and a host of
"Indian killers," "Poem" alludes to a host of pioneers who expanded the
boundaries of the United States. Boone opened the first road to Kentucky,
while Clark was instrumental in establishing American power over the region
that became known as the Northwest Territory. In this respect Williams's text
commemorates the expansion of the early nation and celebrates the violence,
curiosity, and wildness of American frontiersmen and soldiers. On the face of
it, "Poem" appears to commemorate its list of soldiers, hunters, and cowboys
in order to celebrate the American initiative and independence that verge on
anarchy, as the references to "Simon Gerty, the White Savage," and "Wild
Bill" Hickok suggest.

In other respects, however, "Poem" may be poking fun at the traditions it
evokes. At times, "Poem" reads like a list of dime-novel characters ("Califor-
nia Joe," "Texas Jack," "Captain Jack"). Long before Williams wrote his poem,
the series of pamphlets describing the adventures of Davy Crockett that had
been published during the pioneer's lifetime had already made Crockett, Kit
Carson, and Boone into legendary, quasi-mythical figures. "Poem" evokes the
folklore and romance surrounding these men as much as it does the historical
events in which they participated. Together with the wry title, moreover,

Williams's evocation of frontier mythology reflects an awareness of the rhetorical mediations of his names and the histories he intends them to signify. "Poem" flaunts its rhetoricity to such an extent that one may be forgiven for taking its rousing language with a grain of salt. The romantic rhetoric Williams employs in his reference to "Molly Finney, the beautiful Canadian Captive," is similarly secondhand, so it is impossible to determine the tone of the reference in any definitive way. If Williams means to celebrate the heroism of Daniel Boone, he must also confront his belatedness with respect to Byron's treatment of the legendary hero in *Don Juan* and with respect to early mythic treatments of several figures his "Poem" names.

By foregrounding the rhetorical quality of his language through the provocative, possibly ironic title ("this is a poem, even though it might not look like one") and through his deadpan quotation of traditional epithets ("the father of Kentucky," "the Indian killer," "the intrepid pioneer," "that heroic pioneer"), Williams may be parodying the blandness of routine public discourse. If Williams's text makes the artistic claim that some forms of prose ought to be considered as "poems," it also questions the history represented by the figures it identifies and the public vocabulary in which it is couched. Whether "Poem" criticizes or celebrates such rhetoric, however, is unclear. It may in fact do both at the same time.

For all its experimental parody, for example, the poem initially appears somewhat conventional in its imitation of odes to American forefathers, offering as it does a résumé of rugged individuals committed to the expansion and defense of their republic. Except for the single female ("Molly Finney," who is a "Captive"), all the figures named in the poem are energetic men. In addition, most of the epithets applied to them refer to some military deed. As a bare list of names and deeds, "Poem" apparently aims to impress its reader with the character of the men who contributed to the building of the nation, especially by subduing Indians. Williams offers the names of such men as examples of the American spirit in a way that echoes *American Grain* (which includes chapters on Sam Houston as well as Daniel Boone). In this regard, "Poem" seems to champion the American culture described by Williams in "The American Background" and *American Grain*. Nevertheless, "Poem" can be read as a parody as much as a sincere elegy. Williams presents an Emersonian series of Representative Men, but his drastic reduction of the text to mere name and deed suggests either that the name itself suffices to convey the inspiration a good citizen is supposed to feel when he or she learns the relevant stories of each man, or that it flatly fails to do so. Williams imputes an almost magical potency to these names, for in the form of the various epithets, even actions are turned into substantives ("killer," "conqueror," "explorer," "rider," "hunter").

The potency of such names and noun-phrases derives from their cultural contexts. "Poem" depends on the meaning of the myths embodied in the figures it represents, but since some of the names are obscure, the scant information given about their deeds fails to bring them alive for the reader. Because Williams's "Poem" may be read ironically just as easily as it may be taken "straight," it ultimately avoids (like Cortez in "The Destruction of Tenochtitlan") the simple categories of praise or blame. Williams's disruptive parody of generic conventions in "Poem" renders a black-and-white moral dichotomy inadequate. By virtue of its ambiguity "Poem" reconceives the sweep of American history in such a way as to provide a meaningful alternative to familiar myths of American development. It raises as many questions about America, its history, and its heroes as it resolves.

In the same way, moreover, the potentially parodic qualities of "Poem" may satirize the pomp and circumstance associated with the public elegy. While Williams's list includes a number of unfamiliar names, it also includes names of legendary figures so famous that many if not most Americans would immediately recognize them: Daniel Boone, Davy Crockett, Sam Houston, Kit Carson, George Custer, Buffalo Bill, and Wild Bill Hickok. Williams depends on his reader's familiarity with these names to situate the poem in the context of the American frontier; in this respect his poem evidently projects a specifically American audience. Williams's references to "Captain Jack, the poet scout," "Buffalo Bill," and "Wild Bill" may also be theatrical renditions of himself, as if to suggest that he is not above the joke he may be making on the bourgeois ceremonies of commemoration that reinforce American patriotism in a tradition-bound, "pedagogical" manner, or that he, like Whitman before him, sounds his "barbaric yawp" over the rooftops of his genteel neighbors. The fact that Williams also closes his poem with a military "Crook," who was "the conqueror of the Apaches," further suggests that "Poem" may well be satirizing as much as celebrating the wild vivacity of its characters.

If "Poem" simultaneously celebrates and criticizes the public rhetoric that it flaunts, a better-known poem by Williams provides a personal perspective on the complex variety within U.S. history. "Dedication for a Plot of Ground," an homage to the poet's maternal grandmother, may be read as a "feminine" version of the pilgrimage to the New World and of Williams's mostly masculine catalogue in "Poem." From this perspective, "Dedication" represents American history as more varied than the pedagogical accounts of the nation often rendered in grade-school textbooks. Whereas "Poem" turns all potential verbs into heavy-handed nouns, "Dedication" pulses with pungent verbs and rhythms. Moreover, the work of dedication referred to in the title consists in a lively reenactment of the actions of Williams's grandmother. The poem begins by facing toward "the waters of this inlet," orienting itself in the direction of the Atlantic and beyond it to the Old World from which the poet's grandmother came. The first part of "Dedication" is a headlong sentence detailing the personal hardships Emily Dickinson Wellcome had to overcome in establishing herself and her family in a new land:

This plot of ground
facing the water of this inlet
is dedicated to the living presence of
Emily Dickinson Wellcome
who was born in England; married;
lost her husband and with
her five year old son
sailed for New York in a two-master;
was driven to the Azores;
ran adrift on Fire Island shoal,
met her second husband
in a Brooklyn boarding house,
went with him to Puerto Rico
bore three more children, lost
her second husband, lived hard
for eight years in St. Thomas,
Puerto Rico, San Domingo, followed
the oldest son to New York,
lost her daughter, lost her "baby,"
seized the two boys of
the oldest son by the second marriage
mothered them—they being
motherless—fought for them
against the other grandmother
and the aunts, brought them here
summer after summer, defended
herself against thieves,
storms, sun, fire,
against flies, against girls
that came smelling about, against
drought, against weeds, storm-tides,
neighbors, weasels that stole her chickens,
against the weakness of her own hands,
against the growing strength of
the boys, against wind, against
the stones, against trespassers,
against rents, against her own mind. (CP 1: 105–6)

"Dedication" looks toward the East of the Old World, imaginatively echoing the Columbian voyage to America. The first section of the poem presents a tele-graphic travelogue identifying the vicissitudes of the journey. In fact, the language of this section recalls that of Columbus's journals in "The Discovery of the Indies" chapter of *American Grain*, which narrates a series of storms and other mishaps that confronted him.

In "Dedication," Williams portrays his grandmother as an independent and charismatic woman, thereby recasting masculinist narratives of national development. The words he uses to describe his grandmother's emigration are energetic, with verbs placed at the beginning of many lines in the first half of the poem ("lost," "sailed," "ran adrift," "met," "went," "seized," "mothered"). Equally lively verbs appear elsewhere too ("lived hard," "fought for," "brought them here," "defended"). In contrast to Molly Finney in "Poem," Wellcome's character is sharply defined, and her action lies at the center of the poem in which she appears. As a result, "Dedication" may be profitably read against the traditional paeans to the Republic's forefathers that "Poem" presupposes. In his poetic "Dedication," Williams creates a forceful portrait of a memorable female ancestor. Williams's grandmother emerges as a revered family matriarch who successfully established a lineage in a new land.

"Dedication" commemorates the trials his grandmother went through in making a home and a place for her family in the New World. "Between the performative act of the title and the descriptive act of its conclusion," writes John Lowney, "the poem reenacts the biography of the subject who has made the ground responsive to *her* performative act of dedication" (39). As her descendant, the poet honors her memory and accomplishment, praising in her the same commitment to the land that he admires in Daniel Boone:

> By instinct and from the first Boone had run past the difficulties encountered by his fellows in making the New World their own. As ecstasy cannot live without devotion and he who is not given to some earth of basic logic cannot enjoy, so Boone lived to enjoy ecstasy through his single devotion to the wilderness with which he was surrounded. The beauty of a lavish, primitive embrace in savage, wild beast and forest rising above the cramped life about him possessed him wholly. Passionate and thoroughly given he avoided the half logic of stealing from the immense profusion. (*American Grain* 136)

Like Boone (and unlike the "colonial" of Frost's "The Gift Outright"), Williams's grandmother devotes herself wholeheartedly to the earth of her new home and thereby finds herself possessed by it. The ground that embraces her body "is dedicated to" her "living presence," a presence that comes to live, of course, through the testament of her grandson's text. In her peregrinations, she has indeed come well to a new place, making a home for herself and her progeny by living on the land and getting a living from its substance. As Barry Ahearn comments, Williams's "poem credits Grandmother Wellcome with those qualities celebrated in official histories of American pioneers" (97). By recounting the pioneering action of this matriarch, Williams transfigures Ezra Pound's "Patria" into a heroic motherland.

"Dedication" narrates not only Williams's family history but also his genealogy of American culture. Just as Williams devoted himself in his poetry to the land and people of Paterson, New Jersey, so his grandmother "grubbed this earth with her own hands" and "domineered over this grass plot," staking her claim to a property and homestead in the New World.

Lowney points out that "Dedication" not only honors the poet's grandmother but works out a poetic lineage for himself:

> If "the passion, the independence and the determination of this woman born Emily Dickenson in Chichester, England" [Williams, *Autobiography* 167] represent those qualities Williams chooses to identify with his genealogical descent, by insisting on the *i* in "Dickinson" he simultaneously constructs a literary grandmother, whose structurally warped, rhymeless lines resemble Williams's "beginning" to compose in the "American idiom." In conflating the "plot" of Williams's grandmother's life with the plot of reinventing that life, "Dedication for a Plot of Ground" rewrites the past to subvert any nativist "grounds" for constructing models of ethnic, national, or aesthetic purity. (42)

As Lowney suggests, Williams lets the narrative of his grandmother's experience stand for that of the nation, for it both authorizes his poetry and exemplifies immigrant experience. Ahearn makes a similar point, characterizing the note of warning on which the poem closes as "a sort of no trespassing sign" that demonstrates "Wellcome's success in finally attaining a plot of ground from which she cannot be expelled and from which she can exclude others. Thus the end of the poem exemplifies her proprietary determination" (98). Ahearn's assessment reveals Williams's concern to articulate the experience of an "other"—and his powerful success in becoming a "mouthpiece" for the voice of his ancestor. At the same time, his words acknowledge the violence involved in the colonization of an inhabited land, and they show that Williams's celebration of his grandmother's success does not completely suppress the shortcomings involved in it: Wellcome "still has a potent spirit, but . . . has she anything else?" (98).

On one hand, then, the poem is a personal document about the poet's familial and literary lineages. On the other hand, because Williams's poem echoes conventional homages to heroic forefathers, its heroine and her narrative are situated within a familiar public context. In "Dedication," Williams portrays his contradictory commitments to romantic idealization (of the pioneer myth) and brave revelation (of colonial costs) in a single text—though the idealization dominates in this case. In "Dedication," Williams articulates an individual and complex view of his country and its history through the lens of his grandmother's epic experience. The poem evokes familiar national narratives of pilgrimage and settlement, but it does so from the perspective of an exceptional woman. In piecing together its narrative of an American matriarch, "Dedication" presents a dimension of national history that has been overlooked in the past. Williams's homage to his grandmother reminds its readers of the important contributions women have made in American culture at the same time that, as Ahearn suggests, the poem acknowledges the human costs of the grandmother's "grubbing" emigration. It is both as celebration and criticism that "Dedication" functions as Williams's poetic alternative to traditional narratives about America.

In "To Elsie" Williams advances a similarly personal view of the United States, a view that is unnerving, even shocking. With the startling maxim that opens the poem—"The pure products of America / go crazy"—Williams provides an unappealing picture of the most pure-blooded of Americans. While the poem defends the purity of the lineage it depicts (thereby participating in the larger cultural debate about the identity and heritage of "true Americans" that Michaels discusses in *Our America*), its defense of "pure" Americans seems hardly complimentary. In fact, one reading of "pure products" suggests that Williams is ridiculing the endogamy proverbially associated with small towns. Although his "devil-may-care men who have taken / to railroading / out of sheer lust of adventure" remind one of the railroading hoboes depicted by Crane in *The Bridge*, Williams's portrayal of such vagrants is perhaps less sympathetic than Crane's. The "young slatterns" with whom these men mate are as indecorous as the men, for they are "bathed / in filth" all week long and on Saturday are "tricked out . . . with gauds / from imaginations which have no / peasant traditions to give them / character" (*CP* 1: 217). To complete his scandalous portrait, Williams suggests that the male "promiscuity" to which these women fall prey borders on or constitutes rape.

Despite his harsh portrayal of her heritage, the speaker appears to harbor genuine sympathy for Elsie. However condescending this sympathy might at first appear, the speaker acknowledges that Elsie's "broken brain" is the "product" of particular and limiting conditions in America. The opening lines of the poem flatly damn pretensions to purity—racial, sexual, moral, or otherwise. From the perspective of the poem, "American purity" is a contradiction in terms. In this respect, "To Elsie" is of a piece with Williams's *American Grain* broadsides against the inhibitions of the Puritans. The "truth" that Elsie expresses "about us" is a painful one, for Elsie's "broken brain" reveals the destructive character of the purity it embodies. Williams associates the degraded sexuality of the railroad adventurers and the filthy "slatterns" who begot Elsie with the textures of her body itself:

her great
ungainly hips and flopping breasts

addressed to cheap
jewelry
and rich young men with fine eyes (*CP* 1: 218)

As the product of such liaisons, Elsie's body assumes a semiotic quality, for her hips and breasts register her origins by addressing themselves both to the "cheap / jewelry" that echoes the "gauds" of her mothers and the "rich young men" whose "fine eyes" glow with the same "lust of adventure" that motivated her fathers.

While Elsie's "broken brain" testifies to her having gone "crazy," the speaker's intimation that her parentage may have included "a dash of Indian blood" suggests that her purity is compromised by miscegenation, a miscegenation that, according to Michaels, figuratively underwrites the conception of American culture that developed in the early decades of the twentieth century. Elsie is paradoxically both "pure" and the "product" of intermarriage. In Williams's figuration of her, the Indian reverence for the earth confronts what James Breslin considers to be a Puritan view of the world as a loathsome "excrement of some sky" (*CP* 1: 218). Against this view, Williams loves the world and finds it (and Elsie) attractive. Instead of exemplifying the nativism Michaels describes, Williams expresses his appreciation for Elsie's hybridity. As Peter Halter points out, moreover, Williams's

> "pure" can also mean "genuine," "unadulterated," with a cynical undertone: The trueborn offspring of Puritan America are doomed, raised with a religion that denies the rights of the body and turns the wilderness in which they find themselves into the "squalid, horrid American Desart." This rural America is a cruel parody of any genuine pastoral vision. It is a world in which all things physical and natural have been for so long bedeviled that the Promised Land has been turned into a prison and its fruit into "filth," so that mind and body, spirit and senses alike now starve. (140–41)

The situation of America is an impoverished one, subjecting its citizens to a humiliating hunger. Although "the imagination" conjures visions of deer to fill the void of this desire, unsatisfied appetite still overwhelms the speaker. "Somehow," he laments, "it seems to destroy us" (218).

Since most of "To Elsie" employs the third person, the emergence of a communal voice at this point in the poem is surprising. In the face of Elsie's arresting figure, the speaker can no longer maintain the comfortable distance he imposed between himself and the "mountain folk" he described in the first half of the poem. Because she is "denied subjectivity for reasons of race, gender, and economic condition," as Brian Bremen points out, "'Elsie' occupies a threatening position not only within Williams's 'poetry,' but also within the confines of his own domestic space" (61). Stephen Tapscott makes a similar point, characterizing Elsie as a "nexus between public and private worlds" (5). In fact, it turns out that the beleaguered "we" of these stanzas represents not only "some doctor's family," but the entirety of the nation to which that family belongs. "To Williams [Elsie's] . . . story is inescapably his, everyone's," writes James Clifford (4). But the nation suffers from a lack of creative and moral direction because it remains hostile to Elsie's "truth," including the mixed ancestry of much of the country's population.

Williams figures that lack of direction in the closing three lines of the poem:

> No one
> to witness
> and adjust, no one to drive the car. (*CP* 1: 219)

Clifford reads the poem not only as Williams's parable of "modernity's inescapable momentum," but as his effort to record something of cultural value. In his view, Williams resists sentimentalizing Elsie's cultural "predicament" by recognizing that he, too, "shares her fate" (5). His attentive witness brings something promising into being, for by recognizing that he cannot adjust circumstances or "drive the car" of history in the direction he might want to, Williams fashions a voice to represent a silenced people's experience. It is a voice the poet contrives to figure as inchoate, not one that he claims to proclaim with authority. Unlike the knowing speakers of such earlier poems as "Tract," "Foreign," and "Riposte" (*CP* 1: 72–74, 79–80, 95–96), who unceremoniously buttonhole their fellow townsmen, the voice that ends "To Elsie" is passively "given off" like the "isolate flecks" in the penultimate stanza. There is a crestfallen quality to the final lines, but the very existence of the poem argues against a total despair, for it records the "witness" whose absence it laments. In doing so, it advances the project of rendering America articulate without completely appropriating "the other" in the process. Through the strategic distance of its witness, the poem represents an "other" without eclipsing her subjectivity. "Elsie is still largely silent," Clifford writes, "but her disturbing presences—a plurality of emergent subjects—can be felt" (7). In "To Elsie," then, the speaker moves from abstract speculation about "mountain folk" to a specific expression of his relationship with a particular individual. He moves from a description of this people's social background to an assertion of connection between "Elsie" and "us."

• This expanding vision of the national community is evident in different forms in a number of other lyrics by Williams as well, such as "The Forgotten City," one of the several poems Williams entitled "Pastoral," and "It Is a Living Coral." In "The Forgotten City," Williams pays homage to a marginalized community of "curious and industrious people," while in "Pastoral" he honors the ingenuity and endurance "of the very poor." The speaker of "It Is a Living Coral" is a citizen visiting his nation's capital. In each poem, Williams investigates the concept of the nation, and it is possible to argue that in each case, the poet's vision of what constitutes the nation undergoes a transformation, one that criticizes the concept in the very act of constituting it. In each poem, Williams represents aspects of the life and meaning of his nation's citizens that "the news" fails to reflect.

In "The Forgotten City," Williams describes his experience of a detour forced upon him by the depredations of a hurricane. His discovery of the city as a result of the detour he takes is characterized by an eerie wonder in the face of a region that he finds unfamiliar but that is nevertheless near to both his home and New York City. "The Forgotten City" exists in some hidden pocket of the nation. Williams writes:

> I passed through
> extraordinary places, as vivid as any
> I ever saw where the storm had broken
> the barrier and let through
> a strange commonplace: Long, deserted avenues
> with unrecognized names at the corners and
> drunken looking people with completely
> foreign manners. Monuments, institutions
> and in one place a large body of water
> startled me with an acre or more of hot
> jets spouting up symmetrically over it. Parks.
> I had no idea where I was and promised myself
> I would some day go back to study this
> curious and industrious people who lived
> in these apartments, at these sharp
> corners and turns of intersecting avenues
> with so little apparent communication
> with an outside world. How did they get
> cut off this way from representation in our
> newspapers and other means of publicity
> when so near the metropolis, so closely
> surrounded by the familiar and the famous? (*CP* 2: 86)

In "The Forgotten City," the places through which the poet passes are "extraordinary" and "as vivid as any / I ever saw," yet at the same time oddly "commonplace."

This paradox corresponds to the title, which clarifies it, for the only way the city can be both extraordinary and commonplace for the speaker of the poem is for it to have been formerly known, at least to some degree, and yet entirely removed from the consciousness of the man who confronts it. The poem remembers and resuscitates its forgotten landscape, bringing to light that which would otherwise have remained out of view. Although in the Freudian formulation, this definition of the uncanny applies to the personal experience of an individual, in the poem, an entire city acts as an instance of the uncanny. The "decision" that this city "should" remain hidden from sight is the function of a community and not an individual. In other words, it is a political form of the uncanny that the poem unearths, and the poet shows that the repressive burial of this "strange" yet common place is a function of culture and ideology. He makes this clear when he asks how the inhabitants of "The Forgotten City" got "cut off this way from representation in our / newspapers and other means of publicity." Like Bhabha's emphasis on culture as enunciation (and hence on the social contexts of signification) in "The Postcolonial and the Postmodern," Williams's focus on the institutional production of knowledge by the mass media in "The Forgotten City" reveals the ways in which "the news" shapes and restricts its audience's knowledge of the world and its inhabitants.

The poem projects its view of the nation as an imagined community when it identifies the mass media as belonging to a unified "we"; such media are "*our* newspapers and other means of publicity." Nevertheless, the inhabitants of Williams's forgotten city somehow exist as a "they" apart from the communal "we" implied by the word "our." Williams's discussion of the cultural and economic development of the early United States in "The American Background" provides an explanation that accounts for this divorce between urban center and suburban or rural periphery. In this essay, Williams argues that "wealth, by the influence it wields, may become the chief cause of cultural stagnation" (*Essays* 146–47). He elaborates on this point, arguing that

> the decay of the small community was an actual decay of culture; it was a sack by invisible troops, leaving destruction for which the gains—and they were considerable—did not compensate. It was a loss which degraded, which was compelled by circumstances but which posited a return to sources in some form later on . . . . In small communities, being drained of wealth by the demand for it in the cities, men died like rats caught in a trap. And their correctly aimed but crude and narrow beginnings died with them. (*Essays* 147–48)

In "The American Background," Williams locates the influence of European culture—something he identifies as "borrowed," or "secondary"—in the metropolis, whereas he situates the category of the "native," or "primary," in rural areas (*Essays* 135). As David Frail argues, "Williams's confrontation with 'modernity'—the transformation of America from a small-community economy and culture to an urban, centralized, mass economy and culture—was the locus of his politics" (*Early Politics* 3). Because the Jeffersonian "small community" slowly fostered a crude but "authentic" culture through its own self-sufficiency, it embodies the truly American. In this regard, "The Forgotten City" might be said to occupy the place of the lost pioneering ideal in Williams's imagination: "It was the reality of the small community which settled the territory in the first place, but from behind came the wave which blotted that out. And it was the culture of immediacy, the active strain, which has left every relic of value which survives today" (*Essays* 148). From this point of view, the landscape depicted in "The Forgotten City" (and in "Pastoral") is the modern descendant of such settlements, yet this heritage only compounds the city's uncanny power over the speaker. Williams's poem exemplifies a fundamental contradiction in the culture of the national community it represents by dramatizing the cognitive dissonance of the speaker when confronted by such "extraordinary" yet forgotten "places."

The instance of the "political uncanny" that the poem uncovers brings into focus an ideological rift in the poet's culture, for this culture claims to be a democratic union representing all of its citizens, yet the instruments whereby that union mediates and knows itself is not universally representative. The eerie quality that suffuses the poem is (among other things, of course) a function of this rift; the poem's instance of the uncanny is the result of the fissure between the democratic ideology of the national communion and the practice of media organized and controlled by capital. As James A. Delle points out,

> Cities, highways, nations, and continents are culturally created phenomena that simultaneously create culture. This recursive or interactive definition of space has a very significant implication: Those who can exert the most control over the creation of space can control the context of human relations. Although the meanings of space are continuously produced by each individual who perceives and interacts within each space, access to that space is mediated by political and economic forces over which most individuals have very little control. (Leone and Silberman 18)

"The Forgotten City" reveals its speaker's discovery that the cultural organs of capital actually create the categories of "the familiar and the famous" through which he understands the world. "To be cut off from representation," writes Knapp, "is to have fallen outside of the limited set of discursive patterns which society seeks to reproduce. It is to exist, if at all, only as powerless Other to the dominant culture" (100).

As a reproducible text in its own right, however, "The Forgotten City" combats the cultural amnesia perpetuated by the partial and uneven coverage of "our / newspapers and other means of publicity." The poem demonstrates the "constructedness" of the "we" it projects, showing how such rhetoric is emptied of meaning when it is abstracted to the extent required to imagine a country spanning half a continent. The people represented by this "we" are born from the dissonance the speaker feels between that which he thinks he knows about his community and nation (the pedagogical) and that which the poem discloses about this place and people (the performative). Williams's city slips through the cracks of official representation. The poem honors the forgotten by bringing it back into view and reminding readers of its value and existence.

In "Pastoral" ("When I Was Younger"), Williams similarly registers the disjunction between a bourgeois, big-city view of the nation and its inhabitants and the reality of an overlooked place. Like Moore's "People's Surroundings," Williams's poem draws inferences about the personality of people by meditating on their possessions and environment. With Moore, Williams recognizes that the objects he describes "answer one's questions." In line with Williams's dictum "no ideas but in things," the speaker of "Pastoral" proceeds from the sense perception of observation to the cognition of personal insight; his idea of the inhabitants of the houses he sees is grounded in the material substance of those houses.

In tracing these steps from perception to insight, "Pastoral" brings to light another instance of the political unconscious, of the uncanny truth that a prevailing ideology represses:

When I was younger
it was plain to me
I must make something of myself.
Older now
I walk back streets
admiring the houses
of the very poor:
roof out of line with sides
the yards cluttered
with old chicken wire, ashes,
furniture gone wrong;
the fences and outhouses
built of barrel-staves
and parts of boxes, all,
if I am fortunate,
smeared a bluish green
that properly weathered
pleases me best
of all colors

     No one
will believe this
of vast import to the nation. (*CP* 1: 64)

The apocalyptic tone that characterizes "The Forgotten City," with its earth-shattering storms and eerie landscape, is absent from "Pastoral." An appealing modesty pervades the perspective, the textual shape, the cropped lines, and even the title of Williams's ironic urban "Pastoral." All the same, it makes a poetic and political statement quite similar to that of "The Forgotten City," for it shares the latter poem's distinctive journalistic quality; it simply does so in a different way—a way Rod Townley characterizes as backhanded (80). Its parodic title and rhetorical understatement work together to expose the differences between the American dream of financial and professional success and the imposing reality of poverty. The ironic distance between the idyllic rural world evoked by the title and the actual quasi-urban landscape of the poem doubles the opposition between the speaker's youthful commitment to an ethic of success on one hand and the professional devotion he displays in his maturity to the medical needs of the very poor on the other. The poem's understated rhetoric culminates in the quiet jeremiad of its final sentence, which its sensitive line breaks delicately enhance.

The speaker's view of the "houses / of the very poor" is admiring and leisurely. If he does not belong to the social world of this neighborhood's inhabitants or even address those inhabitants directly, he nonetheless participates in that world and honors it with a profound and honest homage. The poem also constitutes "the nation" in a particular way, suggesting that although both the speaker and the people who live in the houses he describes are members of the nation, they are also isolated from it in much the same way as the inhabitants of "The Forgotten City" are. In other words, the poem articulates a discrepancy between the ideology of the United States as a democratic state and the reality of the United States as an economically and politically divided society. In his personal and poetic representation (and hence mediation) of an alienated national constituency, Williams demonstrates the conflict between Bhabha's categories of performative and pedagogical dimensions of national discourse. "Pastoral" reveals the distinction between the lived reality of "the very poor" and the political values of "the nation" they inhabit.

Williams rejects distinctions between the aesthetic and the utilitarian through the language he uses to describe the material condition of poverty (for the "bluish green" patina that covers the paupers' possessions "pleases [him] best of all colors" when it is "properly weathered") and through the attitudes expressed by his speaker, who finds beauty and meaning in the shabby landscape he describes. Most of the poem is devoted to a careful description of the objects it admires, but the rationale for this description lies in the political statement that closes the poem. As I have suggested, the poem embodies Williams's motto "no ideas but in things," for it works hard to represent the physical condition of poverty rather than an abstraction of it. While the speaker focuses on his experience rather than on the people who inhabit the houses he enjoys, the poem insists on the value of the experience of the people who dwell under the difficult conditions it identifies.

The poem's opening contrast, for example, between the perspectives of the speaker's younger and older selves provides an important context for the images that follow. Williams offers a self-deprecating portrait of his changing self by humorously contrasting the passionate attempts of his younger days to "make something" of himself with the loitering enjoyments of his older, now accomplished self. The contrast mocks the speaker's youthful confidence ("it was plain to me") and the earnestness of his earlier self-fashioning. It is clear that the speaker takes himself less seriously than he used to, and that he no longer respects the upward mobility he pursued in his youth. As Ann Fisher-Wirth observes, moreover, he "seems quite content, but in terms of his early dreams, a little pitiful and humbled; the brokenness of the lines, the aimlessness of the journey, make him appear to be as imperfect and unfinished as the neighborhood he wanders" (88). This suggests that Williams's speaker regards himself and his interests as being aligned with the people his poem audaciously "speaks for." "Pastoral" lampoons the American myth of the self-made man. Like Whitman, moreover, Williams's persona shamelessly relishes idleness. The modest eloquence of the second half of Williams's contrast ("Older now / I walk back streets / admiring the houses / of the very poor") gently testifies to the speaker's sense of wisdom gained through experience. What he sees from this more mature perspective is something that is easy for anyone to miss: the dignity, ingenuity, and endurance of the poor; the unexpected beauty inherent in the natural processes of decay; and the striking effects brought about by an un-judging juxtaposition of such human and natural forces.

The poem closes with a mordant judgment concerning the moral, aes-thetic, and political meaning of the scene it earlier depicts. While the poet finds in "the houses / of the very poor" an occasion for meditative wonder ("admiring") and delight ("pleases me most"), he realistically frets that others will fail to recognize and respect the efforts of the poor to survive and live with a peculiarly human grace. In his reading of the final stanza of "Pastoral," Lowney writes that it

> contains a deictic indicator, "this," that can refer to both the descriptive act and the things described. Not only is the urban slum ignored by the "nation," but Williams's poetic treatment of such a topic presumably is ignored as well. The use of "import" accentuates the difference. In addition to suggesting "importance," *import* also suggests something imported. Williams's celebration of the urban slum implicitly celebrates the immigrants who inhabit this slum, however absent they are from the "houses" described in the poem. This celebration of immigrant brico-lage celebrates the poem's own structure, itself "of vast import" not only to the national poetic tradition but to the pastoral tradition. (60–61)

Lowney's characterization of the "houses" as belonging to immigrants situates Williams's poem within the anti-immigrant context described by Michaels in *Our America* and denounced by Moore in "The Labors of Her-cules." Lowney's reading indicates that Williams, like Moore, defends the place of the recent immigrant in American life and culture. For those Americans possessed of an imperial vision, the unglamorous people al-luded to in Williams's poem afford no interest. In the aspiring American effort to support and protect foreign investment, Williams might be sug-gesting, an important domestic resource has been overlooked. Williams's famous remark that he "tapped" his language from the mouths of Polish mothers would seem to confirm this view, while the portrayals of hybrid peo-ples in "To Elsie" and "The Forgotten City" also reflect the poet's celebration of the cultural differences that characterize his country (*Autobiography* 311).

By closing his encomium to the ingenuity of the poor with the quiet yet telling comment that "No one / will believe this / of vast import to the na-tion," Williams indicates the political significance behind the poem's rever-ently delineated surfaces. In his attentive portrayal of such surfaces—

> roof out of line with sides
> the yards cluttered
> with old chicken wire, ashes,
> furniture gone wrong;
> the fences and outhouses
> built of barrel-staves
> and parts of boxes, all—

Williams directs the attention of his readers to the character of the people who gave rise to such surfaces and surroundings. In their need, these people constructed "fences and outhouses" from "barrel-staves / and parts of boxes," and in their stubborn will to survive, they persist despite sagging roofs, dilapidated furniture, and the ashes of spent fires, making do with the "old chicken wire" and other items their wealthier neighbors discard. The poem is a respectful effort to awaken its readers to the "vast import" of such people and their condition. It is an attempt to revise the meaning and the polity of the poet's "nation."

The rubble of Williams's landscape—the scrapped and fragmentary elements that compose the architecture of the poor—corresponds to a telling passage from Bhabha's "DissemiNation." In it, Bhabha describes the way the disparate elements of everyday life are turned to use in a coherent ideology that undergirds the nation as a working political community:

> The scraps, patches and rags of daily life must be repeatedly turned into the signs of a coherent national culture, while the very act of the narrative performance interpellates a growing circle of national subjects. In the production of the nation as narration there is a split between the continuist, accumulative temporality of the pedagogical, and the repetitious, recursive strategy of the performative. (145)

As in "The Forgotten City," where Williams demonstrates a disparity between an individual's imagination of his community—local as well as national—and his lived experience of a forgotten pocket of that community, "Pastoral" at once constitutes the poet's nation, as a pedagogical object to be reproduced in schools and other venues of nationalist ideology, and at the same time dramatizes its tenuous existence, as a fundamentally split entity that needs to be constantly, repeatedly "performed" by its citizens in order to survive. In "The Forgotten City" and "Pastoral," Williams expresses the tension between these two poles of national formation by unearthing an entire city in the face of its discursive erasure and by celebrating the "scraps, patches and rags" of the poor who matter for him despite his nation's coolly official indifference. In this way, the two poems recuperate the "gains" of the small pioneer communities Williams celebrates in "The American Background," gains "which posited a return to sources in some form later on." "The Forgotten City" and "Pastoral" supply viable versions of this promised later form. They commemorate and transfigure the incipient culture of the early settlers, acting by turns as both archive and alembic.

"It Is a Living Coral," like "The Forgotten City" and "Pastoral," offers a view of the nation and its existential meaning for the poet and his reader. In this poem Williams reflects on public art as a way of communicating his view of the nation. With its metaphor of "living coral" and its quotation of the motto *"E Pluribus Unum,"* the poem represents the nation as a pluralistic union teeming with variety but dubs it nonetheless "a trouble" that is

archaically fettered
to produce

E Pluribus Unum an
island

in the sea a Capitol
surmounted

by Armed Liberty— (*CP* 1: 255–56)

The poem is a celebration of the restless energies of "the masses"—the many different peoples who make up the national populace. At the same time, it is an acknowledgment that the nation is a "trouble" that is "archaically fettered" or restrained by the constitution that federally unites its various states (in the linguistic performance enacted by its law) and by the civil war that defended the union it redefined through its force. As a testament to the contributions of various peoples to the United States, the poem characterizes the true center of American culture and society as a muscular vitality located in its ordinary citizens. As energetic as Whitman's athletes, "It climbs / it runs" and it "fetches naked / Indian / women from a river." The exhilarating sweep of that action includes the sexual ardor of Whitman's poetry as well as the rape of land and women that spawned the political unions of the colonies and the republic that replaced them. Such rapine extends not only to the "Indian / women" confronting the pioneers but also to the vast "natural resources" presented by the territories. This is the story told by the successive waves of "men felling trees" that rise and fall within the speaker's mind.

As a meditation on the making of political art for public consumption, "It Is a Living Coral" reviews the architecture of the Capitol building and the painting and sculpture housed within it:

painting

sculpture straddled by
a dome

eight million pounds
in weight

iron plates constructed
to expand

and contract with
variations

of temperature
the folding

and unfolding of a lily.
And Congress

authorized and the
Commission

was entrusted was
entrusted! (*CP* 1: 256)

The repeated exclamation that closes this section refers to a government com-
mission established to oversee the art purchased for public monuments. The lan-
guage and punctuation suggest the speaker's shock at the prospect of the govern-
ment's dealings with art of any kind. It perhaps implies that art is one public
trust the government does not merit. The committees and the political dickering
that goes on in them contrast with the organic image of the lily Williams intro-
duces as a metaphor for the dome of the Capitol building. Although the dome,
like the legislation of congressmen, is the work of human hands, it inspires awe
in those who behold it, whereas the committee work performed among the rep-
resentatives and senators below is often ridiculous and contemptible. The bathos
of Williams's switch from the dizzying height and splendor of the rotunda to the
bemused exclamation indicates the disparity between human aspirations and
the political reality that underlies yet so often undercuts them.

Nevertheless, the organic metaphors of the state as a living coral and of
the dome as a lily convey the driving energy Williams perceives in the life of
his republic. So do the poem's lineation, rhythm, and diction, which features
so many active verbs. Williams's mythic nation is vigorously alive. "It climbs"
and "it runs," yet it is also protean in its restless metamorphoses, for like a
coral it is made up of groups that include both public figures (Jefferson, Gen-
erals Marion and Lee, George Shoup, Admiral Perry) and anonymous "Indian
women" or dead seamen. "The metamorphic disruptions of this 'It,'" writes
Ahearn, "seem much the most significant elements in the poem" (155–56).
Williams renders his panorama of historic figures and scenes with a simple,
vivid clarity that honors the spirit of his nation and its founders.

Yet Williams interrupts his review of public pictures and monuments with
an ironic comment that both upholds the central truth embodied in them and
criticizes their artistic flaws, including some they mean to conceal or simply are
not bothered by. "[T]his scaleless / jumble," Williams writes, "is superb / and ac-
curate in its expression / of the thing they would destroy—" (*CP* 1: 257). Damn-
ing the lack of proportion and order in such art, he nevertheless finds something
in it to cherish, championing against the feckless onslaught of an ominous
"they" some enigmatically unidentified "thing." That "thing" would appear to
be the nation's vital spirit, its traditions of self-reliant creativity and indepen-
dence so often embodied in the figure of the pioneer (and so passionately de-
fended by Williams in "The American Background"), while the ambiguous pro-
noun "they" appears to refer to the moralistic officials who commission and
oversee the art that Williams depicts.

The poem describes political, aesthetic, and perhaps spiritual forms of order and organization, and it contrasts varieties of chaos and control in order to make some judgment about the aesthetic and political states of the union. "It Is a Living Coral" investigates and critiques the genre of the public monument, questioning the patriotic values that sponsor unaccomplished art. Yet by focusing on an art meant to instill the civic virtue necessary to the health of a republic, Williams asks his reader to consider the meaning of this genre and of the experience it is intended to celebrate. This genre honors the bravery of Mrs. Motte and the virtues of political leaders, yet the pictures and statues described in the poem lack the pluck and vitality such art means to praise. Despite themselves, however, the works somehow evince the very "thing they would destroy." If we read that "they" as the bourgeois public fathers (scheming and unscrupulous politicians?) who commissioned the art, or even as the artists and the artworks themselves, then Williams's poem registers a rebellion against a complacent and self-serving concept of the nation as a living embodiment of democracy. As a consequence, no easy division of art or people will do, for like coral, the public art Williams reviews is at the same time both dead and alive. The poem makes a plea on behalf of a newly imagined world and a fresh start at justice and freedom for a vigorous all instead of some ruling few. It carps at the cramping conventions of a public art that stultifies by slavishly praising the dead without imagining relevant alternatives.

The exuberance that courses through "It Is a Living Coral" draws up short in its abrupt ending, violently contrasting with the last picture it presents: the "dead / among the wreckage / sickly green." Although, in Robert Cirasa's words, Williams presents this "suddenly transfigured, ghoulish marine image" as though it were an objective description of a painting (44), the contrast between the vitality of so much of the poem and the picture of the dead at the end results in the formation of a new meaning, a surplus that exceeds simple description. "Let the dead bury the dead," the poem seems to say. The "sickly green" features of the dead must be transfigured if the coral is to remain alive. Although coral may look inanimate, it grows and changes, for it is a union made from many cells and fissures *("E Pluribus Unum")*, and its many arms flexibly bend with the waves. Its strength and durability depend on a dynamic adaptability. So too must the nation, Williams suggests, adjust itself to changing circumstances, honoring the accomplishments of its founders in the form of a living art. The poem's final, brief remembering of the dead acknowledges the role of a people's ancestors in winning and defending the freedom whose legacy the painting is supposed to dramatize. In its different manner, the poem reconfigures this legacy of freedom in order to revitalize it, to "make it new" and robust. Nevertheless, "the poem leaves open . . . the question of whether any coherence can result from [the] transformative, restless 'It'" that Williams never names (Ahearn 155). It is as if the poem were acting out the difficulties of articulation that become Williams's explicit theme in *Paterson*.

• In a set of later lyrics and in sections of *Paterson*, for instance, Williams records his impressions of both ancestral and latter-day Amerindians as well as his opinions about the violent relations between European Americans and Native Americans. Although Williams had offered the name of a famous "Indian killer" for his reader's edification, mystification, or scorn in "Poem," he offers a more explicit and often more sensitive response to Amerindian people in such later poems as "Navajo," "Graph," and "The Testament of Perpetual Change." In "Navajo," Williams recalls encountering an Indian woman and reports his feelings about her:

> Red woman,
>> (Keep Christ out
>> of this—and
>> his mountains:
>> Sangre de Cristo
>> red rocks that make
>> the water run
>> blood-red)
> squaw in red
> red woman
> walking in the desert
> I suspected
> I should remember
> you this way:
>> walking the brain
>> eyes cast down
>> to escape ME!
>> with fixed sight
>> stalking
>> the gray brush
>> paralleling
>> the highway . . .
>> —head mobbled
>> red, red
>> to the ground
>> sweeping the
>> ground—
>> the blood walking
>> erect, the
>> desert animating
>> the blood to walk
>> erect by choice
>> through
>> the pale green
>> of the starveling
>> sage (*CP* 2: 150–51)

Williams stresses the tense relation between himself and the Navajo woman, who is "walking the brain / eyes cast down / to escape ME!" He foregrounds this detail by capitalizing "ME" and following the personal pronoun with an exclamation point, suggesting his sense of the way America's colonial history informs and mediates their encounter. The early reference to the Sangre de Cristo Mountains and the red coloring that unifies the poem also establish a geographic context for the speaker's encounter with the woman. The vast backdrop of the desert similarly reinforces the transpersonal significance of the scene, even as it brings the dignity of the woman's "choice" into emphatic relief.

In "Navajo," the poet addresses the Indian woman, but the tone of the poem suggests that Williams himself never directly spoke to her. In accordance with lyric tradition, the poem supplies an account of the speaker's feelings about the event he describes, so while the syntax of the poem indicates that the words are directed toward the anonymous "Red woman," the reader nevertheless interprets the poem as a kind of soliloquy. The poem exemplifies John Stuart Mill's definition of the lyric as the overheard words of someone thinking aloud ("Lyric" 461). This intense focus on the mental and emotional processes of the speaker is one way in which the poem indicates the racial and "civil" distances between the speaker and the "Red Woman" his poetic naming brings into being.

The several references to blood, however, serve not only as an image of race and proud vigor when the Navajo woman is characterized as "walking the blood / erect," but as a sign of the history of bloodshed between Europeans and Amerindians. Red designates race, but as the companion poem "Graph" shows, centuries of intermarriage have undercut the viability of race as a stable ethnographic category. Yet Williams's first statement to the "Red woman" he addresses suggests the poet's possible recognition of the artificiality of his memory. In writing "I suspected / I should remember / you this way," Williams acknowledges the deliberation that went into the making of his poem. The lines eschew the conception that the poem is an organic outgrowth of experience, for in confessing his suspicion that his future memory would take the shape it does in the poem that expresses it, the lines admit the poet's conscious manipulation of his "material" in advance of the scene of composition. The poem belies the Wordsworthian formula of "the spontaneous overflow of emotion recollected in tranquility," for it implies that even perception and emotion are mediated by consciousness and that the composition of the poem involves a series of conscious manipulations.

The significance of the phrase lies in more than just the fact that it shows the artificiality of poetic composition. For the phrase dramatizes the role of racial and political preconceptions in determining the poet's response to the particular woman before him. In this regard, Williams focuses on the social context of his poetic enunciation in a way that corresponds to Bhabha's discussion of "culture as enunciation" in "The Postcolonial and the Postmodern." "[T]he enunciative," Bhabha writes, "attempts repeatedly to reinscribe and relocate the political claim to cultural priority and hierarchy (high/low, ours/theirs) in the social institution of the signifying activity" (177). The text of Williams's poem dramatizes the interplay between the speaker's expectations about the Indian woman and the nature of his meeting with her, and on the other hand, the speaker's awareness of the role played by expectations in the particular formulation of one's perception of a person or event. In addition, Williams's description of the "Red woman" as "monumental" marks her as his representation and not the "thing itself" (which is in any case impossible, of course, since language must symbolically "reduplicate" its referent in order to communicate it). The self-awareness of Williams's language is not simply an example of modernist style, however, because that self-awareness is not based on the formal aspects of the poem or an exclusive emphasis on its language. The suspicious self-awareness of "Navajo" arises from the speaker's sensation of his own social and historical position as a white man with respect to the Amerindian he meets, not from an explicit commitment to the poem as an autotelic object. What is potentially suspect in the poem, in other words, is the underlying structure of the speaker's preconceptions rather than—or every bit as much as—the slippery play of language within it. Despite Williams's characterization of the poem as a self-sufficient "machine made of words," this poem pushes the reader "beyond" its purely formal aspects to the social and political worlds its language finely registers (*Essays* 256). In the personal drama it portrays, the poem recapitulates the history of conflict between European and Native Americans.

The poem's overtones of sexual menace perform this history in a particular way, for they imply the asymmetrical relations of power between men and women in European society and they figure the European conquest of the New World as a succession of rapes. As in "To Elsie" and "The Young Housewife," Williams "confesses" his complicity in such conquests, and it is the knowledge of such asymmetry that the speaker recognizes in the downcast countenance of the Indian woman before him. So in some ways, perhaps, this poem gives an interesting twist to the mechanism of the male gaze as it is postulated by film theorists in the wake of Laura Mulvey's groundbreaking essay "Visual Pleasure and Narrative Cinema." For this speaker displays his knowledge of the imbalance of power between the sexes as well as his awareness of the shameful mistreatment of Indians by whites. Instead of simply reproducing a gaze that subordinates its female object, the poem represents a speaker suffused with an awareness of the political and historical forces that ground and shape his vision. It is possible to argue that (for the reader as well as for the speaker) the speaker's knowing suspicion gives birth to a moral consciousness that undoes or critiques the epistemological foundations of the "classical" male gaze. He displays his knowledge, but he also puts it in play.

I have been arguing that the precision of Williams's formulation "I suspected / I should remember / you this way" underscores the mediated quality of perception per se as well as the speaker's profound awareness of such mediation, but it also demonstrates his understanding that such mediation is a social as well as a physiological and linguistic phenomenon. The verb indicates that the speaker has a hunch that preceded his actual experience, but it also suggests that the hunch itself may well be suspect. The poet leaves it to the reader to determine the basis and nature of the speaker's suspicions, even as he emphasizes the way in which such suspicions condition both his encounter with a sexually and racially "foreign" person and his representation of that encounter.

The opening lines of "Graph" suggest that it is meant to be read as a companion piece to "Navajo":

> There was another, too
> a half-breed Cherokee
> tried to thumb a ride
> out of Tulsa, standing there
>
> with a bunch of wildflowers
> in her left hand
> pressed close
> just below the belly (*CP* 2: 151–52)

The title of this lyric implies that the figure depicted in it functions for the poet as a kind of hieroglyph or cipher. The "half-breed Cherokee" stands in an emblematic pose, clutching her wildflowers "close / just below the belly." The poem is a graph, or index, of the Indian woman and perhaps also of the precarious civil status of Amerindians in general: the woman depicted is anonymous and/or mythological, trying to get somewhere else by bumming a ride. Like the displaced hoboes of *The Bridge*, this woman is a marginalized citizen. She may have exercised even less choice than they, however, in determining her current circumstances. While merciless economic factors may well have contributed to the nomadic impulse of Crane's hoboes and the devil-may-care men of Williams's "To Elsie," a different range of economic, social, and historical circumstances contributed to the Cherokee woman's situation, the Trail of Tears not the least among them.

"The Testament of Perpetual Change" is another poem that addresses the situation of Native Americans. In it, Williams intercalates his poem with lines from a poem by Robert Bridges, "The Testament of Beauty." In doing so, he invites his readers to look for relationships between the two texts, so that the "Mortal Prudence" and "divine Providence" that inform the sea journey of the Bridges poem correspond to Williams's evocation of the merchant Walgreen as he "carries Culture to the West." As he appears to do in "Poem," Williams mocks certain generic conventions in a flagrant, disorienting way. In "Perpetual Change," the "virus" of Williams's perspective enters and alters the "host" of the Bridges poem:

> *Mortal Prudence, handmaid of divine Providence*
>   Walgreen carries Culture to the West:
> *hath inscrutable reckoning with Fate and Fortune:*
>   At Cortez, Colorado the Indian prices
> *We sail a changeful sea through halcyon days and storm,*
>   a bottle of cheap perfume, furtively
> *and when the ship laboreth, our stedfast purpose*
>   but doesn't buy, while under my hotel window
> *trembles like as a compass in a binnacle.*
>   a Radiance Rose spreads its shell-thin
> *Our stability is but balance, and wisdom lies*
>   petals above the non-irrigated garden
> *in masterful administration of the unforeseen*
>   among the unprotected desert foliage.
>
> *'Twas late in my long journey when I had clomb to where*
>   Having returned from Mesa Verde, the ruins
> *the path was narrowing and the company few*
>   of the Cliff Dwellers' palaces still in possession of my mind (*CP* 2: 152)

In remarking that "the ruins / of the Cliff Dwellers' palaces" remain "still in possession of my mind," the speaker reverses the historical appropriations of land by white pioneers. Williams's separation of the last four lines of "Perpetual Change" marks them off from the rest of the text and thereby emphasizes their significance. The final two lines of unitalicized type provide a counter not only to Bridges's lines but to the picture of Indian degradation presented near the beginning of Williams's poem. The garden is not irrigated, yet the Radiance Rose somehow blooms. It survives "among the unprotected desert foliage" of "Cortez, Colorado." Like the Indian inhabitants, pushed to the badlands of the "desert" by advancing settlers, the desert foliage is "unprotected" and vulnerable, yet adaptable and able to live despite overwhelming adversity.

The Bridges poem features images of sea travel and spiritual ascendancy. Williams's splicing of his lines with lines from "Testament of Beauty" perhaps suggests that the sea travel refers to the voyage of Columbus and subsequent voyages of conquest. Williams parodies the antiquated language and symbolism of Bridges, but he also pairs the sea voyage with his own vision of American Indians degraded by the market culture ushered in by the colonists and fostered by their heirs. And this parallel is matched by one that ends the poem, in which Bridges's coterie of moral aristocrats attains its spiritual summit and the mind of Williams's speaker still lingers on the majestic heights of "the Cliff Dwellers' palaces." Such an intertextual pairing suggests that Williams intends his pueblos to occupy the same moral high ground enjoyed by the speaker in the Bridges poem: "'Twas late in my long journey when I had clomb to where . . . / the path was narrowing and the company few." Even as Williams's picture of the Indian's furtive "pricing" of "a bottle of cheap perfume" risks appearing to repeat a racist portrait of "the shifty savage" as a thief, it locates the Indian's action within a larger historical and eco-nomic context. In his contrast between the enduring pueblos of the Cliff Dwellers and the gaudy commerce of Walgreen's "cheap perfume," Williams communicates his contempt for the latter and his admiration for the cultural achievements he associates with the impoverished Indian he spies "pricing" perfume. Out of the dissonance between Walgreen's cheap perfume and the Cliff Dwellers' architectural achievements, and between the modern Indian and the desert rose, Williams coaxes a subtle satire. The poet prefers the odor of the desert rose, whose survival surprises and pleases him, to the adulterated scent of Walgreen's perfume. At the same time, the poet's aesthetic pleasure in the rose aids him in sympathizing with the beleaguered circumstances of the Indian he describes. In contrast to his idealization of discovery elsewhere in his writing, Williams here criticizes reductive views of post-Columbian conquest and its legacy. "The Testament of Perpetual Change" portrays the United States as a country informed by philosophical expectations and ways of thinking that un-derlie its ideological origins and its cultural practices: just as the Bridges poem glimmers through the lines of Williams's text as some fabulous palimpsest, so the expectations that guide the speaker of "Navajo" frame and shape the rela-tions between white Americans and red.

• Williams undertakes a similarly critical survey of colonization and repre-sentation in *Paterson* as part of that poem's quest for meaningful speech. Joseph Riddel characterizes this work, for example, as "a poem dedicated to effacing the Europeanized or western subject, the father (Pater) language, in order to free the son to father a new world language" (*Turning Word* 62). Like the other poems discussed in this chapter, *Paterson* figures Williams's poetry as a searching alternative to the news, for it presents its reader with a reevalu-ation of his nation's psychic state and culture—a reevaluation it enacts partly through its juxtaposition of stories adapted from old newspapers. Bhabha's "shift from the cultural as an epistemological object to culture as an enactive, enunciatory site" in "The Postcolonial and the Postmodern" suggests that Williams's desire to unleash a new speech for his nation in *Paterson* represents his own effort "to provide a process by which objectified others may be turned into subjects of their history and experience" (178). In his figuration of Paterson's inhabitants as "a thousand automatons," Williams diagnoses the cultural illness he seeks to heal as a form of alienation or dispossession. He goes on to argue that "because they / neither know their sources nor the sills of their / disappointments," they "walk outside their bodies aimlessly, / for the most part, / locked and forgot in their desires—unroused" (*Paterson* 6). They are people who are disconnected from themselves, who lack the lan-guage necessary to know and compose, or articulate, themselves. The next move in the poem ("—Say it, no ideas but in things—") involves the poet's rousing of himself to speak. The formula, which Williams repeats, is an im-perative that functions like an incantation or prayer to the Muses, summon-ing powers beyond himself to elicit the powers of language. Looking to the restless "recoil of spray and rainbow mists" of the Passaic Falls as the source of these powers, he poses the question that motivates the poem:

> (What common language to unravel?
> . . combed into straight lines
> from that rafter of a rock's
> lip.) (*Paterson* 7)

Like "Apology," then, *Paterson* represents itself as a quest for a liberating language. From the very outset of the poem, Williams links his concerns about language with his concern about his nation.

In her reading of *Paterson,* Kinereth Meyer focuses on the tension between Williams's motto "no ideas but in things" and the unbridgeable disparity between word and thing. Despite his concern to foster the articulation of his nation, Williams's quest for a viable language reflects his own awareness of the impossibility of establishing, once and for all, the adequacy of language to experience. "Because of the insufficiency of the word," Meyer writes, "the poet can only gain what Williams calls a 'partial victory'" (154). Meyer explores the ways in which Williams may be said to repeat the gesture of his forebears in attempting to possess or appropriate the landscape of his nation for his literary benefit, but she also notes the tension between this attempt to recover the "unknown shore" that greeted Columbus and the poet's concomitant effort to eschew possessiveness. For Meyer:

> *Paterson* enacts [a] struggle between possession and nonpossession by involving the reader in a general problematics of representation. *Paterson* grapples not only with the belatedness of a twentieth-century effort to repossess the already named and possessed landscape, but with what is conceived of as an inevitable belatedness of word to thing. Throughout the poem, Williams tests the sufficiency of language. (154)

Nevertheless, even as he acknowledges the limits of the word, Williams emphasizes the political stakes of his effort to enunciate a liberating word in *Paterson*.

One can argue, in fact, that it is by means of its confession of the inadequacy of language that the poem achieves its ends, for the disparities between prose and poetry in Williams's epic collage and the obscurities of the prose excerpts demand the reader's active effort in working out the meanings not only of individual passages but of the often dissonant relationships between them. "In many ways," Kathleen Matthews argues,

> Book One of *Paterson* is Williams' virtuoso performance. He defies tradition by using prose and poetry together. He creates a lyrical myth and undercuts the very creation of myth at the same time. He dips into local history to turn it in one direction until it becomes myth and in another direction until it becomes satire. He begins to roll up a devastating picture of the literary landscape and a mock-heroic picture of his own local landscape. (259)

It is by virtue of the various differences in the poem—between expectations about the past and discoveries that belie them, between prose and poetry, between signifier and signified, and between one morpheme and another just enough like it to permit a pun—that Williams enunciates his representative word. The poem shows the strain of the process of this articulation in order to overcome that strain. An analysis of one passage from *Paterson* will indicate what I mean.

In "The Delineation of the Giants" section of Book 1, as in his meditations in "To Elsie" and "Graph," Williams includes an account of a hybrid, marginal community. The group he describes in *Paterson* lived in the Ramapo Mountains and came to be known as "Jackson's Whites." "The inhabitants of the Ramapos," writes Benjamin Sankey, "exemplify the miscellaneousness and meagerness Williams found characteristic of American local culture" (40). In contrast to the "pure products of America," these people spring from a rich "mongrel" mix of many "bloods"—despite Williams's clear association of Elsie with this group (which reflects, as I have suggested, the truth that "purity" is mythic rather than actual). Hunted, they haunt the hills of America:

> If there was not beauty, there was a strangeness and a bold association of wild and cultured life grew up together in the Ramapos: two phases.
>
> In the hills, where the brown trout slithered among the shallow stones, Ringwood—where the old Ryerson farm had been—among the velvet lawns, was ringed with forest trees, the butternut, and the elm, the white oak, the chestnut and the beech, the birches, the tupelo, the sweet-gum, the wild cherry and the hackleberry with its red tumbling fruit.
>
> While in the forest clustered the ironworkers' cabins, the charcoal burners, the lime kiln workers—hidden from lovely Ringwood—where General Washington, gracing any poem, up from Pompton for rest after the traitors' hanging could be at ease— and the links were made for the great chain across the Hudson at West Point.
>
> Violence broke out in Tennessee, a massacre by the Indians, hangings and exile—standing there on the scaffold waiting, sixty of them. The Tuscaroras, forced to leave their country, were invited by the Six Nations to join them in Upper New York. The bucks went on ahead but some of the women and the stragglers got no further than the valley-cleft near Suffern. They took to the mountains there where they were joined by Hessians from the British Army, a number of albinos among them, escaped negro slaves and a lot of women and their brats released in New York City after the British had been forced to leave. They had them in a pen there—picked up in Liverpool and elsewhere by a man named Jackson under contract with the British Government to provide women for the soldiers in America.
>
> The mixture ran in the woods and took the general name, Jackson's Whites. (There had been some blacks also, mixed in, some West Indian negresses, a shipload, to replace the whites lost when their ship, one of the six coming from England, had foundered in a storm at sea. He had to make it up somehow and that was the quickest and cheapest way.)
>
> New Barbadoes Neck, the region was called.

> Cromwell, in the middle of the seventeenth century, shipped some thousands of Irish women and children to the Barbadoes to be sold as slaves. Forced by their owners to mate with the others these unfortunates were succeeded by a few generations of Irish-speaking negroes and mulattos. And it is commonly asserted to this day the natives of Barbadoes speak with an Irish brogue. (*Paterson* 12–13)

In this account, Williams contrasts the "two phases" of early American culture—that of the mansion at Ringwood and that of the Ramapo people. Sankey correlates Ringwood to the "secondary culture," which is "derivative from Europe," that Williams contrasts with the "primary culture" of pioneers in "The American Background" (41). The Ramapo people, on the other hand, inhabit the forest and, displaced though they are, have put down roots into the soil. Sankey quotes Williams's notes for this section from a manuscript in the collection of the State University of New York at Buffalo: "This conglomerate manned the early iron furnaces, brought in the lime and burned the wood to make the necessary charcoal" (40). The labor of "this conglomerate" provided the economic basis for a local, or "primary," culture.

Williams's hill people, moreover, correspond to the varied community Moore defends in the final lines of her antiracist poem "The Labors of Hercules" and in her various images of hybridity in "Virginia Britannia." These people also present an interesting analogue to the wandering hoboes represented by Crane in *The Bridge*. Jackson's Whites form a hidden creole community that the poet seeks to reveal to the nation of his readers. Williams's odd narrative of their history accurately represents Bourne's picture of a "Trans-National America":

> Whatever American nationalism turns out to be, we see already that it will have a color richer and more exciting than our ideal has hitherto encompassed. In a world which has dreamed of internationalism, we find that we have all unawares been building up the first international nation. . . . America is already the world-federation in miniature, the continent where for the first time in history has been achieved that miracle of hope, the peaceful living side by side, with character substantially preserved, of the most heterogenous peoples under the sun. Here, notwithstanding our tragic failures of adjustment, the outlines are already too clear not to give us a new vision and a new orientation of the American mind in the world. (258)

Williams's "delineation" of the hybrid face of Jackson's Whites corresponds to the "outlines" of Bourne's immigrants in the passage above. In the faces of these people, the phantom of racial purity weirdly glimmers, only to disappear in the complex "cross pollinations" of wildly disparate groups. The "colorful" heritage of such strange bedfellows, Williams seems to say, remains the repressed secret of American history.

As Williams's ironic account shows, this group's name is something of a misnomer, for they are not entirely nor exactly white. But the mythic provenance of the name in the unseemly trade of the mythical white man who had power over these people's ancestors makes the name stick. In this respect, the irony of the name and its history corresponds to the Columbian naming of American aboriginals. The inaccuracy of their designation as "Indians" has been no real bar to its widespread currency and permanence since the Conquest. Fablelike, Williams's miniature history of Jackson's Whites demonstrates the fact that linguistic practice registers the social effects of political and economic power. Williams's appended explanation ("There had been some blacks also, mixed in") nicely conveys the unspoken assumptions behind the events it describes, for it gainsays the appellation by supplying the information in the subordinate grammar of the parenthesis. In this manner, the name both is and is not mitigated. It lets the reader guess something of the legendary circumstances of this people through the irony of its innuendo.

It is significant that Williams's prose inset is preceded by poetry about his chief concern in the early books of *Paterson:* "the language!" (12). The prose passage itself, moreover, ends with a focus on the language of Barbados. Such references to language reflect Williams's concern to articulate the experience of the Ramapo people. According to Sankey, in fact, the "truth about us" that Elsie tells in the poem addressed to her is that "we have never successfully fostered a 'primary' or 'related' culture" in America. "The poet of Paterson, attempting to find a language for his subject, is in effect attempting to make up for this cultural deficit. The prose . . . describing life in Ramapos, illustrates the incoherence and inarticulateness of our local culture" (Sankey 42). Williams presents the plight of Frank's inarticulate nation with pathos:

> The language is missing them
> > they die also
> > incommunicado. (*Paterson* 11)

Their lack of a language deprives them not only of expression but of identity itself. In the poem Williams laments this tragedy, but in the prose statement, he attempts to correct it. Williams's disturbing configurations of poem and prose "rearticulate" American culture by reshuffling fragments of history with pictures of the present. As Anelise Corseuil argues, in the paratactic unions between poetry and prose in *Paterson,* "Williams offers a new perspective on history," one that "undermines the ideas of prosperity, or progress that prevail in much of the discourse of his time" (50–51). Corseuil's remark may be transposed to the more specific terms of Williams's views about the way his nation's culture should be represented and interpreted.

In reference to the verses about language that precede the Jackson's Whites passage, moreover, Williams offers his prose report as what Moore might have considered the "raw material" of a new poetry (Moore, *Complete Poems* 267). The account of the Jackson's Whites supplies the preliminary rudiments of a history necessary for the development of an expressive language. Without the ground of such history,

The language, the language
　　　　fails them
They do not know the words
　　　　or have not
the courage to use them　.
　　　　　—girls from
families that have decayed and
taken to the hills: no words.
They may look at the torrent in
　　　　their minds
and it is foreign to them　.

They turn their backs
and grow faint—but recover!
　　　　Life is sweet
they say: the language!
　　　　—the language
is divorced from their minds,
the language　.　.　the language! (*Paterson* 11–12)

The "decayed" families of the girls here appear to echo "To Elsie," for the descendants of Jackson's Whites are at once "the pure products of America" and a marginal, motley lot. Like Moore's popularization of the mule in "The Labors of Hercules," Williams's picture of Jackson's Whites acknowledges and honors the heterogeneous heritage of modern Americans. Together, the poem and the prose account proclaim the existence of an invisible portion of the modern American populace (in a way reminiscent of "The Forgotten City"). They also commemorate this group's history and attempt to prepare for it a means of finding its own voice on its own terms within both the republic of letters and the country's democratic polity. In this respect Williams's juxtaposed prose and poetry answers Frank's call for an articulate speech in *Our America*—at the same time that this strategy of collage testifies to his modernist doubts about the adequacy of speech. Williams's inclusion of so many different voices in *Paterson* reflects his generous interest in fostering his country's ability to express itself.

David Cohen argues that Williams's account of the Jackson's Whites is the stuff of legend. He argues that there is a lack of documentary evidence for the group's Indian ancestry and that the term "Jackson's Whites" is most likely a written conflation of the phrase "jacks and whites," "'free jacks' being a slang expression for 'free blacks'" (*Folk Legacies* 18). In his study of this group, whom he designates the "Ramapo Mountain People," Cohen notes that the various dialect meanings of *jack* also included "prostitutes," "convicts," and "tramps." In addition, the "term *John* or *Jack* is found in the mumming tradition in the West Indies associated with the *Jonkanoo* or *John Canoe* figure," a kind of clown who "wore white false faces" as part of the performance (*Ramapo* 21–22). This meaning of Williams's term widens the scope of his mythic genealogy, and the various definitions point to the historic conflicts between different groups throughout U.S. history. In Williams's account, the designation paradoxically includes an expansive gamut of red, black, and white "races." This confusion indicates the ascendancy of race as a primary category in American social life. But Williams's legend is even more complicated by the fact that the documented responses of the Ramapo people to the myth of their genealogy includes a range of contradictory attitudes and beliefs that have changed over time. Cohen points out that there seem to have been two distinct Ramapo groups, one white and one black, that each group spurned the other, and that the Indian heritage claimed by both groups cannot be verified by documentary evidence.

Cohen's rejection of the historical basis of the narrative of the Jackson's Whites, however, does not preclude readings of the figurative truth behind Williams's version of the story, for it evokes the genuinely historical conflicts among European, African, and Native Americans. Like the other passages about local history in *Paterson,* the account of the Jackson's Whites functions as a kind of exemplary tale about the nature and conflicts of American history. In registering the lack of freedom of marginalized groups and the prejudice against them, the story questions narratives of colonization and nation-building that forget or suppress the limits and contradictions of American history in favor of a merely celebratory view of its democratic achievements. My purpose in introducing Cohen's findings is to show that the central conflict of race in American history is as complicated in Williams's legendary version as in Cohen's anthropological account. In each case, the issue of racial hybridity appears as a marked feature of the stories about the descent of the Ramapo people. The protean quality of these people, their history, their lineage, and the conflicting beliefs about them reflect the centrality of race in the colonial origins and postcolonial history of the United States. Williams's account combines the renegade heritage of "jack" as convict, the miscegenation and profiteering associated with the mythical Jackson's procurement of prostitutes, and the thoroughgoing ambivalence about race figured in the very name of the people. (This list of spurned people echoes many similar ones in the poetry of Whitman. Williams's concern to create a contemporary voice for the various peoples of his nation follows Whitman's lead but seeks to modernize his effort in the characteristically American way of the independent individual.) Williams's effort to create a language appropriate to this heterogeneous people can be symbolized in the punning denotations of the name Jackson's Whites, for if language cannot embody the word in the way the poet wants, it may nevertheless be bent and split to refract the unsuspected meanings lying hidden in its syllables. At the same time, the legend and the name commemorate the violent appropriation of the labor and land of nonwhite peoples on the part of European settlers.

Sankey and Corseuil make this point quite clear. Corseuil writes that Williams's "collage of historical facts, for the most part selected from historical documents, offers a pattern of disruption and violence" (50), and Sankey points out that in an earlier draft Williams had drawn the contrast more sharply between "the reassuringly quiet scene at Ringwood" and the violence of the "events of the area's history." The earlier draft warrants quoting:

> Certainly you would say under these calm trees—
> There's no violence here: rapine, harlotry,
> disease and abandonment—
> engrafted on the wild. Hamilton, violence at
> his birth, drawn toward violence, to die also
> by violence. Violence in the earth. Iron
> lightnings from the earth. Thunderbolts of steel—
> dug by the primitives, by slaves—enkindled
> by strange fires, illicit, unrecognized—the
> Jackson Whites—and the first horseman of
> his day sleeping at the Mansion—Ringwood—after
> the executions at Pompton— (Buffalo MS) (Sankey 50)

This poetic treatment of the material shows the disparity between a citizen's expectations about the nation's history and the painful truth about that history. "Certainly you would say under these calm trees— / There's no violence here," yet violence is so completely "engrafted on the wild" that it becomes invisible. Williams heightens the effect of his antithesis between "calm trees" and "violence" by splitting the line as he does and accenting "no," as if to indicate by his rhythm the tendency to deny the shocking truths about the nation's past. In providing his vignette about the Ramapo people, Williams calls attention to the often unremembered violence that suffuses his nation's heritage. His account of these people in *Paterson* does not merely present an alternative to yesterday's news; it recomposes that news.

• In the first book of *Paterson,* Williams writes that "Leadership passes into empire; empire begets in- / solence; insolence brings ruin." Williams offers this statement as a reply to Pound's remark that "Your interest is in the bloody loam but what / I'm after is the finished product" (*Paterson* 37). Matthews reads Williams's prophetic formulation as a parody of "Pound's expansive theories of civilization" in *The Cantos* (259). The formulation is also an epigram that can be applied to the international roles the United States was coming to play more and more during the course of Williams's lifetime. The insolence described in Williams's proverb applies not only to the arrogance of European power, but to events and attitudes (such as the Trail of Tears, Manifest Destiny, the institution of Indian reservations, and the Monroe Doctrine) that had already come into existence on (and beyond) American soil. In this respect, the adage comes to be as politically self-reflexive as it is satirical toward Pound. Williams's accounts in *Paterson* of colonial atrocities against Amerindians bear this out in the historical and domestic terms to which the poem commits itself, for what makes the accounts so horrifying is the attitude of the Europeans toward the events they perpetrated. Williams's epigram draws on the links traditionally made between the American and ancient Roman republics, and it alludes to the arguments attributing Rome's fall to a serious moral decline. An American empire is vulnerable to the same ruinous insolence and dissipation that, according to such arguments, destroyed the Roman empire. The driving energy of Williams's cropped clauses build up to convey a powerful prophecy, one that warns of the dangers to a republic too enamored of the power and wealth brought by empire. If Williams's warning seems unaware of a view such as the one advanced by William Appleman Williams that the American republic was already an embryonic empire at birth, it can nevertheless be meaningfully related to the historian's thesis. For imperial insolence too easily forgets the domestic and moral costs of empire.

As my discussions of the Columbus passage from "Asphodel," several of the poet's lyrics, and the passages from *American Grain* and *Paterson* suggest, "All of Williams' figures from the American past . . . can be read as ideograms of the poet; all Williams' writing about that past can be read as covert dissertations on poetics, even the original documents which he inlaid into his own text" (Frail, "Fourth of July" 2). Williams's writing provides one kind of answer to Frank's call for the cultural awakening of the nation and for a corresponding language to illuminate and communicate that awakening—even as it parodies and transforms Frank's neo-Romantic and mystical assumptions through its vigorously self-reflexive language, its fine-spun ironies, and its varied forms of satire. Through his forays into the past, Williams elaborates a poetics based on the invigorating embrace of a new and unknown world, but he also reveals the ways in which the European conquest of the Americas "ended so disastrously" (*CP* 2: 323). In the tension between his undiminished Romanticism and his journalistic reportage, Williams produced a vernacular in his poems that made a new American form of articulation possible. His work celebrates the poetic promise of a distinct new language, even as it expresses the limits and contradictions of representation itself. By conveying his interest in the lives of other people in each of the texts I have discussed, Williams produced a valuable record of otherwise hidden histories. Through their innovative performances and unexpected perspectives, Williams's poems bring into being salutary new views of his country.

Chapter 3

NATIONAL FORGETTING AND REMEMBERING

IN THE POETRY OF ROBERT FROST

• "Forgetting," wrote the French historian Ernest Renan, "is a crucial factor in the creation of a nation. . . . Indeed, historical enquiry brings to light deeds of violence which took place at the origin of all political formations, even of those whose consequences have been altogether beneficial. Unity is always effected by means of brutality" (11). In the case of the United States, the conquest of Native Americans exemplifies the violence that according to Renan must always be forgotten in the formation of a nation. A number of Robert Frost's poems reflect this necessary forgetting, but many of them also engage in acts of remembering that honor the past without subverting any particular ideology. As a poet, Frost is both settled and unsettling, a writer who composes without resorting to simplistic moral categories or the easy romanticization of Indians as noble savages. While his poems testify to their conflicting positions within the Joycean nightmare of history, Frost himself "distrusted progressive models . . . and was apt to see certain of his inheritances as natural and unchangeable" (Rotella 242). In his thinking about national history and empire, Frost adopts a Virgilian perspective, assuming that injustice is in the nature of things and that in the long-term perspective of history, the European conquest of the Americas merely gave rise to the world's most recent empire, which in its turn, too, would someday fall. In particular, Frost's treatment of the theme of the American Indian shows that, despite the willed forgetting entailed by narratives of national formation, the memory of the brutality that founds the nation persists in the imagination of European Americans. Several of Frost's poems show how that memory haunts otherwise confident expressions of patriotism, troubling complacent formulations of American history as a straightforward progress toward freedom and equality.

Benedict Anderson explicates a particular passage from Renan's essay in order to convey the odd temporality of the process of "national forgetting." "The essence of a nation," writes Renan, "is that all individuals have many things in common, and also that they have forgotten many things. No French citizen knows whether he is a Burgundian, an Alan, a Taifale, or a Visigoth, yet every French citizen has to have forgotten the massacre of Saint

Bartholomew, or the massacres that took place in the Midi in the thirteenth century" (11). Anderson zeroes in on the French phrase translated in this excerpt as "has to have forgotten." To him, the phrase "suggests, in the ominous tone of revenue-codes and military conscription laws, that 'already having forgotten' ancient tragedies is a prime contemporary civic duty. In effect, Renan's readers were being told to 'have already forgotten' what Renan's own words assumed that they naturally remembered!" (200). Anderson accounts for this paradox by arguing that the citizens of modern nations must undergo "a deep reshaping of the imagination of which the state was barely conscious, and over which it had, and still has, only exiguous control" (201). This reshaping exacts a forgetting in order to reconfigure the bloody events of the past as disputes between common members of a nation—as fratricidal or civil conflicts instead of wars between enemies unrelated by blood. The process of remembering-through-forgetting gives birth to a conception of the nation as an extended family. In his effort to account for the necessity of already having forgotten something one may be expected to know, Anderson writes that

> the creole nationalisms of the Americas are especially instructive. For on the one hand, the American states were for many decades weak, effectively decentralized, and rather modest in their educational ambitions. On the other hand, the American societies, in which "white" settlers were counterposed to "black" slaves and half-exterminated "natives," were internally riven to a degree quite unmatched in Europe. Yet the imagining of that fraternity, without which the reassurance of fratricide can not be born, shows up remarkably early, and not without a curious authentic popularity. In the United States of America this paradox is particularly well exemplified. (202)

Forgetting past events in order to reconfigure the nation as a family, the citizens of the United States of America nonetheless confront themselves (as the plural name of their country suggests) as a diverse, even fragmented, population that is anything but a family. Despite American society's being more gesellschaft than gemeinschaft, Anderson suggests, the need for a sense of national unity is so great that it overcomes (or seeks to overcome) fragmentation by figuring the social contract (gesellschaft) of the U.S. Constitution in the kinship terms of family or tribe (gemeinschaft). The conflict between these two views of social relations may inform the conflict in Frost's poetry between the dutiful forgetting that accepts the metaphor of the nation as a fraternity or family and the sometimes less sociable act of remembering that troubles this metaphor. However, unlike Anderson's examples of fraternal partnerships from nineteenth-century American literature (Natty Bumppo and Chingachgook, Ishmael and Queequeg, or Jim and Huck Finn), Frost's poems offer no soothing view of American history as "reassuring fratricide" or peacefully fraternal companionship (Anderson 199–203). Frost's speakers might sympathize with Native Americans, but they ultimately avoid the sentimentality of transfiguring them from threatening "others" into comforting brothers.

Indeed, the specter of the Indian, with all the fascinated anxiety it engenders, possesses Frost's imagination in a powerful way. D. H. Lawrence offers an illuminating comment on this anxiety in his *Studies in Classic American Literature:*

> A curious thing about the Spirit of Place is the fact that no place exerts its full influence upon a newcomer until the old inhabitant is dead or absorbed. So America. While the Red Indian existed in fairly large numbers, the new colonials were in a great measure immune from the daimon, or demon, of America. The moment the last nuclei of Red life break up in America, then the white men will have to reckon with the full force of the demon of the continent. At present the demon of the place and the unappeased ghost of the dead Indians act within the unconscious or under-conscious soul of the white American, causing the great American grouch, the Orestes-like frenzy of restlessness in the Yankee soul, the inner malaise which amounts almost to madness, sometimes. (40–41)

As Lawrence suggests, the figure of the Indian haunts the collective memory of his conquerors' progeny. Moreover, while Lawrence's "Spirit of Place" corresponds to Frost's play on "possession" in "Gift Outright," his references to the "Orestes-like frenzy of restlessness in the Yankee soul" and of "madness" could be applied to the speaker's uncle in "A Servant to Servants," the speaker of "The Witch of Coös," Frost's ancestor Charles in the unpublished poem "Genealogical," or perhaps most accurately, to the Miller in "The Vanishing Red." In his poetry Frost demonstrates his ambivalence about nationalism and its requirement of forgetting, sometimes satisfying this requirement, but often enough evading it. The subtle and penetrating modulations within the poems (be they linguistic, perspectival, or dramatic) celebrate American accomplishments at the same time that they question them. In his work, remembering becomes a way of both articulating national responsibilities and critiquing forms of patriotism he found too easy.

As he insisted in his reflection upon his practice as a writer, the category of the nation was fundamental to Frost's sense of the artistic process. "'Nationality,'" he told an audience at Middlebury College in 1943, "is something 'I couldn't live without'" (Reginald Cook 34). For Frost, nationality and individual personality were parallel terms. In "Education by Poetry," he explains what he means: "Look! First I want to be a person. And I want you to be a person, and then we can be as interpersonal as you please. We can pull each other's noses—do all sorts of things. But, first of all, you have got to have the personality. First of all, you have got to have the nations and then they can be as international as they please with each other" (*Collected Poems, Prose, and Plays* 727).[1] In a letter to Régis Michaud, Frost wrote that "I am as sure that the colloquial is the root of every good poem as I am that the national is the root of all thought and art. It may shoot up as high as you please and flourish as widely abroad in the air, if only the roots are what and where they should be" (*Selected Letters* 228). Frost's comments to Michaud and his remarks in

"Education by Poetry" show that getting one's national and metaphysical bearings—knowing who and where one is, as "A Cabin in the Clearing" puts it—intimately informs his practice as a poet. This knowledge, Frost's work shows, emerges from the dialectic between remembering and forgetting the circumstances of one's country's origins.

Frost shows his interest in national matters quite clearly in a number of poems. For example, some of his juvenilia ("La Noche Triste," "The Sachem of the Clouds") as well as a few of his mature poems (such as "The Vanishing Red" and "A Cabin in the Clearing") and one unpublished poem ("Genealogical") deal with the subject of Native Americans, while some of his light verse ("America Is Hard to See," "The Vindictives," and "The Discovery of the Madeiras") reflects upon the European conquest of the New World and slavery. Moreover, in more famous poems such as "Mending Wall," "The Death of the Hired Man," "Home Burial," "The Hill Wife," "The Need of Being Versed in Country Things," and "Directive," together with "The Black Cottage," "The Generations of Men," "The Birthplace," "Beech," and "Triple Bronze," Frost offers meditations on the topics of place, property, self, and boundary that can be related to the role of national issues in his career. More specifically, Frost's portraits of abandoned, haunted, or ruined homes foreground the role of property and settlement in American history in uncanny ways that destabilize the concepts of property and self. As Andrew Lakritz argues, the Frostian "ruin is evidence of . . . an original birth, and acts in nationalist terms as guarantee of the identity for the American, as against any other claims for identification" ("Frost in Transition" 213). While Native Americans do not haunt all of Frost's landscapes and domestic interiors, the eerie quality of many of their appearances reveals the unstable character of personal identity and human relationships in a culture crucially defined, as "Build Soil" makes clear, by the conflict between the individual and the communal. In a way that corresponds to Moore's depiction of the contrasting attitudes toward land and property between natives and colonists, to John Locke's distinction between "civilized" land enclosure and "savage" land use, and to Frantz Fanon's association of proper self and property ownership, Frost's investigations of American property and identity show their historic interrelation. For Tom Paulin, in fact, "Frost's status as a national poet" partly derives from his anxious sense of the powerful connection between the two (172). Finally, one of Frost's most famous short poems, "The Gift Outright," addresses the matter of the nation's origins, demonstrating the way in which key elements of colonial history must be forgotten in the process of constructing a coherent national narrative.

Frost simultaneously remembers and forgets the colonial origins of his nation in unexpected and indirect ways through his descriptions of property and homes. While property is a defining term in Frost's lexicon ("Good fences make good neighbors"), a fact that aligns him with Locke, the poet frequently questions the legitimacy and adequacy of property and its boundaries, especially through the metaphor of deserted or decaying homes.

"Mending Wall" famously broaches these issues by pitting two proverbs against one another ("Something there is that doesn't love a wall" versus "Good fences") and comparing the enclosure-committed neighbor to "an old-stone savage armed" (40). By likening the property-defender to the figure of the savage, whom Locke defined as having no conception of property, Frost ironically suggests that the alliance between property and personal identity lacks absolute coherence. Like "Blueberries" (about people competing to pick fruit on another man's property), "Stopping by Woods on a Snowy Evening" (whose speaker acknowledges the absent owner of the woods while enjoying his view of them), and "Trespass" (which comically transfigures an act of trespassing into the opportunity for human exchange), "Mending Wall" imagines ways in which personal freedom can exist outside the imperious limits of property. On a somewhat starker note, the "Witness Tree" of "Beech" marks out the territory of the "Moodie Forester's" private domain, simultaneously asserting its boundaries against a surrounding "world" of "dark and doubt" and acknowledging the limits of those boundaries (301).

"Mending Wall" and "Stopping by Woods" are only two of the more famous poems that address divisions between people and property, for Frost repeatedly questions the permanence of boundaries by calling attention to their permeability. In "Death of a Hired Man," for example, he depicts the intersections between the private space of the home and the social world outside. The poem supports Bhabha's claim that "The recesses of the domestic space become sites for history's most intricate invasions. In that displacement, the borders between home and world become confused; and, uncannily, the private and the public become part of each other, forcing upon us a vision that is as divided as it is disorienting" (9). In "Death of a Hired Man" (as in Williams's "To Elsie"), for example, an outsider brings the conflicts of the public world into the family household. Like Williams, Frost shows how a hired laborer becomes part of the family and thereby changes it. "Death" revolves around definitions of home that reflect the openness of the domestic space to the social world in which it is embedded. In the conversation between the householders Mary and Warren, Frost foregrounds the meaning of *home* by offering competing definitions of the term in a way that recalls the debate about fences in "Mending Wall." For Warren, *home* means "the place where, when you have to go there, / They have to take you in," while for Mary it means "Something you somehow haven't to deserve" (43). The fact that both definitions are prompted by the presence of Silas, an outsider, reflects the permeability of "home" to the world. By means of the debate between Warren and Mary, the poem becomes a public meditation on the meaning of home in general, even though it is set within the privacy of their particular home. Mary introduces the word in relation to Silas, and Warren echoes it ironically as they each express their views regarding his arrival. The poem makes clear the initial position of each member of the couple, but it does so in the context of Silas's foreign presence in order to dramatize his "place" within their family and the relevance of his implicit claim to their hospitality. Although the poem is not an allegory about the relations between employees and family employers, the fact that other poems (including "The Code," "A Servant to Servants," and "Two Tramps in Mud Time") feature similar relations suggests that the poem does have a representative status within Frost's oeuvre. This poem remembers the communal obligations that American individualism often forgets or represses by emphasizing, through the tense balance of Mary's and Warren's opposing views, the affection for Silas that Warren ultimately joins his wife in acknowledging. The poem's focus upon the opposition between community and individual recalls the analogous conflict between familial and contractual social relations that Anderson sees as central to the dynamic of national remembering and forgetting. In addition, its domestic setting links it with Frost's many other poems about homes, including "A Cabin in the Clearing" (which I discuss later in relation to America's pioneer history).

Like "A Cabin in the Clearing," "The Birthplace" also evokes America's pioneer mythology, and like the more famous "The Need of Being Versed in Country Things," "The Birthplace" presents the site of a former dwelling:

> Here further up the mountain slope
> Than there was ever any hope,
> My father built, enclosed a spring,
> Strung chains of wall round everything,
> Subdued the growth of earth to grass,
> And brought our various lives to pass. (243)

The poem's title and plot commemorate the founding of the speaker's childhood home, but it also shows how the pioneering efforts of the ancestor were at odds with the "mountain slope" on which he built his property. The walls of this poem recall the one in "Mending Wall," but in "Birthplace," Frost takes pains to represent walls as property-bounding "chains" that the founding father used to subdue his plot of ground. In addition, the poem highlights the fact that those efforts eventually fell to nothing: "The mountain pushed us off her knees. / And now her lap is full of trees" (243). "The Birthplace," like Moore's "Virginia Britannia," emphasizes the limits of human history by contrasting its achievements with its losses in the face of powerful natural forces. The conclusion it reaches, like the territory it maps, is ultimately unsettled, for the boundaries between nature and human culture have dissolved. Such poems as "Storm Fear," "Now Close the Windows," "Mending Wall," "Home Burial," "An Old Man's Winter Night," "Locked Out," "The Sound of Trees," "The Lockless Door," "Tree at My Window," "The Thatch," and "Beech" engage a similar dichotomy between external and internal spaces, and they exhibit the same suspicion of the border that divides them. In doing so they reflect an uneasiness between human beings and the landscape or social world with which they interact. A similar anxiety about place informs "A Cabin in the Clearing" and "The Gift Outright."

"The Black Cottage" also plays with the division between a domestic interior and the outside world, but it does so in order to meditate on national history in an explicit way. The action of the poem takes place in an abandoned house that recalls the ruined homesteads of "Ghost House," "The Generations of Men," and "Directive." As the speaker and his guide roam through the cottage, the guide, a clergyman who knew the woman who inhabited it, begins to ruminate on her "idea of things." In doing so, he articulates national values that she embodied for him. For the guide, the cottage functions as a monument to the nation's founding ideals because it reminds him of his friend's devotion to her husband who died in the Civil War and to the democratic principles of freedom and equality. "'One wasn't long in learning,'" he explains to his companion,

> "that she thought
> Whatever else the Civil War was for
> It wasn't just to keep the States together,
> Nor just to free the slaves, though it did both.
> She wouldn't have believed those ends enough
> To have given outright for them all she gave.
> Her giving somehow touched the principle
> That all men are created equal." (60)

The minister's language describing his dead friend's sacrifice connects this poem to "The Gift Outright." The "lady" remembered in the poem embodies the founding values of the republic, but she has both sacrificed her husband to a war that reunited it and surrendered any social standing she may have had by deliberately withdrawing from it. Like the setting of "The Death of the Hired Man," "The Black Cottage" is uncanny in the way Bhabha describes, for the poem opens the private space of the house to the public values it represents for the minister.[2] While the poem romanticizes Jeffersonian democracy by rendering it remote, beleaguered, innocent, and heroic from the sentimental perspective of the admiring minister ("'I shouldn't be surprised if in this world / It were the force that would at last prevail'"), it also clearly articulates a commitment to republican values (61). Of the claim that "'all men are equal,'" the minister admits,

> "That's a hard mystery of Jefferson's.
> What did he mean? Of course the easy way
> Is to decide it simply isn't true.
> It may not be. I heard a fellow say so.
> But never mind, the Welshman got it planted
> Where it will trouble us a thousand years.
> Each age will have to reconsider it." (60)

The minister's concession about the truth of Jefferson's thesis yields to his triumphal sense that the goal of democratic equality is worth pursuing, even in the face of imperious dismissals and abridgments of it ("'it simply isn't true'"). For Jonathan Barron, "The Black Cottage" shows that "Frost's nationalism" was "defined" by "deeply considered, deeply felt individual choice" (151).[3]

This view places "The Black Cottage" at the heart of the republican tradition of U.S. history, but Frost's overall fame as a poet rests not only on his exploration of individualism (as the popularity of "The Road Not Taken" similarly demonstrates), but also on his success at registering the nuances of American speech and his ability to entertain conflicting positions in singular turns of phrase.[4] In "Mending Wall," "The Code," and "Home Burial," for example, Frost depicts physically vigorous but laconic men very much like the pioneer described by Waldo Frank in *Our America*, and he does so in order to articulate their outlooks, which for him are representative American ones. In such poems as "Good Hours," "The Hill Wife," "Once by the Pacific," "Bereft," "Acquainted with the Night," and "Desert Places," the confident, imperial self of the Emersonian imagination gives way to an anxious loneliness that is one of the keynotes of Frost's lyric poetry. At the same time, the Dickinsonian or Thoreauvian defiance of, say, "Into My Own," "In Neglect," and "Not Quite Social" represents another characteristically Frostian stance. Along different lines, Frost's intimations of conflict or violence in poems from "A Hundred Collars," "The Code," and "The Self-Seeker" to "'Out, Out—,'" "The Witch of Coös," "The Subverted Flower," and "The Draft Horse" provide a relevant field of reference for the poems about Indians and national consciousness that form the basis of this chapter. Although many of Frost's less-known poems are the focus in what follows, I consider them in the context of his work as a whole by attending to the issues of property, identity, place, and conflict that inform his most accomplished poems.

• Frost once remarked to Sidney Cox that "one of his passions in boyhood was angry sympathy with the American Indians" (Cox 21). Two pieces among Frost's juvenilia reflect this early interest in Native Americans. "La Noche Triste" (1890), Frost's first published poem, recounts the attack on the Aztec capital Tenochtitlan by Cortez and the rout of his army by Montezuma's army. In hindsight, Frost described the subject of "La Noche Triste" as the "bad night the Indians gave the Spaniards to my gratification when they drove them temporarily back from Tenochtitlan" (Thompson and Winnick 297). "My sympathies were with the Indians," he told Louis Mertins. "I had been grieving about the way Cortez treated Montezuma and his people. I remember it was a windy, dusty March day in Lawrence. My thoughts kept coming back to the Indians trying to escape from the Spaniards" (44). Although much of the poem is devoted to the excitement of the battle and the dangers of the Aztec defense and the Spanish retreat, it ends on a note of memento mori when, in the penultimate stanza, it reminds the reader that "The flame [that] shines brightest e'er goes out." In its context within Frost's ballad, the Aztec victory, which its readers know was reversed in subsequent engagements with the Spanish, exemplifies the truth that all things human die, including nations. If there is a pleasure on the speaker's part in the early Indian victory, there is also the acknowledgment that all empires are doomed to fall:

> The Montezumas are no more,
> Gone is their regal throne,
> And freemen live, and rule, and die,
> Where they have lived alone. (488)

Even in his celebration of a rare Indian victory, Frost keeps in mind the tyranny of the Aztec regime. Frost's concern for the well-being of Native Americans does not prevent him from recognizing the flaws of those whom he favors. His "asystematic immersion in the age of pre-colonial exploration," writes Lesley Lee Francis, "was a specific and integral part of the larger, intuitive search for the signs of man's passing and did not stop with . . . the publication of 'La Noche Triste' in the *High School Bulletin*" (15).

Frost's publication of "The Sachem of the Clouds" (1891) in the Lawrence *Daily American* only a year and a half after "La Noche Triste" confirms Francis's claim. The poem clearly evinces the sympathy for American Indians that Frost also articulated in a class debate the same year. In this debate, Frost defended "a bill for removing the Indians from Indian Territory to more fertile districts and ceding said districts to the tribes forever; and for giving them some compensation for the losses already suffered," drawing on "extensive factual information from Helen Hunt Jackson's impassioned indictment, *A Century of Dishonor: A Sketch of the United States Government's Dealings with Some of the Indian Tribes*" (Francis 10). Subtitled "A Thanksgiving Legend," "The Sachem of the Clouds" enacts a fantasy of revenge on behalf of the Indians. Its commemoration of American aboriginals reflects the white speaker's mournful regret concerning their defeat at the hands of his ancestors. The poem communicates this mourning through the figure of the sachem, who commands the elements and calls upon them to wreak vengeance on behalf of his people:

> "Come, O come, with storm, come darkness! Speed my clouds on Winter's breath.
> All my race is gone before me, all my race is low in death!
> Ever, as I ruled a people, shall this smoke arise in cloud;
> Ever shall it freight the tempest for the ocean of the proud.
> 'Thanks!' I hear their cities thanking that my race is low in death.
> Come, O come, with storm, come darkness! Speed my clouds on Winter's breath!"
>   (494–95)

As in Frost's later poems (and in such nineteenth-century poems as Lydia Sigourney's "The Cherokee Mother" and "The Indian's Welcome to the Pilgrim Fathers"), the voice of the Indian haunts the landscape of "The Sachem of the Clouds," unsettling the complacency of his white usurpers: "Thus his voice keeps ringing, ringing, till appears the dreary dawn" (495).[5] Yet the enthusiasm for warfare and the awareness of the injustices of the Aztec empire in "La Noche Triste" also reappear in Frost's later work, showing that contradictory perspectives on Indians and European colonization persist throughout his writing.

Assuming the perspective of "The Sachem of the Clouds" in "Genealogical" (1908), a poem he included in a letter but never published, Frost demonstrates something of this boyhood passion by writing about his ancestor, the "Indian killer" Charles Frost. In a letter dated January 1908 to Susan Hayes Ward, Frost ironically refers to his forebear as "my bad ancestor the Indian killer" and calls the poem "some Whitmanism of mine" (*Selected Letters* 42). Frost refers to the poem again in a letter of December 19, 1911, calling it "that authentic bit of family history I once promised you" (43). The poem links Frost's national and family history in a comic and ironic bond that evokes without resolving the tensions between Native Americans and European settlers:

> It was my grandfather's grandfather's grandfather's
> Great-great-grandfather or thereabouts I think—
> One cannot be too precise in a matter like this.
> He was hanged the story goes. Yet not for grief
> Have I vowed a pilgrimage to the place where he lies
> Under a notable bowlder in Eliot, Maine,
> But for pride if for aught at this distance of time.
> Yearly a chosen few of his many descendants
> At solemn dinner assembled tell over the story
> Of how in his greatness of heart he aspired
> To wipe out the whole of an Indian tribe to order,
> As in those extravagant days they wasted the woods
> With fire to clear the land for tillage.
> It seems he was rather pointedly *not* instructed
> To proceed in the matter with any particular
> Regard to the laws of civilized warfare.
> He wasted no precious time in casting about
> For means he could call his own. He simply seized
> Upon any unprotected idea that came to hand. (514)

The clearing of land in this passage corresponds to the title and theme of the later poem "A Cabin in the Clearing," and as in that poem it subtly implies a connection between the cutting down of trees and the mowing down of men. "Genealogical" contemplates a "pilgrimage" "for pride" to the "notable bowlder" marking the tomb of Frost's ancestor, articulating at the same time a mock repudiation of his deeds. Like the ruined dwellings in Frost's more famous poems, that "bowlder" marks the ancestral tomb as an uncanny site, for the poet's imagined pilgrimage instead turns out to be an account of the ancestor's grim pillage of the Indians and their land. His already ironic pride turns into amused chagrin.

With his joking repetition of ancestral grandfathers (which corresponds to the comic train of "greats" describing a grandmother in "The Generations of Men"), his admission that "One cannot be too precise in a matter like this," and his colloquial aside ("He was hanged the story goes"), Frost suggests the legendary character of the narrative that follows. Given the vagaries of oral transmission resulting from the changes that creep into a story as it gets passed from generation to generation, Frost's casually dropped remark turns out to be more significant than it may first appear. It hints at the legendary quality of the narrative, provoking the reader's desire for an entertaining tale at the same time that it subtly undercuts the veracity of the events it recounts. Like "The Vanishing Red," "The Witch of Coös," and "Paul's Wife," "Genealogical" has an air of the tall tale about it. While maintaining the reader's suspended disbelief, the narrator of this poem delivers his account with a nod and a wink. Part of the pleasure of the poem is in the narrative performance, including any touches of excess that may embellish the story line here and there. In the process of this performance, inherited views about the colonization of North America and the origins of the United States are scrutinized, challenged, and reshaped.

"Genealogical" is thematically linked not only to Frost's youthful "Sachem of the Clouds" but to the later poems "The Generations of Men" and "The Vanishing Red." It is significant that the association of eating with murder occurs in both "Genealogical" and "The Vanishing Red," an association that figures colonial dispossession as a form of cannibal savagery. The angry rapacity of the Miller in "The Vanishing Red" (discussed later) figures the colonial dispossession of indigenous inhabitants by white invaders. This conflict between hospitality and individuality, moreover, recurs in "Love and a Question," "The Death of the Hired Man," "Snow," and "Two Tramps in Mud Time." In "Genealogical," Frost depicts his ancestor's massacre of the Indians at the banquet to which he had invited them. Once they arrived, Frost writes, "he fell upon them with slaughter / And all that he didn't slay he bound and sold / Into slavery where Philip the Chief's son went" (515). Motivated as it is by the desire for the lands they inhabit, Charles Frost's ruse of a "barbecue" (a word derived from Taino, a Caribbean Indian language) represents his assault as a devouring violence, for after the ambush, we are told, he remained a "good sleeper and eater" and "serenely forgot" those who escaped his power.[6] Frost undercuts the "heroism" of this betrayal by following up the report with the offhand remark that "He doubtless called the place something and claimed the victory" (515). The intentional vagueness of "doubtless" and "something" deflates the significance of the event, translating the victor's ritual from a sublime naming that affirms the heroism of action into a satiric travesty of triumph, while the second half of the predicate ("claimed the victory") may be read as a buoyant announcement of conquest or a doubting account of the Major's version of events. As so often in Frost's poems, the imagined tone of voice is crucial, for a stress on "claimed" suggests that what the Major claimed as a great victory was in fact a grave ignominy. And the claim he stakes is for the land formerly used by the Amerindians he has vanquished.

While Charles Frost's ploy of a dinner is echoed in the Miller's treachery in "The Vanishing Red," it also makes his ambush a murderous violation of the rites of hospitality. This violation is on the disastrous order of the grisly feast Atreus gave his brother Thyestes, for it too entails a painful legacy. In provisionally conceiving of American history as family history, Frost's poem echoes the consequential events of another family's tragedy. In the same way that Atreus's betrayal of his brother left a curse on their family, the ancestral Frost of "Genealogical" leaves a curse that marks the history of the United States. The dinners Charles's scions sponsor in his honor ritually repeat his treachery. In this regard, Frost's reference to his family's banquet echoes "The Sachem of the Clouds" by ironically revising traditional Thanksgiving narratives of pilgrim-Indian cooperation, replacing them with a less felicitous but more accurate account of the nation's origins.

Frost's burlesque rendering of his ancestor Charles's death, burial, exhumation, and reburial in "Genealogical" suggests that he very much enjoys debunking his progenitor: the poet evokes the figure of his forebear, kills him off, grants him a sodden resurrection in the form of a desecrating disinterment and posthumous hanging, and finally returns him to the earth of his "eternal" rest. "All that detracted from the glory of" the Major's "achievement," Frost writes,

> Was the escape of a few of the devoted tribesmen
> Either by running away or staying away
> An awkward remnant that would have lain, methinks,
> Even upon my somewhat sophisticated conscience
> Given to the sympathetic fallacy of attributing to savages
> The feelings of human beings,
> More heavily than those who were slain.
> He good sleeper and eater serenely forgot them.
> But here again he just missed greatness as a captain.
> For these waylaid him one Sunday on his way home
> From the proper church completely edified
> And slew him in turn with great barbarity
> And left him outspread for filial burial.
> His sons with dignity dug him a decent grave
> And duly laid him to rest.
> But the Redskins, not quite sure they had done enough
> To satisfy the eternal vengeances,
> Returned and had him out of the ground and hanged him up.
> And so he was hanged!
> The indefatigable sons cut him down and buried him again,
> And this time to secure him against further disturbance,
> With the help of their neighbors at a sort of burying bee
> They rolled a stone upon him that once it was sunk in place
> Not strong men enough could come at together to lift it. (515–16)

Frost satirizes the self-righteous religion of his ancestor when he reports that the survivors of his attack "waylaid him on Sunday on his way home / From the proper church completely edified" (515). Frost means us to share his delight in the "great barbarity" of the Indian reprisal and his scorn for "the proper church" from which Charles exits (and that no doubt countenanced the white mistreatment of the Indians). Whereas the dead obtrude on the living as an eerie irruption of the netherworld in Robert Lowell's "At the Indian Killer's Grave" (a poem that shares a similar theme but treats it somewhat differently), "Genealogical" is an irreverent exhumation, for it digs up the dead ancestor not once but twice in order to defame him. Frost performs his own revenge against his ancestor by evoking a poetic effigy of him in order to malign and shame it. The poem reverses the conventions of elegy by denigrating the life of the dead man. Instead of honoring Charles, Frost looks back at his example with an ironic mix of chagrin and humor: "And there he lies in glory the ancestor of a good many of us. / And I think he explains my life-long liking for Indians" (516). Although it is a private joke fraught with oedipal impudence, "Genealogical" squarely plants Frost the poet in "the bloody loam" of his nation's history, for in a sense he is the descendant of his ancestor's deceit. While the poem remained a private joke in the corpus of his writing, a piece he consciously excluded from his published work, its appearance in a letter might suggest, if we follow the logic of Mark Richardson, that it offers a less diplomatic but more "sincere" version of Frost's view of the relationship between poetry and society than his published poetry does (54–75).

Frost's reference to his "somewhat sophisticated conscience" conveys the sense of guilt regarding colonial injustice against Native Americans that often remains unspoken in his published works. The stylized humor of the phrase expresses Frost's irony regarding the putative superiority of his conscience, ridiculing his self-righteous stance even as he deconstructs the racism that regards Amerindians as "savages" who lack "the feelings of human beings." Frost's wry formulation suggests that he is aware of historicity as well as history. He seems to imply that in the end his sense of things may be no better than that of his ancestor Charles, recognizing how easy it is to condemn aspects of a past in which one has not participated but from which one has nonetheless benefited. Charles Frost's atrocity was only one in a larger pattern of dispossessions upon which the possessions of his scion's famous poem "The Gift Outright" depend. Frost the poet also knows the story he inherits is not an unusual one. His relation to the account demonstrates his larger-than-American sense of man's inhumanity to man, which puts him at odds with the view that American empire is somehow exceptional. For Frost, the American imperium is neither more nor less monstrous than previous forms of empire. His commemoration in "Genealogical" of the brutality of colonial history demonstrates his awareness of the unsettled, conflicting nature of his country's origins and history. It provides an account of the dispossession of Native Americans that "The Gift Outright," with its self-conscious ceremony and celebration, will be obliged to forget.

In "Genealogical," Frost situates himself as a reader of his forefather's act by comparing his own identity as a poet to the Major's identity as renegade statesman and de facto soldier:

> I will not set up the claim for my progenitor
> That he was an artist in murder or anything else
> Or that any of his descendants would have been
> Without the infusion of warmer blood from somewhere.
> Were it imperative to distinguish between statesman and artist
> I should say that the first believes that the end justifies the means
> The second that the means justify the end. (514–15)

The phrasing here ("an artist in murder or anything else") is comic, suggesting that Frost is joking as much about his own artistry as his progenitor's military maneuvers. The "infusion of warmer blood" he deems necessary to account for his poetic temperament separates him from the cold-blooded killing of "the Major," but it also draws on stock racial stereotypes that associate southern climates with passionate dispositions. Moreover, Charles Frost's strategic scheming is not categorically different from the cool-headed calculation his descendant practices in his craft as a poet. Frost's phrase betrays his sense that art is in fact a kind (but only a kind) of murder. Perhaps when he composed the line he was thinking of his wife, Elinor, who disliked his publishing (Meyers 160–61, 165).

More significant, perhaps, is the chiasmus that Frost relies on to define the differences between politics and poetry, and between Charles Frost and himself. The Major does not quite earn the title of statesman, but the poet's identification of him as such nonetheless reflects the careers of the many soldier-statesmen who won U.S. elections after having served in wars against Indians. According to the poet's discriminating definitions, the "statesman" believes "that the end justifies the means," whereas the "artist" believes the reverse, that "the means justify the end." If the poet does not quite achieve his desired end in "Genealogical," it is the fault of his artistic means and not of his ancestor's bloody ends. The Major's dispossession clears the ground for his people's settlement, but the unsettling memories of colonization persist amid the benefits he bequeathed to his descendants. In "Genealogical," the logic of a lineage becomes the figure for a nation's history, though this logic works differently from the mythology that Renan and Anderson describe, which recasts conflicts between conquerors and conquered as conflicts between kin. The war Frost depicts is not a civil one.

• Frost's arch homage to his family patriarch ends up honoring the Indian victims of his ancestor more than the ancestor himself. This unsentimental twist leaves as its legacy a sense of the Indian's persisting presence in America even at the moment of his supposed eclipse. In this respect "Genealogical" serves as a thematic counterpart to "The Vanishing Red," while its meditation on the issues of settlement and dispossession link it to the later poems "The Gift Outright" and "A Cabin in the Clearing." In "The Vanishing Red," published in the 1916 collection *Mountain Interval,* Frost renders a shocking portrait of racial hatred in twenty-nine brief, compelling lines. The voice of the poem's narrator is extraordinarily intimate and colloquial. In the first two lines, the narrator twice repeats the verb phrase "is said to," affirming the secondhand basis of the narrative that follows, as Karen Kilcup notes when she says that Frost's repetition "highlights the poem's . . . legendary framework" (56).

Both the poem's title and the hedging declaration of its first sentence refer to the decimation of Amerindian peoples by their white supplanters. They simultaneously remember and forget, in other words, the colonial displacement at the heart of American history. The poem's title makes its reference metonymically, by virtue of its racial designation. This identification by color is reinforced and clarified by the phrase "the last Red Man," but it also implies that the Miller's vision is colored by blood. Cox writes, "He saw red," not only in his assessment of the Indian according to the color of his skin rather than the content of his character, but in the bloody visions of his murderous plan (22–23). The narrator introduces his two chief characters in the evasive language of the first three lines of the poem:

> He is said to have been the last Red Man
> In Acton. And the Miller is said to have laughed—
> If you like to call such a sound a laugh. (136)

The reductions of the characters of the story to the racial and professional designations that identify them establish the legendary anonymity that characterizes the poem as a whole, indicating (despite its meter) its ballad-like quality. It also throws into relief the violent tension that will erupt between them.

The Miller's defensive repetition of the interrogative phrase "Whose business" in the following passage characterizes the Miller's as-yet-undescribed deed in terms of a familiar idiom that makes his murder of the Indian part of his profession, or "business":

> But he gave no one else a laugher's license.
> For he turned suddenly grave as if to say,
> "Whose business—if I take it on myself,
> Whose business—but why talk round the barn?—
> When it's just that I hold with getting a thing done with." (136)

The Miller is indeed a man of business; he prefers acts to mincing words. In repeating his rhetorical question regarding the interest of others in his affairs ("Whose business . . . ?"), he insists that his murderous activity is clearly his own. In rendering the Indian a literal grist to his mill, Frost figures the white man's act as an expression of commercial voracity. Frost's answer to the

Miller's question would be the same he attributes to Terence in "The Constant Symbol": "all human business is my business" (787). Frost proves this claim in the text of his poem, for part of the artist's ethics is to reveal to his audience all dimensions of human experience—even those we label "inhuman." Frost's fable tropes the industrial capitalism of his own day as a deadly machine that a white proprietor turns to his own racist ends. It is in this sense that the fate of "The Vanishing Red" is most fully consumed in the Miller's personal business.

In the second stanza of the poem, the narrator situates his tale in the context of the historical conflicts between European invaders and Amerindian inhabitants. Yet in doing so he also insists that the story about the Miller is the result of something more personal and complicated than the ongoing conflicts "between the two races." In reporting his tale, the narrator seems to invite a sympathetic or at least nonjudgmental perspective toward the Miller. "You can't get back and see it as he saw it," the narrator insists:

> It's too long a story to go into now.
> You'd have to have been there and lived it.
> Then you wouldn't have looked on it as just a matter
> Of who began it between the two races. (136)

The narrator contradicts himself in claiming "It's too long a story to go into now" and then denying that the murder was "just a matter / Of who began it between the two races." On one hand, the narrator's first "it" would appear to refer to the relationship between Europeans and Amerindians in all its sweep and complexity. Hence the pronoun implicitly remembers the dispossession of Native Americans inaugurated by the establishment of the United States. On the other hand, the second "it" is much more clearly delimited, apparently referring to the Miller's specific act, and so it represses the memory of that original dispossession. The second pronoun, however, is literally circumscribed by syntax that refers to the colonial conflict between whites and reds: "This story that is 'too long' 'to go into now,'" writes Kilcup, "is in fact what the poem unfolds" (56). Despite the mystifying apologia of the narrator, then, the appalling history of relations between conquering pioneers and indigenous occupants clearly contributes to the Miller's animosity. In a manner that conforms to the pattern described by Renan, his malevolence at once evokes the origin of the United States and willfully forgets it.

That his ill will takes a bodily form, moreover, is a testament to the powerful sway of racist ideology over the individual mind. In this case, the Miller's visceral response to the "guttural exclamation" of his Indian visitor probably reflects his belief that race is a matter of blood. If over time the conception of race as a biological category has fallen into scientific disrepute, it nevertheless exercises a powerful hold over the Miller's imagination. It is noteworthy that the Miller's disgust is triggered by a not fully verbal expression on the part of the "Red Man":

> Some guttural exclamation of surprise
> The Red Man gave in poking about the mill,
> Over the great big thumping shuffling millstone
> Disgusted the Miller physically as coming
> From one who had no right to be heard from. (136)

The indirect discourse of the last line of this passage registers the Miller's prejudice, as does the description of the Red Man's inspection of the mill, an act that clearly offends the Miller. Masking his umbrage, the Miller invites him to have a closer look. Like the narrator of Poe's "The Cask of Amontillado," the Miller ushers the Indian "down below a cramping rafter," leading his guest to a carefully premeditated death.

The narrator's details are lavished upon the circumstances of the Miller's disgust and the spectacular dash of the mill's "water in desperate straits like frantic fish," but he characterizes the "Red Man" only very sparingly, rendering him inscrutable. This inscrutability proves to be a cynosure of the Miller's prejudicial malice, for he ascribes to the Indian an emptiness he fills with his own bigoted beliefs. Because of his preconceptions about Indians in general, he attributes to this particular individual an unflattering imbecility. The Indian, moreover, does not even speak; his "guttural exclamation of surprise" at the sight of the mill, about which he surreptitiously pokes like an awkward animal, suggests that in the view of the Miller he is not even capable of speech. In attributing to the Indian a bestial or childlike speechlessness (a true form of infancy, if one recalls that the Latin root of that word, *infans*, means "speechless"), the Miller reduces the Indian to something like a cipher of the white man's prejudice (Kilcup 56). The Indian is not even granted a distinguishing appellation; one feels that the Miller's addressing him as "John" is done with a total disregard for the man's actual name (although this anonymity may of course also be part of the poem's generic conventions).

When the narrator makes his final grisly report, he reinforces the suggestions of cannibal commodification evoked by the Miller's vocabulary of "business":

> [The Miller] took him down below a cramping rafter,
> And showed him, through a manhole in the floor,
> The water in desperate straits like frantic fish,
> Salmon and sturgeon, lashing with their tails.
> Then he shut down the trap door with a ring in it
> That jangled even above the general noise,
> And came upstairs alone—and gave that laugh,
> And said something to a man with a meal-sack
> That the man with the meal-sack didn't catch—then.
> Oh, yes, he showed John the wheel pit all right. (136)

While the Europeans, as Cheyfitz and others point out, convinced themselves that there were cannibals to be found everywhere among the Amerindians they had "discovered," such beliefs were not accurate. The disparity between expectation and actuality did not, however, prevent Europeans from corrupting the designation *Carib* into *cannibal* and thereby inventing a phenomenon through a process of willful misnaming (Cheyfitz 41–44). Such misnaming reflects the way European assumptions shaped colonial assessments of the New World. Like the "tapestried landscape" of expectation to which Elizabeth Bishop alludes in "Brazil: January 1, 1502," the conventions of Indian behavior and of relations between Amerindians and Euro-Americans that Frost evokes and reconfigures in "The Vanishing Red" conform to familiar preconceptions.

Jeffrey Cramer points out that Frost used a local tale as the basis of "The Vanishing Red." "According to an annotation made by Frost in a copy of *Mountain Interval*," Cramer writes, "the story was told to him by someone from Acton" (59). In this tale that Frost recasts in poetic form, the Miller reverses that earlier pattern in which whites accused Indians of being cannibals, for in his unreported remark "to a man with a meal sack," the Miller suggests that he has converted the Indian from grist to gristle, making him into a food commodity, a horrible flour of bone meal and blood. The Miller moves, then, from the physical disgust he felt before the living Indian's "guttural" outburst, to a grotesque appetite for his dead and mutilated body. The Miller's "wheel pit," writes Robert Faggen, is Frost's "metaphor for a machinery that inexplicably allows one creature to extirpate another" (121). The poem's association of machinery with destruction, moreover, echoes similar associations in "When the Speed Comes," "The Self Seeker," "'Out, Out—,'" "The Line-Gang," and "The Grindstone."

The narrator of "The Vanishing Red" does not merely reproduce some more or less expected prejudice against Native Americans, however. Just as he identifies "the last Red Man" by his race, he names the white man by his occupation. Hence both red and white are identified by impersonal categories. In the language and generic conventions of the poem, both men remain types, distanced from the reader by a mist of time and anonymity. In addition, the narrator modifies his opening description of the Miller's reputed laugh with the modifying line "If you like to call such a sound a laugh." That parenthesis finesses even further the narrator's already tentative report. The narrator's hedging rhetoric suggests the limitations of his knowledge about the tale he so carefully retails (or, as the etymology of this verb intimates, "cuts up" into the meaty parcels of a poetic account for his readers' eager consumption).

The narrator does not even know what the Miller "really" thinks. He has to infer his motives and emotions from his laughter and his sudden gravity, for we are told that "he turned suddenly grave *as if* to say, / 'Whose business,—if I take it on my self,'"—not that the Miller actually said these words (emphasis added). The poem evokes from its readers a series of expectations that are based on a shared knowledge of American culture and history—and it plays with such expectations with gothic glee in order to expose them. It resists the reader's efforts to pin down the narrator's perspective, while it invites the reader to condemn or condone her perspective rather than the Miller's racial bigotry—or even the reader's own prejudices. For this reason, a reader risks misreading the narrator's function in the poem, which is to elicit the reader's emotions about the event described without committing too demonstratively to either the position of "John" or "the Miller." This aspect of the poem's diegesis, or account of events, constitutes not only part of the wit and fascination of the poem but also part of the political content of its style, or "performance." While it is not clear that the narrator speaks, as Kilcup argues, "from the point of view of someone who has not only heard the story but also been present during its actual enactment" (maybe he was, maybe he wasn't), her claim that "the narrator intimates the responsibility of the voyeuristic audience, himself included, in the murder that transpired" does seem accurate. The poem implies the Miller's murder of the red man, but the narrative of that murder itself "remains painfully unspoken" (Kilcup 57). "If in 'The Vanishing Red' John is hardly noble," Kilcup writes, "then, in a supremely ironic twist, the Miller [just like the nativist bigots in Moore's "The Labors of Hercules"] becomes the savage" (59).

In a poem that bespeaks the genocidal plight of Amerindians without presuming to speak for them (either those who are dead or their survivors), Frost articulates a central tension of American history through a powerful and telling silence. While for the Miller, John's "guttural exclamation" signifies his insuperable distance from language, for Frost's reader the poem turns on the Miller's (initially) "illegible" laugh. Articulation disappears down the well of his laughter—the poet figures his effort to voice Frank's "mystic word" of "America" (in all its polyglot variety) in the inscrutable terms of both the Indian's "guttural exclamation" and the Miller's enigmatic laugh. But it disappears only momentarily, to reappear with a vengeance in the implications of the poem as a whole. Frost's articulation in "The Vanishing Red" resides as much between the lines of the poem as it does in the words that constitute it.

Hayden Carruth may be right to argue that "the heart of the poem is the Miller's laugh," but if he is, it seems to me that he makes this argument for the wrong reason (34). Carruth reads the Miller's laugh as an existential response to the absurdity of "Man destroying himself, held in the absolute need to destroy himself," but that laugh is in fact the sign of something more reprehensible. After all, the poem depicts one man destroying another man, not himself. The laugh—or something approaching a laugh—actually expresses the Miller's defensive complacency regarding his murderous "business": "the Miller is also uncomfortable, of course, laughing off his own feeling of guilt. What he has done is more savage than anything the red man . . . ever did" (Cox 23). In this sense, "The Vanishing Red" temporarily buries language in a cacophonous cackle. Carruth's perceptive reflection on the role of New England understatement in the poem shows how language is both defeated and redeemed, or made to speak beyond its limitations, in "The Vanishing Red." "There is rarely a shriek in Frost," Carruth writes. "The Red Man just vanishes—not a word. The trap door says it, and then the Miller's laugh" (35).

Kilcup also comments on the poem's silences, but she does so in order to decipher the moral and political issues that the poem as a whole both bespeaks and obscures. "The ultimate horror of the murder," she writes, "is its concealment, both concretely and linguistically" (58). In this concealment, the narrator's attempt to maintain some sort of objectivity fatally fails:

> The speaker himself intimates and covers the violence with ostensibly detached and shockingly ironic language like "a *manhole* in the floor" (emphasis added). Next it is muffled by the noise of busyness, of business, and then the final line of the poem buries the Miller's guilt in a metaphoric and linguistic hole that renders it even more abhorrent because of the vacuum of moral responsibility it conceals . . . . The auditor inside the poem—like the speaker and the reader—shares the Miller's guilt, for he "didn't catch" what the latter tells him until much later. (Kilcup 58)

Like Kilcup, Cox reads the poem as an indictment of the reader's complicity in the Miller's act: "those who shared the Miller's civilization," he points out, "never did anything about the murder of the Indian" (24). In its dissolution of the narrator's attempted distance between himself and his story lies the performative power of Frost's poem. It undoes the appropriative lust figured by the miller's murderous mill.

• As with the work of Moore and Williams, the cultural nationalism that flourished in the early decades of the twentieth century informed the work that Frost produced not only during but well after those decades. His effort to reimagine the colonial moment of his nation's history, like that of his colleagues, pervades his career. In various poems such as the ones I have discussed, Frost dramatizes the pattern of forgetting that characterizes nation-building, but he also remembers events from history in order to parody received notions and to rearticulate them in a newly meaningful way for his own era. In poems that may be considered central to his elaboration of the national myth of the United States, such as "A Cabin in the Clearing" and "The Gift Outright," he similarly demonstrates the contradictory elements of this important historical paradigm.

In "A Cabin in the Clearing," which was circulated in 1951 as Frost's Christmas poem to friends, Frost evokes the pioneer tradition of U.S. history. By relating the issue of place to the matter of self-knowledge, Frost repeats the trope of "The Gift Outright" (first published in 1942) and suggests that the settlements of American history are vexed ones that need to be worked out more justly. Although the question of knowing who and where the cabin dwellers are is ultimately metaphysical, Frost grounds the philosophical considerations of his poem in the material settings of a representative American "clearing." National heritage and the pioneer ethos, after all, provide the basis of the metaphors in "Cabin." In "A Cabin in the Clearing," writes J. Albert Robbins, Frost "employs a metaphor uniquely American," even though he means that metaphor to speak "for all men" (62). In "Genealogical"—as he considers the life and behavior of a family ancestor in relation to the Native Americans that ancestor displaces and kills—Frost interrogates national history through the metaphor of his family ancestry, revealing the internal divisions of the nation and calling attention to its bloody origins. In "The Vanishing Red," which functions as a fable of white-red relations in North America, he shows that the still unresolved tensions of settlement persist in the unsettling specter of the subjugated Indian. The resonant metaphors of possession in "The Gift Outright" can be related to the historical dispossession of the Indians of North America; the experience of existential displacement in "The Gift Outright" and "A Cabin in the Clearing" is symbolically linked to the bodily "displacement" acted out in "The Vanishing Red," which represents the wholesale dispossession of Indians from their "land of living" by European colonizers.

This phrase, "land of living," is a biblical one that Frost uses in "The Gift Outright," and I use it here to refer to the land that aboriginal Americans cultivated in order to get their living before they were pushed into other regions or defeated in battle by settlers. At one end of the social spectrum, the colonial rapacity for land reflected the wealth and prestige of landownership in European culture, while at the other end, the tenure of land by pioneer farmers simply represented their need for sustenance—for "making a living." Both conditions account for the pathos commonly associated with the pioneer homestead. The figure of the settler is so powerful in the symbolic iconography of America because it embodies the American ideal of self-sufficiency. Nevertheless, Frost's poems often remind us that the rugged individual of the American frontier won his independence through violent displacements that not only have hurt Amerindians but have haunted the conscience of the pioneers' descendants ever since. In this way, Frost's poems continually raise the unsettled questions of American settlement.[7]

"A Cabin in the Clearing," for example, presents its reader with a pioneer vista discussed by the personified smoke and mist surrounding the cabin. As Robbins notes, "the metaphor of wilderness and clearing is made to carry much of the poet's meaning, whether we read the lines psychologically, historically, or spiritually" (63). Frost uses dialogue to make statements that are in one sense about the metaphysical "place" of the cabin's inhabitants and at the same time about their sense of themselves as participants in a specific nation. As in other poems that foreground the permeability of boundaries, in "Cabin" Frost links the human and natural world by characterizing Smoke as the by-product of the domestic activities of the cabin dwellers: over the course of the poem, Smoke functions as both a sign of domestic warmth and the airborne matter given off by human efforts to win a living from the fruit of the now tilled American wilderness. It is also the by-product of clearing land by fire. Similarly, Mist is the hovering cloud of water that "cottons to their landscape." It saturates that landscape, furnishing one of the ingredients necessary to the growth of the foodstuffs that sustain the cabin dwellers.

The representative of doubt, Mist, begins the poem by asserting,

I don't believe the sleepers in this house
Know where they are.

Smoke, the defender of the cabin's inhabitants, adopts a more optimistic outlook, stressing the accomplishments of the people whom Mist recognizes only as "sleepers." Smoke points out that

They've been here long enough
To push the woods back from around the house
And part them in the middle with a path.

Mist, the inveterate questioner, repeats his claim: "And still I doubt if they know where they are. / And I begin to fear they never will" (427). The debate broached by Frost's two speakers turns on their view of the settlers who inhabit the cabin and the clearing over which the speakers hover. As "the guardian wraith of starlit smoke, / That leans out this and that way from their chimney," Mist's interlocutor literally flows from the interior, domestic space of the settlers he describes. Smoke's defensive posture derives from his closer proximity to the cabin dwellers, but it turns out that Mist, too, is involved in their lives and livelihood. Although Mist's existence is external to their hearth, he is

the damper counterpart of smoke
That gives off from a garden ground at night
But lifts no higher than a garden grows.

Mist may be outside the house but, as he tells Smoke, "I cotton to their landscape" and "I am no further from their fate than you are" (428). Taken together, then, Frost's interlocutors represent products of the labor of the cabin's inhabitants and natural features of the landscape. Like the natural forces described by Moore in "Virginia Britannia," these forces speak from a vantage "above" that of the human beings they discuss. The perspective Frost attributes to these personified elements is broader than that of the humans they describe. And fond as the speakers might be of these settlers, they also see their shortcomings.

At one point, for example, Smoke remarks of the cabin dwellers that "They must by now have learned the native tongue. / Why don't they ask the Red Man where they are?" (428). Smoke's question, alluding perhaps to the cliché of Indian smoke signals, implies that the Indian offers a clue to the identity and destiny of the cabin's inhabitants. Mist's reply—"They often do, and none the wiser for it"—provides an ironic rejoinder that hints at the possibly misguided outlook of those inside the cabin. Mist's remarks affirm the characterization of the Indian as a knowledgeable forebear whose relationship to the land offers an important form of wisdom that could mitigate the spiritual disorientation of their colonial successors. In this poem, however, Frost does not follow Michaels's paradigm of appropriating an Indian heritage for the cultural benefit of the white settlers represented by Smoke. The poet shows instead that the settlers are distinct from their Indian predecessors. "A Cabin in the Clearing" explicitly associates the Amerindian with the genius loci of the New World, but it also satirizes the effort to recapitulate the Indian as a trope for indigenous national culture by portraying the pioneer inhabitants of the cabin as "none the wiser" for having sought out the Native American for his wisdom. "Cabin" shows that the Native American is a permanently haunting feature of the landscape of the American consciousness, but it shows at the same time that the pioneers inhabit a world that is not commensurate with the Native American one. The ghost of the Amerindian can roam through the dreams of Americans only because, as Lawrence argued, their numbers have so drastically dropped.

Smoke agrees that the cabin dwellers may never clearly comprehend their identity or destiny. The settlers, it seems, have lost their bearings, and this fundamental disorientation may prove to be permanent. For his part, Mist concedes that the occupants of the clearing spend a lot of energy trying to learn the qualities of their location and the nature of their relationship to it, and he ambiguously characterizes their piecemeal approach as "fond," meaning foolish as well as affectionate. Taking up the thread of Mist's thought, Smoke goes on to consider the history of these newcomers. "If the day ever comes when they know who / They are," says Smoke,

> they may know better where they are.
> But who they are is too much to believe—
> Either for them or the onlooking world. (428)

In an interesting shift that approximates Mist's skepticism, Smoke observes that such people "are too sudden to be credible." As latecomers to the stage of world history, Americans remain blind to their true status in the world (for "who they are is too much to believe"—their status outstrips their credibility). Yet in another sense, too, they are beleaguered by being "too sudden"—for "sudden" in this context can mean both historically belated and spontaneous (or impulsive). Spontaneity is a quality that corresponds to the similarly ambiguous "mettlesomeness" attributed by Moore in "England" to the characteristic American. Frost's commentary on the dilemma of his rustic Yankees also echoes Moore's "heat which may appear to be haste" (*Complete Poems* 47). The heat which may be the fever of inspiration may also be the wasted energy of frenetic but not especially thoughtful activity. Appearance may accord with reality, or it may belie it. Being "too sudden" implies belated youthfulness but also reckless immaturity. No opprobrium attaches to the fact of Americans' late emergence in the world, however abrupt, but the want of tact and deliberation associated with immaturity is a more serious matter. Like the nation's "first flag" to which Moore refers in "Virginia Britannia," a "too sudden" manner may be both "dashingly undiffident" and the "tactless" sign of one's citizenship in a self-consciously "new republic" (*Complete Poems* 110). The ambiguity of Frost's phrase both grants and withholds its sympathy, for it at once countenances and condemns the anonymous inhabitants it describes. On one hand, these obscure pioneers are "too sudden" in appearing in the clearing and before the audience of "the onlooking world," through no fault of their own; on the other hand, their "too sudden" behavior is embarrassingly precipitate.

Mist concludes the colloquy by inviting his partner to listen in on the settlers "talking in the dark." This scene dramatizes Frost's exemplary scenario in a famous letter to John Bartlett, in which he tells his friend, "The best place to get the abstract sound of sense is from the voices behind a door that cuts off the words. . . . It is the abstract vitality of our speech. It is pure sound—pure form" (*Selected Letters* 80). If the sleepy speech of the inhabitants ultimately amounts to so much "haze," their words are nevertheless all they have, for in this context they approach Frost's "abstract vitality," which he conceives of as a Platonically "pure form." Frost's witty play on "eavesdropping" pleases him so much he repeats it. In doing so, he underscores his characterization of the poem as a critical but baffled inquiry into the meaning of the inhabitants' location and identity in the couplet that rounds it out: *"Who"* is *"better"* equipped, asks the newly introduced narrator, *"than smoke and mist"* to *"appraise / The kindred spirit of an inner haze"* (428). Frost's choice of verb is quite precise, and yet the judicious connoisseurs this verb prompts one to expect turn out to be the murky interlocutors of the poem. Smoke and Mist "appraise," or review and evaluate, the moral worth of the cabin's inhabitants. The "inner haze" of the dwellers corresponds to the material haze of Smoke and Mist.

One way to read this short exchange is in the context of the other poems discussed here, as, that is, a meditation on the nation and its history, including the people's sense of itself, its location, and its position in the world beyond its borders. As a dialogue, it involves some give and take, and although it ends on a negative note, it offers a modicum of sympathy and hope regarding the inhabitants of "the clearing." Frost's decision to include "A Cabin in the Clearing" as the title poem of his 1962 book indicates the significance that the myth of the pioneer held for him. Despite the widespread urbanization of the country by the 1950s and the imperial forays that multiplied in the wake of the Second World War, the picture of the nation as a wilderness inhabited by a hardy people lingers as a powerful icon for the poet and his readers.

Yet Mist's insistence that the cabin dwellers neither know where nor who they are makes "all the difference" to one's understanding of the poem, for this insistence transfigures received notions of the nation. The poem evinces an affection for the people inside, but it also questions and criticizes their circumstances. Although these circumstances have existential dimensions, they also have political ones. Frost's language is broad enough in its implications to allow for all of these meanings. "A Cabin in the Clearing" figures the cultural and political issues associated with the country's settlement in the simple image of an isolated cabin. Frost's homestead resonates more or less immediately within American culture, or at least it did so for a period of time that extended through Frost's cultural moment. Because of this legacy, it is still possible to interpret the poet's clearing as a representative American settlement, and therefore as a space that engages the issues of national remembering and forgetting.

While the cabin dwellers discussed by Mist and Smoke may be interpreted as the American common man and woman, Frost portrays contemporary Americans as the descendants of pioneers much more explicitly in "The Gift Outright." In this poem, in fact, Frost makes use of the same unifying "we" that Moore, Williams, and Crane do in various poems. Like them, Frost enunciates a communal vision of the history and destiny of the United States. The voice adopted by the speaker of this poem is confidently representative, for there is no breach between the national "we" inscribed in the poem and the individual who pronounces that "we." In fact, the poem dramatizes the nation's constitution of the speaker and of readers as citizens:

> The land was ours before we were the land's.
> She was our land more than a hundred years
> Before we were her people. She was ours
> In Massachusetts, in Virginia,
> But we were England's, still colonials,
> Possessing what we still were unpossessed by,
> Possessed by what we now no more possessed.
> Something we were withholding made us weak
> Until we found out that it was ourselves
> We were withholding from our land of living,
> And forthwith found salvation in surrender.
> Such as we were we gave ourselves outright
> (The deed of gift was many deeds of war)
> To the land vaguely realizing westward,
> But still unstoried, artless, unenhanced,
> Such as she was, such as she would become. (316)

As in Louis Althusser's formulation of interpellation, the poem "hails" its "hearers," and in responding to that invocation, listeners acknowledge themselves to be the persons addressed. Through this process, individuals become social beings. In this case, they "remember" their identity as U.S. citizens.

Because the poem takes for granted the centrality of the English perspective on "the American colonial experience," it presents its compressed account of U.S. history as normative. As Harold Bush Jr. observes, Frost's narrator immediately incorporates the reader into some sort of social grouping or identity. The paradoxical nature of that co-optation recalls the simple opening of the U.S. Constitution: "We the people." The immediate assumption must be that "we" represents all true Americans, past, present, and future, and from the beginning of the poem a consensus is posited. The act of positing that collective group, or naming that "we," is a speaking into existence, such as God did at the Creation: "Let there be light." There is also a timeless quality inherent in such a naming because of the implication that "we" includes all Americans at all times, perhaps even those not yet born. (175–76)

In the poem the speaker's contradictory "we" is meant to embrace all the members of the nation, but this embrace conceives its audience as a homogeneous community divided only by its colonial connections to England. A certain blindness informs the speaker's perspective, for his words subordinate the losses of Native Americans, enslaved blacks, and non-British immigrants to the grander narrative of colonial pilgrimage and freedom. In its commemoration of national origins, the poem "forgets" the bloody history that features so prominently in "La Noche Triste," "The Sachem of the Clouds," "Genealogical," and "The Vanishing Red." By assuming its readers' assent to its implicit hailing, "The Gift Outright" deftly pressures one to accept its representation of national constituency, into seeing oneself in the lineaments of its particular formulation of "America." Frost's "we" dramatizes the constitution of its readers as citizens by the national polity. Its assumption of national unity implies that the country is a synergistic social whole that cannot be fully comprehended.

In declaring that "This land was ours before we were the land's," Frost both invokes his readers' already established sense of themselves as American citizens and calls that citizenship into being through an assertion of landownership. The line enacts, or performs (in Bhabha's sense), its version of the national community in its evocation of a "we" defined by what is held in common as "ours." The poem presumes that its audience is unified by common proprietary ties. In order to forge its vision of national unity, it must "forget" the manner in which it became "ours." Frost first presented the poem in public just days before Pearl Harbor was bombed, and the rhetoric of the poem either reflects the strong sense of national unity that solidified among Americans because of the attack, or it promotes such a sense by repeating a defining narrative in a contemporary climate of threatening aggression. Although he may have composed the poem earlier, Frost made it public at a moment when, because of potential threats from the Axis powers, the value of national unity was especially high.

As some readers of the poem point out, however, the definition of the national that Frost assumes in "The Gift Outright" comes at a price. For those readers who cannot claim English heritage, the poem demands an imaginative identification with those founders, so that the audience addressed by the poem must affiliate with the English by proxy, as it were.

Since this is presumably easier to do for some groups of citizens than it is for others, Frost's poem "forgets" something of the cost of the symbolic identification it asks of its readers. Whereas the poem aims to communicate a sense of the unity of the nation through the metaphors of possession, salvation, and surrender, it does so by requiring the imaginative affiliation of all its citizens with the mythic pilgrims who laid the foundations for the latter-day republic. In this respect, the poem conforms to the drama described by Anderson, whereby disparate citizens become filiated kin, although Indians are not overtly included among these kin. To put the matter in Werner Sollors's terms (but in a way that challenges the opposition between them), the symbolism of descent mediates consent in "The Gift Outright." "Allegiance" to America may be "volitional," as Sollors argues, but coercive social pressure often conditions, and sometimes compromises, such choice (150–51).

In addition, the poem ironically transfigures the military surrenders of the Amerindians into the psychic surrender of all "colonials" to America. That gesture unites citizens not only to the land of the New World, but to one another, to the imagined community that constitutes the "nation." Frost reverses expectations when he makes the possessors become the "possessed." Indeed, as Reuben Brower observes, the entire "poem is an expanded pun on 'possession'" (202). Like Williams, who wrote in *American Grain* that "the New World presses on us all" (70), Frost argues that the New World requires a new way of thinking, being, and writing. Unlike "The people along the sand" in "Neither Out Far Nor In Deep" who "turn their back on the land" and "look at the sea all day," Americans must look inland to find their meaning and their place (Frost 274). They must turn from "a conformity of dull staring" backward toward the shores of England (Poirier 244). The progeny of the uprooted colonials had to learn to think of themselves as belonging to America as much as they thought of America as belonging to them. As soon as this process of identifying American rather than English soil as home got under way, the poem argues, the first real Americans were born. In the words of Williams's "Spring and All," a "profound change / has come upon" such settlers and their descendants. In the process of this change, Frost's fellow citizens—like the stubborn "stuff" of Williams's poem—become one with their new land and achieve a consciousness not previously available: "rooted, they / grip down and begin to awaken" (*CP* 1: 183). In Frost's poem, however, the pioneers' surrender to the soil of America paradoxically corresponds to the military surrenders of Indians it leaves unreported. In the process of becoming "rooted," Americans "grip down" into a soil stolen from others; if the sleepers of "A Cabin in the Clearing" ever "begin to awaken" to themselves and their new power in the world, they must—sooner or later—also "awaken" to their part in the continuing nightmare of history. By suggesting the continuities as well as the disparities between the forms of forgetting and remembering that are required to make and sustain a nation, Frost's poems indicate the relationships of American history to longer, larger, and more complex spans of human history. The history of the United States is embedded in human history as a whole, so that it participates in the problems and triumphs of that history in ways that are detrimental or beneficial not only to its own interests but to those of other countries as well.

In the syntax of Frost's poem, the military conflict entailed by the colonials' salvific "surrender" is relegated to parentheses: "Such as we were we gave ourselves outright / (The deed of gift was many deeds of war)." In this formulation, as Paulin has suggested, one kind of surrender erases or covers over another (172–73). In the topsy-turvy whirl of meaning enacted by the poem's puns, colonial "surrender" (together with postcolonial military action) becomes an act of possession, and Indian dispossession goes unmentioned. The line implies such dispossession but glosses it over in the extravagance of its wordplay, for Frost's punning repetition of "deed" and "deeds" modulates in meaning from a legal document conferring or affirming possession to acts of military conquest. Nevertheless, Frost's artful ambiguity keeps in play the unmentioned menace of Indian inhabitants: the alienating displacement of the colonials in "Gift" ironically corresponds to the Indian experience of displacement in "The Sachem of the Clouds." In the end, the significant political and historical links between the two meanings are underscored as well as obscured by the equivocation.

The poem's identification of surrender as salvation further compounds the complexity of the metaphor, moreover, for the finding of salvation presupposes the need for it. The poem suggests that salvation is a form of deliverance from the dilemma of physically living in one place while spiritually inhabiting another. The conflict between the heritage associated with the colonist's remembered place of origin and his commitments to his current circumstances prevents him from achieving a true sense of home: "mere presence," writes Hamida Bosmajian, "was not enough to achieve national identity. The colonial American was still in an existential limbo" (98).

This unsettling aspect of settlement is perhaps conceptually akin to Bhabha's theory of the "unhomely moment" he finds in postcolonial experience (*Location* 9–18). Alluding to Freud's German word for the uncanny in his essay of that name, Bhabha's version of the *unheimlich* names a specific kind of unwelcome irruption. It designates the intrusions of the public upon the private, the improper upon the proper, and the foreign other upon the native self. Frost's poem evokes all of these intrusions in one way or another. In the speech of the poem, for example, the private individual assumes the voice of the public "we," and the puns on "possession" signify both ideological allegiance and colonial ownership of property. Both occupying a land that is foreign and remembering a distant nation that is no longer home, moreover, the colonist feels himself disinherited, spiritually dispossessed. Yet he feels this way at the same time that his colonization has entailed the dispossession of an indigenous population that he experiences as alien.

Frost's poem dramatizes the legal enactments behind the European conquest of the Americas in a manner akin to Moore's representation of this process in her allusions to English and Indian place-names in "Virginia

Britannia." The acts of naming and mapping the regions of Virginia were part of the English administrative process of taking title to the region—a process Frost figures through his puns on "deed." Naming and mapping are ways of laying claim, as much in Frost's poem as in Moore's. From a Foucauldian perspective, these instruments of knowledge double as the disciplinary technology of power—the means of securing and maintaining possession. In "Gift," Frost's representation of property approximates that of "Beech" rather than that of "Mending Wall," for it anxiously shores up ownership through its wordplay on "deeds" in a way that is analogous to the doubt-besieged "Witness Tree" and "iron spine" that marks the property described in "Beech" (301).

A deed is something done, but in the plural form it takes in the poem ("many deeds of war"), it is—like the Latin *gesta*—also the record of things done. In this regard the word registers the two principal meanings of history. On one hand, history refers to the sweep of actual events through time, but on the other, history is the preserved record—either oral or written (as in the text of the poem itself)—of those past events. Frost's first use of the word to refer to a legal document conferring possession roughly corresponds to the definition of history as record. His reference to "deeds of war," however, corresponds to history as event, the actions of a person or group that affect the course of future events. As a document, a deed has an illocutionary effect—it is a speech act, an example of language that can make something happen. A legal deed extends title to its bearer, and Frost's line makes it clear that the price of that transfer of ownership is paid in military deeds. Given the correspondences I have outlined, it follows that the poem implies that such acts of aggression make up an important part of a nation's history. As the record of these acts, the poet's text becomes the entitling deed of Frost's nation, its virtual performance in the medium of language.

As Richardson points out, Frost explicitly linked poetic performance and enacted deed in a brochure of 1923 entitled *Robert Frost: The Man and His Work*:

> Sometimes I have my doubts of words altogether, and I ask myself what is the place of them. They are worse than nothing unless they do something; unless they amount to deeds, as in ultimatums or battle-cries. They must be flat and final like the show-down in poker, from which there is no appeal. My definition of poetry (if I were forced to give one) would be this: words that have become deeds. (Frost 701)

As Richardson observes, such "brief remarks provide a fine example of a public persona that Frost often adopted as a poet" (51). Frost's mixing of the categories of language and action in these statements clearly corresponds to the language of "The Gift Outright," and it just as clearly evokes the linguistic and theoretical concepts of the performative. The martial rhetoric of the prose passage matches that of the poem, too, suggesting that Frost's sense of poetic creation as a form of manly prowess was also profoundly martial. (This metaphor, moreover, marks an interesting point of similarity between Frost's view of poetry and the view Williams describes in his essay "The Poem as a Field of Action," which symbolizes the making of a poem as a form of battle.) In the context of his recitation of "Gift" at John F. Kennedy's inauguration, the words of Frost's poem became a deed, registering the importance of the poem's meaning in a specific political and social context and repeating the story of the nation's coming-into-being. But the poem also plays with categories in a way that suggests the partialness of such equations.

The rhetorical parallels and repetitions of the poem, its appeal to the common man ("Such as we were we gave ourselves outright"), and its evocation of a common heritage also give the text an oratorical character. It is as if a politician or local figure of authority were reciting the words of the poem as a speech, so that the poem already "inscribes" Frost's recitation of the poem at Kennedy's inauguration before the fact. The implied situation of the poem is that of a public address. In fact, the repetitions in "The Gift Outright" figure in small the iterative quality of "performance" per se. The oratorical repetitions of "The Gift Outright," then, apparently constitute the linguistic trace of Judith Butler's doctrine of iterability that I briefly defined in the introduction. According to this view, structures must be "enacted" on a regularly repeated basis in order to exist at all.

Frost's reading of his poem at Kennedy's inauguration provides another example of such iteration, one that is deeply significant in terms of its political meaning and social ramifications. For Frost had composed his poem about twenty years before the inauguration and had read it in public for the first time "before the Phi Beta Kappa Society at William and Mary College, December 5, 1941." He first published the poem in the *Virginia Quarterly Review* in 1942 (*Poetry of Robert Frost* 565). When Frost recited the poem from memory at the inauguration, he delivered a text that had been rendered public many times, in the published form of his various selected and collected poems (1946, 1949, 1954, 1955) and in the oral form of his many public readings. "In one sense," Philip Gerber writes, "this recital was the very peak of his long career" (27). Although Gerber's phrase "in one sense" is of course an important mitigation of an otherwise overstated claim, a remark about the occasion that Jean Gould attributes to Frost might confirm this view: "It is a proud moment," Frost beamed, "to have poetry brought into the affairs of statesmen" (4–5).

Indeed, Frost became as famous for his crafty public persona as for the careful craft of his poetry.[8] "Like the ancient bards and troubadours," his biographer Meyers writes, "Frost performed his poetry and brought it directly to his audience" (181). "He was certainly," Meyers adds, "a first-rate actor, liked performing and was excited by appearing on stage" (185). As Derek Walcott puts it, "he played the cynical American Horace as carefully as any sophisticated celebrity or rough politician" (109). Frost himself attests to his view of poetry as a skilled performance. He told Poirier in an interview published in the *Paris Review,* "I look on poetry as a performance. I look on the poet as a man of prowess, just like an athlete. He's a performer. And the things you can do in a poem are very various" (890). Poirier's own commentary on Frost handsomely expands on this statement: "Poetry is not life," he writes, "but the performance in the writing of it can be an image of the proper conduct of life. The exercise of the will *in* poetry, the *writing* of a poem, is analogous to any attempted exercise of will in whatever else one tries to do" (9). For Frost, "A poem is an action, not merely a 'made' but a 'making' thing" (Poirier 64).

Frost had of course attained his national prominence before Kennedy's inauguration. In a famous speech in 1959, Lionel Trilling acknowledged Frost's status as a national myth:

> We do not need to wait upon the archaeologists of the future to understand that Robert Frost exists not only in a human way but also in a mythical way. We know him, and have known him so for many years, as nothing less than a national fact. We have come to think of him as virtually a symbol of America. (448)

Despite the controversy engendered by Trilling's speech, it is unlikely any of his critics would have disagreed. Bernard DeVoto, for example, gushed that Frost was "'the greatest living American'" and "the quintessence of everything I respect and even love in the American heritage" (Meyers 270). Indeed, whereas his fellow poets promoted American culture and aspired to contribute to it, Frost came to embody it. During his 1961 visit to Israel, Frost displayed his confidence in his status as a "national fact" (and perhaps his solipsism as well) when he "publicly announced that he did not intend to talk *about* American civilization because," as he put it, "'I *am* American civilization'" (Meyers 325). Its extravagant humor and hubris aside, the statement perhaps has a grain of truth to it.

In any case, Frost clearly styled his image with the same care he invested in his poetry, and his sense of poetry as a performance is of a piece with his knack for sparkling conversation and his vocation of "barding around." The public persona he crafted for himself corresponds to Marianne Moore's cap-and-cape masquerade of George Washington later in her life. Like Moore, Frost associated his public image with his cultural work as a poet, evoking the stereotypes of Yankee independence and hardihood as themes that resonate within his work and his audience. The view that Frost's recitation at Kennedy's inauguration was the summit of his career emphasizes the performative aspect of poetry, and it dramatizes the process by which a national tradition is formulated and perpetuated over time. Walcott's narrative of the event brings these issues sharply into view:

> On that gusting day of the inauguration of the young emperor, the sublime Augustan moment of a country that was not just a republic but also an empire, no more a homespun vision of pioneer values but a world power, no figure was more suited to the ceremony than Robert Frost. He had composed a poem for the occasion, but he could not read it in the glare and the wind, so instead he recited one that many had heard and perhaps learned by heart. (93)

Just as Frost's historic recitation disseminated an inherited narrative of his country's experience, every reading and rereading of "The Gift Outright" presents a new opportunity for either accepting and perpetuating or rethinking and adjusting its version of national history. The ceremonial context for Frost's delivery of his poem to a television audience imparted to its speech an authoritative power it would not otherwise "possess," but (as Walcott's narrative implies) the poem also lent the considerable power of its eloquence to the drama of the new president's inauguration.

While "The Gift Outright" registers a definite history, giving a narrative account of the genesis and development of the poet's nation, it also looks beyond the past and the occasion of the poem's presentation to an open-ended future. The repeated formula of "Such as we were" in line 12 and "Such as she was" in line 16 echoes the phrase "Such was our land" in line 2 and builds up a sense of continuity between past and present that culminates in a vista of the future presented as both hopeful and uncertain. The final line's calm, stately declarations—"Such as she was, such as she would become"—draw the poem-as-speech to a conclusive end, but they also look forward with confidence to a promising future. At the same time, the poem's closing statements characterize an end that, precisely because it is projected into the future, remains necessarily clouded in doubt. Such declarations leave the details of American history vague in ways that recall the forgetting they permit and require. Frost's account of U.S. and colonial history must suppress the injustices that the nation perpetrated in the very process of its constitution.

• If such poems as "The Gift Outright" and "A Cabin in the Clearing" seem to ignore or momentarily forget the Indian genocide entailed in American settlements, the ghosts of Indians nevertheless haunt their landscapes, and other poems by Frost overtly acknowledge the founding barbarities of American democracy. Because the figure of the defeated Amerindian haunts the collective psyche of the colonizer's heirs, the figure of the Native insists upon itself in various ways in the works of American writers. "Inheriting both the guilt of the conquerors and the deprivations of the conquered," writes Spencer, "the American has thus become the split and fearful soul of which his national literature, if astutely read, is the reflection, ineluctably pervaded with haunting imagery of Indians, forests, and the night" (116). The Amerindian may be "The Vanishing Red," but the memory of him stubbornly persists, while the cabin of the settlers' clearing remains haunted by "the native tongue" to the point that its inhabitants must "ask the Red Man where they are" (428). If the new dwellers in the land pursue such inquiries to no avail, they nevertheless express their mingled helplessness and guilt in the land they came to govern. The speaker of "Genealogical" eschews the violence committed by the settlers against the Indians and attempts to atone for it. Despite this Whitmanesque effort to share the position of the disinherited, the poem is brought up short against itself, limited by the fact that it originates in its creator's guilt and longing for reconciliation.

These poems reflect the tensions that constitute settlement and hence the central experience of the nation, and they show that the unsettling aspects of national history inhabit the lives and minds of the conquerors as well as those of the conquered. If the colonizer dispossesses his indigenous rivals, his descendants remain nonetheless dogged by the ghosts of their displaced victims, and their consciousness of those ghosts constitutes as vital a part of the nation as the declarations and documents of the country's famous white "fathers." If, as Harold Beaver claims, "the Indian, from the start, was invisible" to his white conquerors, these poems bring his disavowed specter into sharp and haunting relief (11). They show how the imperial enterprise that forged the nation and pervaded its subsequent existence also, in the process, divides the lives and allegiances of its citizens. The poems lend paradoxical support to Kennedy's posthumous tribute to Frost. "In serving his vision of the truth," he wrote, "the artist best serves his nation" (54).

Chapter 4

EMPIRE AND AMERICA

IN THE POETRY OF HART CRANE

• Like his contemporaries, Hart Crane evokes colonial and national history in order to describe, diagnose, and judge American culture.[1] In his effort to reconfigure his nation's history and meaning through a synthesis of American symbols and experience in *The Bridge,* Crane paradoxically produces an account of the contradictory, internecine character of American culture and society. *The Bridge* dramatizes the social conflicts between European colonists and their descendants on one hand and the aborigines and African slaves they dominated on the other. Crane's poem also underscores the economic disparity between the well-to-do and the working classes of America. In this chapter, I demonstrate the ways in which Crane's poetic quest for transcendence reflects the political and commercial contexts of his career. Whereas Moore, Williams, and Frost also celebrate and criticize aspects of American history, their work achieves an artistic unity that most critics consider lacking in *The Bridge.* I account for this disunity by relating it to the social conflicts of the United States during Crane's lifetime. Through a consideration of the role of place and patronage in the creation and content of *The Bridge,* I show that Crane adumbrated the political, commercial, and military circumstances of his country. In addition, I explore Crane's symbolic fusion of the personal and public spheres (in "The Harbor Dawn" and "Van Winkle") in order to show not only how such circumstances shape individual experience but also how they tyrannize the individual. By including lyrical reports of personal experience (in "Harbor Dawn," "Van Winkle," and "Quaker Hill") as well as imaginary encounters with social outcasts or oppressed groups (in "The River," "The Dance," and "Cutty Sark"), Crane makes a place in narratives of American history for the experience of homosexual men, disenfranchised hoboes and sailors, Native Americans, and blacks.

Crane "used the private lyric," writes R. P. Blackmur, "to write the cultural epic" (305–6). By drawing on lyric values within the context of an epic ethos, Crane hoped, in the words of Alan Trachtenberg, to "alter the larger culture itself, to revise its sense of itself, its dominant values, and especially its idea of its history" (59). In his effort to affect his culture, Crane's work shuttles back and forth between the expansiveness of his rhapsodies and his effort to "condense eternity"—between epic and lyric, public and personal, imperial and domestic. The hybrid form that characterizes *The Bridge* discloses the opposing forces at work in the poem—between the ideal of a unified nation and the historical reality of a fragmented one, and between the imperial gain of free-market forces and the salutary insights of a humane imagination. William Appleman Williams's thesis that the United States was a "republican empire" from its origins offers one way of explaining these contradictions. Through the cracks of its varied structure, *The Bridge* reveals something of the ways in which imperialism constituted America, for the colonization that displaced and marginalized Native Americans is of a piece with the military and economic exploitation of people in other lands for the benefit of a nation whose founding freedoms were predicated upon the health of the market.

Like Williams, who wrote and published parts of *American Grain* while he was in Europe or returning to the United States, Crane drafted many sections of *The Bridge* while living outside his country. As Langdon Hammer points out, "most of Crane's 'mystical synthesis of America' was not written in the United States but on the Isle of Pines in Cuba" (173). In Hammer's view,

> the transcendental aims of *The Bridge* need to be understood in relation to the isolation in which Crane's poem was actually written. In 1923, when he first conceived of *The Bridge,* Crane saw himself as part of a new aesthetic community in the United States; through his relationships with men like Frank and Stieglitz, Munson and Tate, Crane felt "directly connected to Whitman" (Crane, *Letters,* 128).[2] Crane saw himself as part of the nation described in Frank's *Our America,* and he fully expected *The Bridge* to win for him a place in the national literature. By 1926, however, when he arrived in Cuba, Crane's identification with Whitman had permanently divided him from friends like Tate, and he had fled the nation he wished to speak to and on behalf of. Ending in expatriation, [Crane] . . . is symbolically excluded not only from the heterosexual household [of Tate and Caroline Gordon], but also from the nation. (173)

Striking out for a territory beyond the boundaries of his country and literary community, Crane became, like Columbus in "Ave Maria," an "exile" (*Complete Poems* 47).[3] While the circumstances of Crane's coming to reside on the island were personal, his residence there also had important social ramifications that informed the composition of his poem. Removing himself from the ground of his quest by residing on the Isle of Pines, Crane wrote from the outside of America to get at its inside.

Paul Mariani describes the biographical and national factors that contributed to Crane's sojourn on the Isle, pointing out that his family's "decaying plantation" there had belonged to his maternal grandfather, Clinton Hart, who died in January 1913. Mariani sketches the neocolonial circumstances surrounding Hart's acquisition of the property:

When the island, located fifty miles off the southern coast of Cuba, became a U.S. protectorate after the Spanish-American War, a number of enterprising Americans saw their chance to scoop up cheap land on which to grow fruit for American consumption. Clinton had been one of these entrepreneurs, and now that he was dead and the estate in shaggy disrepair, his wife and daughter came to spend their winters there. The plantation had long since ceased producing anything and had been left to decay genteelly in the hands of various caretakers. (*Broken Tower* 25)

The fact that Crane wrote much of his national epic while living on his grandparents' property provides an international as well as a personal context for interpreting *The Bridge,* but the fact that the property was in disrepair when he lived there was also significant for his family and his poem. At the same time that *The Bridge* was materially and metaphorically established on the soil of a quasi-colony, the Hart family's tenure of its property seems to have been precarious (Mariani, *Broken Tower* 356). In 1924, in response to Crane's request for permission to go to Cuba and occupy the house, for instance, his mother, Grace, wrote him, "I never want you to plan to go to the Island or give it another thought. . . . If you knew the troubles & complications that are constantly confronting me with that property, you would want to stay as far away as possible" (*Letters of Hart Crane and His Family* 304).[4]

Despite the fact that Grace's refusal of permission was motivated by her effort to persuade Crane to return to Cleveland, the complications to which she refers in the letter were not insubstantial. As Thomas S. W. Lewis points out,

Cuba and the island were often in a state of turmoil [in 1917], because of a rebellion over Cuban government frauds. Grace had good cause for concern, as the island's political status had been uncertain since the Spanish-American War. Though it was agreed in 1904 that the United States should cede the Isle of Pines to Cuba, special interest groups were successful in delaying ratification of the treaty until 1925. As a result, neither government exercised absolute control over the territory. (*Family* 41–42)

During a significant part of Crane's life, then, the Hart estate was situated in a political limbo brought about by the efforts of Americans with property there, a state of affairs that worked to their advantage by staving off the return of Cuban sovereignty to the island. In a letter of January 1924, Grace wrote:

I am watching with great interest the action of Congress when the Isle of Pines matter comes up before the Senate. We are fighting hard to defeat the treaty which would turn it over to Cuba . . . . I have been writing Mrs. Upton [the first woman member of the Republican National Committee], & some of the women from the Isle of Pines who are now in Washington on the matter. It will mean a big difference in the valuation of our property down there & besides it is known by a few that one of the biggest gold mines in the world has been discovered there. But we do not want to advertize the fact to the Cubans at the present time. (*Family* 257)

Grace's letter demonstrates that her son was aware of the political conflict surrounding American military occupation and properties on the island, and it also reveals the economic motives behind the effort to sustain U.S. control of it. Grace's interest in an El Dorado–like gold mine on the Isle brings to mind not only Columbus's warning to his sovereign to restrain his greed in "Ave Maria" but also the mother's speech recorded in "Indiana." Like the woman in the latter section who "won nothing out of fifty-nine . . . / But gilded promise," Crane's mother may have placed her hopes in the fool's gold of flimsy dreams (66). Although I have suggested that in composing *The Bridge* on the Isle of Pines, Crane traveled outside of America in order to write about its interior, the island was actually both outside and not outside of the United States. Located in a place that defied the neat division of domestic and foreign, it was at once beyond the borders of the nation and nonetheless under its sway.[5]

This nebulous territory leaves its figurative mark in the wandering, unsettled movements of the hoboes, homosexuals, Native Americans, and blacks in the sections of *The Bridge* that Crane composed when he was on the Isle. The ambiguous political status of the territory during this period was part of the aftermath of the Spanish-American War, which many historians interpret as the origin of modern U.S. imperialism.[6] In what follows, I define *imperialism* as the domination of a foreign country for the economic and political benefit of the dominating country. Crane expressed his desire to own the estate in a letter of July 4, 1927, to Mrs. T. W. Simpson, who took care of the property (*O My Land* 342). Crane wrote this letter to Simpson (whom he called "Aunt Sally") after he had lived on the Isle and written several sections of *The Bridge*. His wish to own his grandfather's property reflects not only the freedom and pleasure he associated with the place but also the sense of accomplishment he felt after composing much of *The Bridge* there. "Villa Casas," the name of the house on the island property, provided a genuine home for Crane, who badly needed one throughout his adult life. Sherman Paul writes that for Crane "the island was both family ground (he speaks variously of 'the house my grandfather built,' 'my grandmother's place,' and the 'sure . . . ground' of 'my parents' property') and 'Eden'" (169). At the same time, the property was acquired through an imperial seizure that made it, like the land of the United States itself, a colonial dispossession of previous occupants, and hence a postlapsarian Eden. While Crane sometimes demonstrates his sympathy with those victimized by colonialism, he also shows a desire to own, to possess—both his mother's property and a legitimate place as an American writer. *The Bridge* reflects the neocolonial conflict surrounding the Caribbean property.

In fact, in *The Bridge*, Crane's expansionism is at war with his evident sympathy for hoboes and Indians in such a way as to reproduce, or inscribe, the moral and political conflicts surrounding the ownership and governance of the Isle of Pines. In the course of his poetic quest, Crane reveals some of the domestic effects of contemporary U.S. imperialism in a manner that parallels his commemoration of the colonial defeat of North American Indians. Crane's portraits of hoboes in "The River" and of the drunken sailor in "Cutty

Sark," for example, accord with James Wilson's claim that "The fruits of empire do not rest exclusively in external conquest; they also consist of the labor and capital obtained from the weaker members of its citizenry" (30). Indeed, *The Bridge* reflects the exploitation of others both within and beyond the nation's borders, as if hinting at the connections between the colonial conquest that gave rise to the United States and the imperial domination that helped sustain it.

Although Crane's epic is, in Stevensian terms, "a poem of the act of the mind," its representation of American materials reflects the view that American history has been driven by the repeated effort to win a new frontier. But as the history of the Hart plantation on the Isle of Pines shows, when the formal boundaries of the nation brought domestic growth to a close, advocates of expansion produced new frontiers external to the nation. In *The Bridge,* Crane refers to the subordination of Amerindians and others within the country's borders, but in "Cutty Sark" and "Cape Hatteras," he also alludes to the hemispheric hegemony of the United States. He repeats such allusions in more explicit and critical terms in such lyrics as "Imperator Victus," "Sad Indian," and "Bacardi Spreads the Eagle's Wing," while in "The River" section of *The Bridge,* he ironically alludes to the hoboes he celebrates as "born pioneers in time's despite" who "win no frontier by their wayward plight, / But drift in stillness" instead, "as from Jordan's brow." Across the river—whether the Jordan or the Mississippi—the receding promise of American freedom is somehow never fulfilled. Such lines reveal the imperial flaws of the republic, flaws that manifest themselves throughout the poem in terms that are foreign and domestic as well as (to repeat Bhabha's terms) pedagogical and performative. In the "inviolate curve" of his vision, Crane glimpses the "chained bay waters" that both threaten and protect the "Liberty" he desires. As Jeffrey Walker suggests, "Crane rather ironically presents the original promise of the New World or the American vision of unaccomplished destiny, as splintered, deflected, and distorted in the pursuit of global commerce" (133). In his effort to achieve a "mystical synthesis" of his nation, Crane reveals the disunited state of America.

Howard Zinn offers one perspective for understanding the international context in which Crane composed *The Bridge.* He describes the imperial design of American policy and trade in the first three decades of the twentieth century:

> While demanding an Open Door in China, [the United States] had insisted (with the Monroe Doctrine and many military interventions) on a Closed Door in Latin America—that is, closed to everyone but the United States. It had engineered a revolution against Colombia and created the "independent" state of Panama in order to build and control the Canal . . . . Between 1900 and 1933, the United States intervened in Cuba four times, in Nicaragua twice, in Panama six times, in Guatemala once, in Honduras seven times. By 1924 the finances of half of the twenty Latin American states were being directed to some extent by the United States. By 1935, over half of U.S. steel and cotton exports were being sold in Latin America. (399)

These military and commercial maneuvers represent defining features of the developing foreign policy of the United States during the period in which Crane lived and wrote. Although Crane's letters make it clear he was more interested in transcending American history than in reporting it, his poetry nevertheless reveals some of the domestic problems associated with imperial investments abroad. While Crane's "Revision of history becomes a mode of self-discovery and self-possession" (Trachtenberg 59), his poetic representations firmly register the dispossessions of American history.

If Williams's composition of portions of *American Grain* on his return to the United States reinforces the symbolic dimension of the book as an imagined voyage to the New World, Crane's removal to a different part of the Western Hemisphere to compose *The Bridge* (together with the fatal curtailment of his return to America at the end of his life) has somewhat different implications. The material he composed during his sojourn in the Caribbean reflects not only his commitment to the culture of the New World but also his awareness of U.S. domination abroad. While *The Bridge* does not articulate in any systematic way the relationship between the domestic and foreign effects of imperialism, the varied testimonies that appear throughout the poem may be read in conjunction with each other in order to tease out the relations between such effects. In the punning terms of Crane's poem, Giles points out, "Brooklyn Bridge is . . . [the] 'Terrific threshold'" not only "'of the prophet's pledge' but also '. . . of the *profits'* pledge'" (*Crane* 33; emphasis added). By crossing that threshold, Crane reveals the human cost exacted by imperialism both within and beyond the borders of his nation.

Like the Hart family's plantation on the Isle of Pines, the financier Otto Kahn's patronage of Crane when he was composing *The Bridge* metaphorically informs the poem. As Gregory Zeck explains,

> When Hart Crane first wrote to Otto Kahn [to request a loan], at the urging of his friends Waldo Frank and Eugene O'Neill, he was both impoverished and discouraged. But on December 6, 1925, after a three-hour conference with Mr. Kahn, Crane emerged from the banker's Italian Renaissance mansion, at 1100 Fifth Avenue in New York, with a check for one thousand dollars and the promise of one thousand more to follow. (In all, Crane was to receive $2,400 from Kahn between 1925 and 1930, the year *The Bridge* was published.) (61)

Crane's grant came from a great patron of the arts. The German-born Kahn was a cosmopolitan man who, although he "never got a university degree," was privately tutored and read incessantly (Kobler 11).

Kahn's money came from his work as a financier for Kuhn, Loeb, and Co, a bank that sponsored American enterprises both at home and abroad. His work with the American railroad baron Edward Harriman provides an important historical context for two particular sections of *The Bridge*, "The River" and "Cutty Sark." In "The River," Crane's allusion to the Twentieth-Century Limited explicitly tropes American commerce and technology as a powerful, speeding train. By contrasting the lives of the railroad hoboes with both the train and his father's "cannery works," Crane figures the conflict between American capital and labor. His choice of the train as the metaphor for capital reflects the history of American railroad monopolies, a history in which Harriman played a central role. Moreover, Kahn's work for Harriman as a financier included such extensive travel on his railroads that Kahn came to identify quite personally with the trains running on Harriman's lines. Kahn occupies an important seat on the Twentieth-Century Limited, the train that passes by Crane's hoboes in "The River."

Like his domestic brokering of Harriman's railroads, Kahn's foreign investment can also be figuratively related to Crane's composition. Kahn provided financial assistance to Harriman when he sought, in an instance of American "Open Door" policy in China, to establish a commercial foothold in Manchuria in order to realize his desire to build and control a railroad that would loop the planet (Freeman and Nearing 40–41).[7] Kahn's collaboration with Harriman reflects contemporary American efforts to develop foreign investments; this fact in turn corresponds to Crane's figurations of U.S. trade in "Cutty Sark," where U.S. trade abroad figures in the descriptions of the sailor-protagonist and the American ships involved in the tea trade with China. Crane situates his poem in the context of contemporary commerce by way of Whitman's concept of global "rondure" in "Passage to India," a term that Crane uses several times in "Cutty Sark." Crane's references to *rondure* allude to more than Whitman's work, for they also reflect the efforts of bankers and businessmen in his own era to advance global trade. While Harriman's attempt to establish a railroad that would circle the world exemplifies one such effort, the construction of the Panama Canal provides another. In "Cutty Sark" Crane figuratively evokes Harriman's Manchurian scheme through his references to *rondure,* and he explicitly refers to the Panama Canal, where his drunken sailor once worked. "Cutty Sark" figures a complex network of U.S. commercial ventures abroad, ventures that had a distinctly imperialist cast.

In addition to providing the economic support needed by the poet to complete his project, then, Kahn enters Crane's poem in the punning reference to "the Chan's great continent" in "Ave Maria," in references to the railroad industry in "The River," to U.S. trade abroad in "Cutty Sark," and perhaps also to the businessmen Crane satirizes in "Quaker Hill." In addition, repeated references to coins throughout *The Bridge* (in "Van Winkle," "Virginia," "Cutty Sark," and "The Tunnel") trope both Kahn's generosity and the domestic and global trade of Crane's day. As Miriam Fuchs writes, moreover, "Kahn's loan triggered an extremely productive period of writing" for Crane (47). The poet acknowledges his patron's generosity in his pun on "Chan" and his allusion to Cathay at the same time that his work often implicitly opposes some effects of Kahn's foreign investments.[8] In addition, the poem's recurrent image of the coin symbolizes the global circulation of capital from Kahn's China through the Panama Canal to the United States. In "Van Winkle," as Thomas Vogler points out, "the 'nickel for car-change' that the poet-as-Rip must keep as he begins his trip . . . is the same coin that will play the 'nickel-in-the-slot piano' in 'Cutty Sark,' and it is the coin pressed into the subway slot in 'The Tunnel'" (74).⁹ In an important sense, the coin of imperial commerce buys the poet's entrance into the mysteries he seeks to unfold.

Despite this, Crane's poem resists as well as recirculates the material and psychic investments of his nation's imperial capital. As R. W. B. Lewis points out, "For Crane, . . . Cathay was . . . an attitude of spirit *as against* material conquest" (259). If *The Bridge* participates in the pedagogical formation of its American readers in "Rip Van Winkle" (as I show later), it also subverts the country's citizen ideal through its various representations of hoboes, Amerindians, and African Americans in other sections. Long before receiving his grant from Kahn, Crane reflected his ambivalence about business in a sensationally titled interview ("Millionaire's Son Is Clerk in an Akron Drug Store") with columnist Alice Chamberlain of the *Akron Sunday Times*. In the interview, which appeared in the December 21, 1919, issue of the paper, Crane told Chamberlain "that the artist's creation is bound to be largely interpretive of his environment and his relation to it; and living as we do in an age of the most violent commercialism the world has ever known, the artist cannot remain aloof from the welters without losing the essential, imminent vitality of his vision." While the poet's response to the business world embodied by his father seems defensive (for the poet "must see much farther than the edge of his desk"), Crane also advocates an engagement with the world of commerce, and hence also with history. In the view of the poet, the artist must be "two different people" (Unterecker, *Voyager* 156). Similarly, despite his insistence on limiting the meaning of "Cathay" to the literary and transcendental, the word also functions as a synonym for the real country of China. The various improvements of the twentieth century made global trade easier and more efficient, facilitating the circulation of capital that helped secure U.S. ascendancy in the Western hemisphere, which gave the United States a commercial advantage over China. The economic domination made possible by such developments can be deciphered in the figurations of *The Bridge*. "Confronting the Exchange," Crane's poem ventures the task of "surviving in a world of stocks" (78).

• In the proem, in "The Dance," and especially in "Atlantis," Crane depicts an ideal vision of his nation. In the proem, images of the seagull's "inviolate" flight and the Statue of Liberty (which reappears in "Cutty Sark") convey the "freedom" that Crane attributes to his symbolic bridge and that constitutes the basis for American democracy. In "The Dance," the poet performs a ritual reconciliation between Europeans and Amerindians in the persons of himself and Maquokeeta. Similarly, in "Atlantis" Crane gestures toward a utopian republic that functions, in the terms laid out by Fredric Jameson in *The Political Unconscious*, as a principle of hope and a goal to realize (286). As Edward Brunner writes, "Atlantis is a city that is fabulous in a way other lost cities are not: though presently lost, it will someday return. It therefore stands as a parallel to human hope and desire, which also pursue that which may be recovered again" (180). Nonetheless, while "Atlantis" articulates a utopian ideal, other sections of *The Bridge* reveal the failures of the nation. One way that Crane portrays the conflict between "mystic" ideal and corrupt reality is through his various evocations of "the word." In the frustrated confession of "A Name for All," he declares that "we must maim // Because we are usurpers" (119). While those lines refer to a linguistic usurpation, they can also be interpreted as Crane's unwitting but incisive epigram about America's colonial heritage.

As Tim Dean argues, "Crane subscribed to a poetic ideology that was at once transhistorical and culturally specific" (85). Through his synthesis of epic and lyric genres in *The Bridge,* Crane turns America inside out. As Joseph Riddel writes, "The poet's role in history (or better perhaps, his obligation to history) has a paradoxical effect on Crane's form. For the visionary poet, while he expressly denies history, must acknowledge it in the very act of trying to transform it" ("Poetics" 96). In *The Bridge* Crane evinces the interiority of his lyrics in *White Buildings,* so that actual landscapes take on the charged meanings and emotions of the speaker's personal experience, but he also expresses the ways the world informs the self. By including portraits of various marginal figures, Crane insists upon their epic (and hence national) importance. "Crane's history-making project," writes Suzanne Clark Doeren, includes both "the traditional recalling and the iconoclastic remaking of the past" (21–22). Doeren's "recalling" and "remaking" correspond to Bhabha's categories of the pedagogical and the performative. In the effort to work out its wished-for syntheses, *The Bridge* unsettles the categories of inside and outside.

In the course of that process, moreover, *The Bridge* reveals the manner in which "inside" and "outside" define one another, for in order to be coherent, each term depends on the meaning of the other. Crane's work shows how national ideology shapes and influences the lives of its citizens, but the reverse is also true, for it reveals the rifts between various groups and argues for an account of the nation that addresses these rifts. By dramatizing the performative character of the nation and its traditions, *The Bridge* shows how individual agency presses back (to borrow Stevens's phrase) against the pressures of political as well as psychological reality. Through its fluid forays between boundaries, *The Bridge* links conceptual domains separated by ideology.

In the process of depicting Columbus as discoverer in "Ave Maria," for example, the poem discloses his mercenary motives. As Giles points out, "The Spanish monarchs Ferdinand and Isabella backed Columbus' mission to uncover an alternative trade-route to India only because of the promise of increased wealth for themselves if Columbus were successful. The journey was an archetypal capitalist venture: money invested in the hope of greater returns" (*Crane* 31–32). The venture capital of the Spanish sovereigns circulates in the poet's text as a sign of European conquest and dominion; it corresponds to the repeated image of the coin that appears in many of the sections of *The Bridge* and to Kahn's financial backing of its composition. In the image of the planet as a vast and gleaming ring, which (in one of many echoes of "Passage to India") the poet likens to "pearls that whisper through the Doge's hand," Columbus describes in sensual detail what he insists is "no delirium of jewels." Crane's hero conveys his awe for the New World in a turn of phrase that pits spiritual against economic value. Yet the figure simultaneously posits and denies the equation of the world with jewelry. It allows for real jewels at the same time that it defies the acquisitive delirium Columbus rightly fears will be provoked by his message.

Although Crane's Columbus expresses his awareness of the commercial motives of his mission, he tries to temper them when he admonishes the king to

> Take of that eastern shore, this western sea,
> Yet yield thy God's, thy Virgin's charity
>
> —Rush down the plenitude, and you shall see
> Isaiah counting famine on this lee! (48)

The ambiguous verb phrase "Rush down" implies at least three things: to "hunt" down, or to flush out quarry and kill it; to attack or conquer; and to swallow greedily. In light of the conquest of the Americas that followed Columbus's voyages (and to which Crane refers at the beginning of "Van Winkle"), the phrase seems to be an ironic figuration of successive Spanish attacks against indigenous Americans as a form of hunting. (The cluster of military images in the preceding stanzas reinforces this reading.) In more colloquial terms, the phrase suggests a dog's greedy eating (compare the phrase "wolf down"). Interpreted this way, the phrase construes the sovereign's potential seizure of the New World as a bestial devouring (which makes it like the Miller's voracity in Frost's "The Vanishing Red"). No matter which reading one entertains, the lines flash with a sharp, prophetic irony, given the historical outcome that—according to the fiction Crane creates—they prefigure. In Columbus's counsel to his Spanish patrons, Crane reflects the dangers of growing U.S. imperialism. Writing his national epic on the foreign ground of Cuba, a territory usurped by his family and nation, Crane hints at the similar dangers and possibilities shared by Spanish colonization and U.S. imperialism. As the lyrics "Imperator Victus" and "Bacardi Spreads the Eagle's Wing" suggest, Crane's sojourn in the Caribbean gave to him an increased, if dissonant, sense of the oppressive conditions caused by such imperialism.

The irony produced by Columbus's moral couplet ("Rush down the plenitude . . .") is an effect of the distance between Crane's historical position and that of Columbus. The implicit burden of the couplet is the history that occurred between Columbus's voyages and modern times. Through their ironic remembering of America's original "plenitude," Crane's lines inscribe the intervening conquest of the Americas. Because of its unspoken acknowledgment of events in the interim, linking Columbus's era to Crane's, the couplet reflects the specific historical context of *The Bridge*, including the imperial "rushing down" of other lands (especially in Latin America) by the United States during Crane's lifetime. In the "mystical synthesis" of his poem, Crane consistently "bridges" personal and national experience, but he also implies the alienated disarray of groups within the country victimized by colonization and imperialism. "Columbus' warning," writes John Carlos Rowe, "anticipates Crane's general critique of modern American history, which finds its 'civilized' origin in Fernando's impulse toward exploitation" ("'Super-Historical' Sense" 600). The advice prophetically registers the disunity it would prevent but fearfully foresees.

• "Harbor Dawn" functions as a preamble to later subsections of "Powhatan's Daughter," the section following "Ave Maria," by narrating the slow arrival of light at the beginning of a new day and thereby repeating the "dawn" of the proem. The setting is a bedroom near the New York harbor, which becomes a point of departure as the poet guides his reader through a tour of the nation and its history in "Van Winkle." As a prefatory poem in the "Powhatan's Daughter" sequence, "Harbor Dawn" establishes Crane's method of uniting personal and historical experience. "Crane maintained a hold," writes Janis Stout, "on both sides of the public/private duality, and the critic disregards either of the two at his peril" (179).[10] The memories Crane evokes in "Powhatan's Daughter" are collective and political as well as individual and archetypal. By intertwining the lyric world of the bedroom with the epic world of myth and history represented in the marginalia, Crane furnishes his reader with the first glimpses of an important interplay that structures the rest of *The Bridge*. In this regard, the passage differs sharply from Crane's lyric of 1918–19 entitled "Interior," in which he makes use, and to great effect, of the discrepancy between the public and personal. "Wide from the world," the speaker whispers, "a stolen hour / We claim." Like John Donne, Crane has his speaker defend from profane minds the private space shared by lovers: "none may know / How love blooms like a tardy flower / Here in the day's afterglow" (149). "Interior" sees the world as a threat, but Crane overcomes this threat by subjugating the world, which at last "must bow" to the lovers. In contrast, "Harbor Dawn" conjoins the public and the private.

Recent criticism challenges the dichotomy between the two—by arguing that the public informs the private sphere—and provides a helpful perspective from which to view Crane's mix of genres. Although it is through a mythic treatment of Pocahontas and her sexuality that Crane marries lyric to epic and the personal to the public, some of the consequences of this mixing are nonetheless social and political. The parallel texts of poem and marginalia bring these categories together, but the texts themselves also mix genres and spheres. In the marginalia, for example, the undefined "you" wakes from either a meditation on the history embodied by Columbus's soliloquy in "Ave Maria" or from a pleasant evening's sleep. In either case, this "you" wakes to face both a lover and the consideration of a mythic and mysterious "woman" whose presence blends with the dawn.

In the topsy-turvy perspective induced by Crane's language, one wakes only to another reverie. Inside the bedroom of "Harbor Dawn," the associational world of dream and metaphor holds for both sleeping and waking states. By drawing on "the logic of metaphor," Paul observes, Crane "builds the poem from the inside out, creates the field of meaning upon which its coherence depends" (298). The "you" addressed in the poem itself must be the speaker's lover, whereas the addressee in the marginalia seems to be the speaker. The dual voice produced by these texts offers a layered portrait of the lyric self: to modify John Stuart Mill's formulation, one voice overhears the speaker addressing himself in two different but parallel, even dialogue-like, ways. The vocative speech of the poem addresses a lover in a relatively straightforward manner. The reverie in the margin, however, is much more complicated. The speaker finds himself, in the midst of some Keatsian "waking dream," impelled "to merge [his] seed." Given the bedroom scene of the main text, one expects this impulse to be directed at the speaker's lover. The speaker himself appears to have such an expectation in mind, but after a pause in the text of the margin, he asks himself "with whom?" and follows up this confusing question with another: "Who is the woman with us in the dawn? . . . whose is the flesh our feet have moved upon?" Crane merges the neat formality of the rhyming couplet with the yearning lyricism of an interrogative syntax. Instead of closing his commentary with an epigram, he opens it up with a question whose answer must be intuited. The emotional connotations of the question suggest a compelling desire to "know" this woman. The desire is both for an understanding of her mythic identity and for a mystical union with her that is figured in sexual terms. Crane's speaker plays out what Annette Kolodny calls the "pastoral longings both to return to and to master the beautiful and bountiful femininity of the new continent" (138).

The gap in the margin—a mystifying blank space on the page out of which a confused question emerges—corresponds to an important section of the main text that it parallels. Further indented than the rest of the lines of "Harbor Dawn" and in italics like all of the marginalia, this section may be read as the representation of an especially private experience, the speaker's climactic paean to his lover:

> *your hands within my hands are deeds;*
> *my tongue upon your throat—singing*
> *arms close; eyes wide, undoubtful*
>   *dark*
>   *drink the dawn—*
> *a forest shudders in your hair!* (53–54)

This exultant song of pleasure is doubly framed by the text of the marginalia and the image of the window.

My object in pointing out these aspects of "Harbor Dawn" is to show that Crane conveys through them the interplay between the private and the public, an interplay that suggests connections between national policy and personal experience without explicitly stating them. In a daring gesture, Crane makes this scene between two male lovers the preamble to his subsequent voyage through American history. In taking homosexuals as his representative Americans, he makes the marginal into the central. The glittering "window-eyes" of the "Cyclopean towers across Manhattan waters" wink at the speaker in his bedroom, the trucks and shouting stevedores both disturb the speaker's sleep and "give it back again," and the intruding fog "leans one last moment on the sill" before the lyric draws to its end. Those trucks and stevedores ship the goods imported from foreign centers of trade developed by American financiers like Kahn, and Crane's scene shows how close to home the products of imperialism come. The sound of the stevedores at work on the dock enter into the consciousness of the sleeping poet.

The gap in the marginalia of "Harbor Dawn" corresponds exactly to the climactic burst of speech in the main poem. Hesitation in one text counterpoints confident sexual advance in the other. The interaction between main text and gloss mimics the cognitive dissonance between visionary possibility and painful reality on the speaker's part, between "The long, tired sounds" of the past and the contemporary preoccupation with commerce and gainful labor (53). The one-eyed windows of the office buildings glare their disapproval of the speaker's sleepy debauch, while noisy stevedores push along their products. The dissonance reflects the national disunity (between straight and gay, laborer and loafer, the cultured man and the businessman) that the lyric dreams of superceding.

"The Harbor Dawn" brings lyric and epic conventions together in a dialectic that turns out to be an ongoing one in *The Bridge*. The larger-than-life figure of Pocahontas, whom Crane portrays as an Earth Mother, articulates with the portrayal of Columbus in "Ave Maria," so that she embodies historical experience as well as mythic forces. Although the significance of her appearance is not yet clear in "Harbor Dawn," her importance as the earth goddess blends elsewhere with her status as the ghostly ambassador of a decimated people. In "The Dance" section in particular, Pocahontas's role as a representative member of the native dead parallels that of her male counterpart, Maquokeeta. "Harbor Dawn," however, focuses much more directly on the sexual resonance of the epic world Pocahontas comes to embody in *The Bridge*. Crane makes her the occasion for his interlacing of the exterior and interior when he refers to her in the margin as the woman with the "us" of himself and his lover. While the sexual exchange of the poem seems to be with a male lover, Pocahontas enters the speaker's consciousness as the cognitive ground of his experience, both as a lover and as an American. This conflation of personal and archetypal repeats the effect of the transition from the heroic world of Columbus in "Ave Maria" to the poet's bedroom in "Harbor Dawn." Crane's dialogical articulations in "Harbor Dawn" suggest that the spirit of Pocahontas presides over the whole of the poem rather than individual parts of it. As Crane makes clear in subsequent sections of "Powhatan's

Daughter," hers is "the flesh our feet have moved upon." In an oblique way, this embracing "our" is like the "us" in "Virginia Britannia" and a number of Williams's poems, an "us" that signals these writers' sense of themselves as American citizens of European descent. While Crane's metaphor suggests that "Powhatan's Daughter" supports and upholds Americans, it also implies that Americans subjugate her by trampling her beneath their feet.

In the main body of the poem, the speaker's exuberant encounter is bracketed by the lines describing the window. The window's four sides frame the interlude, ensconcing it in the transparent but hard protective film of its glass. The syntax of the line introducing the interlude is connected to that of the interlude, whereas the syntax of the line following it is cropped and separate: the line "While myriad snowy hands are clustering at the panes—" is punctuated as though it were an interrupted subordinate clause, but in fact several lines of the interlude after it can be read as filling out that syntax. At the same time that the "snowy hands" clutch at the panes, the lovers themselves engage in the tumultuous clutches of love. Crane compounds the warmth and security associated with the bedroom, so that the threatening cold of the snow contrasts sharply with the bedroom's indoor comfort. The triumphant "singing / arms," the erotic "tongue upon your throat—singing," and the shuddering forest of the lover's hair pour forth in the mellifluous tones of an aria, whereas the staccato brevity of the line closing the scene stutters with crisp, repeated beats: "The window goes blond slowly. Frostily clears." The repeated liquids, the excessive stresses, and the pauses of the two completed sentences within the line call the lovers to the "things of this world," intruding upon their thoughts and reminding them of its demands and responsibilities. So engrossing is the outer world in this section that Bernice Slote writes of a "harbored room" in describing it (157).

The window of the bedroom, then, embodies the presence of the public world in the privacy of the bedroom. In Jacques Derrida's terminology, the "pane" of the window functions like a hinge term in the "structural syntax" of *The Bridge,* for it opens on two vistas at once. While "myriad snowy hands" finger the outer face of that windowpane, the inner surface of the pane witnesses a triumphant union between the speaker and his lover. In discussing the pivotal role of the word *hymen* in his interpretation of texts by Plato and Mallarmé in *Dissemination,* Derrida explains that it is the syntax of the texts that determines the undecidability of a word and others like it rather than the word itself (220). The window both separates and connects interior to exterior in Crane's "episode of hands" by virtue of its position within the poem's "structural syntax." The "pane" that demarcates the space between public and private also opens both spaces to one another. Crane's window simultaneously separates and unites two domains, showing how the category of the public informs the private, but also how the private might resist or influence public structures.

While Derrida undermines the integrity of a word that marks the point between two spheres on linguistic and logical grounds, Louis Althusser attacks the legitimacy of their differentiation on economic and political grounds:

The distinction between the public and the private is a distinction internal to bourgeois law, and valid in the (subordinate) domains in which bourgeois law exercises its "authority." The domain of the State escapes it because the latter is "above the law": the State, which is the State *of* the ruling class, is neither public nor private; on the contrary, it is the precondition for any distinction between public and private. (144)

The very boundaries of the division between a private space and a public one are defined by the nation whose development Crane's poem tropes and celebrates. Yet the bay, like the bedroom, is "pillowed" and "darkling"; Crane's lyric presentation of the lovers in the bedroom shows how the realms of the public and private profoundly inform, even permeate, one another.

So does the "Van Winkle" subsection of "Powhatan's Daughter," which features childhood memories of lessons about the nation's founding. In the second and third stanzas of this section, Crane's nostalgic portrait of his school days vividly evokes the historical figures he studied. The speaker communicates his memory of learning about the luminaries he mentions through a direct appeal to the senses, which makes his memories almost tangible:

> Times earlier, when you hurried off to school,
> —It is the same hour though a later day—
> You walked with Pizarro in a copybook,
> And Cortes rode up, reining tautly in—
> Firmly as coffee grips the taste,—and away!
>
> There was Priscilla's cheek close in the wind,
> And Captain Smith, all beard and certainty,
> And Rip Van Winkle bowing by the way,—
> "Is this Sleepy Hollow, friend—?" (55)

If Pizarro might be merely a name "in a copybook," the speaker experiences Cortes as an exciting adventurer, feels Priscilla's seductive proximity, and thinks of Captain Smith in terms of personal charisma. As L. S. Dembo observes, "the figures of the conquest appear," to the boy who learned about them, "to be alive and immediate" (66). The man remembers his schoolboy visions of Cortes' military prowess with a physical immediacy that he conveys with the simile comparing his learning about Cortes to the sharp taste of coffee. He renders Priscilla as a presence manifested in the natural element of the wind, so that this American fairy-tale princess shares some of the mythic stature of Pocahontas. In his characterizations of Priscilla and Captain Smith, Crane mentions a bodily feature of each, and the references to Cortes and Rip Van Winkle include bodily movements that define their different personalities. As Vogler points out, "The first two lines of 'Van Winkle' encompass the whole of the continent, from 'Far Rockaway to Golden Gate,' and the history of the continent is identified with the poet's personal history as the transition to the past is made in terms of the poet's childhood" (73).

European adventurers and conquistadors mapped the planet and claimed the New World as their own to profit from as they pleased. Their tales establish a cultural ethos by purveying values that constitute terms like *democracy* and the *New World* in a particular way. This body of legends is part of what makes for a national character. They contribute to the sense of a national spirit that over time becomes familiar to members of the nation. As a result of this process, individuals come to identify with a community much larger than any of the ones they experience directly. The history of the conquistadors, the account of John Smith, and Longfellow's poem about the courtship of Miles Standish form a cycle of narratives about the country's origin. The myth of rugged individualism is grounded in the historical events of the Spanish adventurers and English colonists, but the continued life of such myths depends, as Bhabha and Butler both point out, upon their being recirculated in every generation. A "structure [in this case, the nation-state] gains its status as a structure," Butler writes,

> only through its repeated reinstatement. The dependency of that structure on its reinstatement means that the very possibility of structure depends on a reiteration that is in no sense determined fully in advance, that for structure, and for social structure as a result, to become possible, there must be a contingent repetition at its basis. Moreover, for some social formation to appear as *structured* is for it to have covered over in some way the contingency of its own installation. (13)

Crane dramatizes this process, the reproduction of nationalism, in the first three stanzas of "Van Winkle." He portrays the way in which the individual becomes a citizen-subject.

For Althusser, the reproduction of nationalism occurs as part of a larger process. Like other dimensions of a country's prevailing ideology, nationalism is disseminated by the "Ideological State Apparatuses" (which include schools) as part of the general ideological reproduction of economic relations. In order for society to perpetuate itself, it must reproduce the conditions of its existence, attempting to guarantee that reproduction as best it can. According to Althusser, such reproduction provides the basis for "the reproduction of labour power" that sustains "bourgeois" hegemony (130), and schools occupy a "*dominant* position" in this process (152). In tracing the historical development of schools, he links schools and families in a pairing that supports the status quo (154). In "Van Winkle," Crane dramatizes the role of this ideological "couple" (in the form of the poet's parents) in the creation of his speaking subject.

The vividness with which Crane renders his memories points to their psychic importance. By describing the speaker's experience of these stories as though they were physically felt impressions, Crane is suggesting something significant about the formation of the individual as a citizen. From one point of view, the narratives register a historical experience that defines the United States as a legitimate nation. From another, the narratives purvey an ideology about the structure and history of the nation to each generation of students who study them. The scene of learning depicted by Crane's speaker represents the reproduction of a particular ideology about the country to which the students belong. It shows the process that creates the feeling of belonging to and participating in the life and community of one's country. The school lessons he singles out constitute the mythic narrative of the nation's origin.

From this perspective, Crane's account of his childhood lessons is an exemplary one. Each of these tales conveys some aspect of the characteristic spirit of the nation. Pizarro's flat, allegorical presence stands for exploration and discovery, whatever forms they take, in American culture, while Cortes' heroic motion conveys his energetic leadership. There may be a hint of the calculating strategy and ruthless savvy Cortes drew upon in his conquest of Montezuma's city, but it is neatly sublimated in the dashing allure of his confidence. Captain Smith's manly bearing provides the English counterpart to Cortes, while "Priscilla's cheek close in the wind" supplies a maidenly love interest. This scene of schooling represents the general experience of coming to know oneself as a citizen. At the same time, Crane shows how these disparate characters are yoked together to produce a unifying national myth. The artifice of this gesture is the "contingency" that for Butler is "covered over" in the repetitions that make any social structure cohere and endure (13). Despite Crane's adoption of the myth of national unity, the fact of its disunity makes itself known, first in the displaced form of the family antagonisms he recounts in the latter half of "Van Winkle" and later in the explicit questioning of national history in "Quaker Hill."

In the second half of "Van Winkle," Crane fuses memories of school with more personal ones of play and family interaction. Through the figure of Rip Van Winkle, Crane turns from the past of his nation to the past of his memory. Just as Crane used the unnamed figure of Pocahontas to fuse the lover's personal experience with the national experience symbolized by Columbus's monologue, so he draws on the literary character of Rip Van Winkle, the man who slept through the revolution that founded the nation, in order to connect the lore of colonial history with the lyric lore of the psyche. This synthesizing gesture both positions Crane within the American literary tradition represented by Washington Irving and reveals the discontinuities within his family that correspond to the disunity within the nation. Although Crane obscures the issue of national disunity in "Van Winkle," he reveals it in other sections of *The Bridge* such as "The River."

Crane makes his transition from school lessons to backyard memories by disrupting the syntax of the quatrain that ends his reprise of legendary Americans. The text that interrupts it sounds like the chant of schoolchildren as they jump rope or skip through hopscotch squares:

> And Rip forgot the office hours,
> and he forgot the pay;
> Van Winkle sweeps a tenement
> way down on Avenue A,— (55)

Crane alludes to Rip Van Winkle's defining experience in this chant—the act of forgetting. An aura of sleepy oblivion surrounds this latter-day avatar of a New World literary tradition. Like the hoboes who appear later in "The River," Crane's Rip occupies a low position on the social ladder. This bathetic drop from the heroism of the previous quatrains provides an ironic commentary on them. In the figure of his derelict Rip, Crane provides an American hero to rival that of the conquistadors and colonists. He characterizes his Whitmanian idler with a significant, defiant affection; "oblivious of the feverish, commercial bustle," writes R. W. Butterfield, Rip "holds the first signpost for those who would jump from the economic treadmill and relinquish the present" (160). In fact, the figure of the loafer effects the ironic fusion of "the School-Family couple" evoked earlier in the section. Rip's incorrigible lassitude is at odds with the disciplined labor of the businessmen who are the heirs of the Puritans and who rule the state, but it is perhaps a desirable alternative to the debauched lapses (depicted in "Quaker Hill") of such businessmen.

In juxtaposing the national history embodied in his lessons with memories of play and parents, the poet again suggests that the public world of politics and conquest is not separable from the lyric world of personal experience. While Crane focuses on the mythic significance attached to each of these scenes, implying that it is the archetypal elements in both that are important and that enact the synthesis he intends, it is also true that the lore of national origin provides a historical context for the speaker's memories at the end of the section. Althusser's conception of the state and family as an ideological dyad suggests that the fragmentation and conflict of Crane's family (particularly regarding the poet's attitudes about his father's business affairs and his mother's property on the Isle of Pines) carries over into his country. As John Irwin argues, "In his role as native son imaginatively present at, imaginatively participating in, the generation of the American self, Crane found that the work of depicting a primal scene of national origin inevitably involved for him a reassessment of the emotions associated with his personal origin" (270). Van Winkle's bridging of the past and present shows how individual experience is situated in a particular time and place that are as divided by conflict as the speaker's family.

The reminiscences of childhood play and parental ministrations occur within a historical context that colors them in ways that are often inscrutable. The national ethos of the school lessons provides a social matrix from which to interpret the deeply personal experience that occurs within it. Two "archeologies" are simultaneously at work within *The Bridge*. The poet searches into the political history of his nation at the same time that he plumbs the inner reaches of his memory. Like the "tongues" of the snakes "That flittered from the ash heap," the mother's remembered smile "flickered." For the speaker and his audience, these subtle motions are equally portentous events. The distance between the legendary "lessons" of "Van Winkle" on the one hand and the hoboes, blacks, and Indians of "The River" and "The Dance" on the other exemplifies the difference between the pedagogical and the performative constitutions of the state described by Bhabha. "Van Winkle," in other words, represents the nation and the experience of citizenship as received lessons, whereas "The River" and "The Dance" portray characters who challenge ideal conceptions of the nation and of the bourgeois white male as representative citizen. Like Moore's "Virginia Britannia," *The Bridge* both celebrates and interrogates the birth of a nation.

In "The River," Crane includes dispossessed hoboes in his epic embrace. In a gesture that ironically echoes Whitman's praise of trains in "To a Locomotive in Winter" and evokes Kahn's economic involvement with the railroad industry, Crane figures his era as a train speeding through a landscape of billboards. The commercial flash of the "20th Century Limited" may have mass appeal, but the speaker's satire suggests that its glitter is gilded, for its promise rings hollow for the three men deafened by the frenetic roar of its progress:

> So the 20th Century—so
> whizzed the Limited—roared by and left
> three men, still hungry on the tracks, ploddingly
> watching the tail lights wizen and converge, slip-
> ing gimleted and neatly out of sight. (57)

Crane expresses the menace posed by fast-track business for the private lives of the hoboes who are left momentarily blinded in its wake. The wandering men whom the speaker remembers having seen "Behind / My father's cannery works" occupy marginal social positions, yet their symbolic position in Crane's poem is central. Their contrast with Crane's patron could not be more extreme, for, as mentioned earlier, Kahn made much of his money through his involvement with the railroad industry and was an important business associate and staunch defender of the railroad baron Harriman, whom Theodore Roosevelt urged the Interstate Commerce Commission to investigate (Kobler 47). Crane's characterization of the train supports Henry David Thoreau's claim in *Walden* that "We do not ride upon the railroad; it rides upon us" (396).

Although the hoboes he remembers in *The Bridge* are shiftless "Rail-squatters ranged in nomad raillery," whose languor contrasts with his father's busy "works," the speaker finds something to admire in them.[11] He portrays them as failed pioneers and infantilizes them, but he can not help enjoying the pleasure they take in their leisured days:

> The ancient men,—wifeless or runaway
> Hobo-trekkers that forever search
> An empire wilderness of freight and rails.
> Each seemed a child, like me, on a loose perch,
> Holding to childhood like some termless play.
> John, Jake or Charley, hopping the slow freight
> —Memphis to Tallahassee—riding the rods,
> Blind fists of nothing, humpty-dumpty clods. (58–59)

Dispossessed and impoverished, Crane's hoboes seem to wander without purpose. "Being homeless," Stout comments, "they are free to find America for themselves, but Crane gives no assurance that they will indeed perform the pioneers' symbolic act of home founding" (190). For all their playful energy and potential labor power, they remain "Blind fists of nothing" and incongruent "clods" in the eyes of their so-called social betters. As the "aimless outcasts of America," Crane's hoboes are one of the groups in his poem who may be classed among the domestic victims of America's commercial imperialism, for the employers who benefit from such imperialism would certainly sneer at these men, perceiving them as at best indigent and shiftless day laborers (Butterfield 162). Kahn's financial backing of railroads and his own travels by train "all through the nation for Kuhn, Loeb," differ sharply from the hitch-hiking lives of the hoboes (Zeck 62). While Crane pays homage to Kahn's patronage in the aristocratic language used by Columbus in "Ave Maria," here this patronage appears as the destructive force of "the 20th Century Limited" that runs roughshod over the lives of three jobless men.[12] If "in the empire of American railroads" Harriman presided as "emperor," the hoboes who ride the rails would find themselves subject to his dominion, as trespassers on his property (Kobler 46).

Nevertheless, although they find themselves in the wake of a dynamo that bypasses them, leaving them at the wrong end of the twentieth century, Crane's hoboes maintain a determined innocence by "Holding to childhood like some termless play," even in the face of class prejudice and the threatening "empire wilderness" ruled by American business. In contrast to the violent speed of the Limited, "some men," Crane informs us,

> take their liquor slow—and count
> —Though they'll confess no rosary nor clue—
> The river's minute by the far brook's year.
> Under a world of whistles, wires and steam
> Caboose-like they go ruminating through
> Ohio, Indiana—blind baggage—
> To Cheyenne tagging . . . Maybe Kalamazoo. (57–58)

Like Whitman's poetic selves, they are constantly afoot, open to the world's vistas and experiences, up to something.

Also like that same poetic forefather, Crane celebrates such despised men, assigning them a prominent place in the "home" of his poem. In a letter to Mrs. T. W. Simpson, whom he addresses as "Dear Aunt Sally" (a sobriquet he uses later in "The River"), Crane explains the structural function of the hoboes in *The Bridge*:

> I'm trying in this part of the poem to chart the pioneer experience of our
> forefathers—and to tell the story backwards, as it were, on the "backs" of hobos.
> These hobos are simply "psychological ponies" to carry the reader across the

country and back to the Mississippi, which you will notice is described as a great River of Time. I also unlatch the door to the pure Indian world which opens out in the "Dance" section, so the reader is gradually led back in time to the pure savage world, while existing at the same time in the present. (*O My Land* 341)

Crane presses the loafing hoboes of his memory into the service of his text, figuring their rhetorical role in the poem as a form of manual labor. As the etymology of *metaphor* suggests, they carry something from one point to another, facilitating the poet's foray into the past. As "psychological ponies," they serve as beasts of burden to convey meaning from the otherwise inaccessible past into the living light of the present. If the hoboes are the impure products of America, the failed counterparts of the nation's industrial and financial magnates, they are also the harbingers of "the pure savage world" embodied for Crane by the Indian.

Despite their lack of social standing, Crane's roving hoboes possess a sacred knowledge of the country beyond the reach of the affluent. As Thomas Yingling points out, "These are figures who, in their constitution of an underground social structure, represent an alternative to the poem's opening vision of America as dominated by commerce" (204). In their defense, Crane suggests their significance:

Yet they touch something like a key perhaps.
From pole to pole across the hills, the states
—They know a body under the wide rain;
Youngsters with eyes like fjords, old reprobates
With racetrack jargon,—dotting immensity
They lurk across her, knowing her yonder breast
Snow-silvered, sumac-stained or smoky blue—
Is past the valley-sleepers, south or west. (59)

Although these wanderers appear as insignificant insects against the stark immensity of the continent, their furtive lurking "across her" puts them in a distinguishing relationship to their country. In the sexualizing language of the poem, they "know" her yonder breast. Unlike the small-souled Puritans of Williams's *American Grain,* who are unwilling or afraid to touch the Indians or the earth of the New World, these hoboes have touched the body of their homeland. Even though this contact gives them a modicum of knowledge, they remain ignorant, for they are reduced to "knowing her without name."

The speaker likens his own knowledge of his nation to the wisdom of the hoboes, juxtaposing their knowing with his:

I have trod the rumorous midnights, too,

And past the circuit of the lamp's thin flame
(O Nights that brought me to her body bare!)
Have dreamed beyond the print that bound her name.

Trains sounding the long blizzards out—I heard
Wail into distances I knew were hers.
Papooses crying on the wind's long mane
Screamed redskin dynasties that fled the brain,
—Dead echoes! But I knew her body there,
Time like a serpent down her shoulder, dark,
And space, an eaglet's wing, laid on her hair. (59)

The speaker claims to know America with the same directness and intimacy as the hoboes. "Pursuing Pocahontas," Dembo writes, "the poet . . . becomes a hobo in imagination, as in 'Van Winkle' he became a child" (70). Although Crane's speaker is clearly a reader, for he dreams of Pocahontas within the charmed circle "of the lamp's thin flame," he sings exultantly (if parenthetically) of "Nights that brought me to her body bare!" and yearns to know the actual and not merely the nominal reality of his nation—to know Pocahontas as America "beyond the print that bound her name." In these passages, Crane's representation of Pocahontas as the symbolic body of the New World points to a conception of the nation as an abstract and figurative essence, a ground to thought that functions as a substrate for the production of the idea of the nation under the auspices of the imagination. "Pocahontas's function," writes Rebecca Blevins Faery, "is to secure the establishment of an American nation in a landscape that is her 'body' and to provide a site where white Euro-Americans can replace Indians in a refigured identity as 'Americans'" (129–30). As a result, Crane's representation of Pocahontas dramatizes the teasing out of ideas about his nation in a way that echoes the lessons of "Van Winkle."

Crane's use of Pocahontas to effect the synthesis of his speaker's consciousness with the New World landscape that surrounds it participates in a general trend of his time. R. W. B. Lewis points out that Pocahontas was a "cliché of popular culture" by the time Crane wrote his poem (313–14), and Giles comments on the conscious artifice through which Crane "punningly refurbishes Pocahontas as a capitalist production of the 1920s" (*Crane* 58). Moreover, as Jared Gardner (following Michaels) points out,

> Many writers at the time were attempting to define an American identity with the Indian as a central symbol . . . . As Frank writes in *The Rediscovery of America* (1929), "our root is in the red men; and our denial of this is a disease within us." Not simply a literary conceit, however, this formulation of the Indian's relation to American identity was one aspect of a social project that sought to claim an inheritance for America that would distinguish it wholly from its European parents. (25)

Artists sought to adopt the Indians as the ancestors of a unique New World culture distinguishing the artistic practice of the United States from that of Europe. They conjured metaphorical genealogies whereby the Indians were their true ancestors, in an effort to claim that a new "American" race had been born from the hybrid fusions of immigrant and indigenous populations in the land that became the United States. Crane's description of an important scene in "The Dance" supports Gardner's thesis: "Not only do I describe the conflict between the two races in this dance," Crane wrote his patron Kahn, but "I also become identified with the Indian and his world before it is over, which is the only method possible of ever really possessing the Indian and his world as a cultural factor. I think I really succeeded in getting under the skin of this glorious and dying animal, in terms of expression, in symbols, which he himself would comprehend" (*O My Land* 347).

A similar impetus seems to lie behind the poet's meditation on history in the following stanza from "Quaker Hill":

> The resigned factions of the dead preside.
> Dead rangers bled their comfort on the snow;
> But I must ask slain Iroquois to guide
> Me farther than scalped Yankees knew to go:
> Shoulder the curse of sundered parentage,
> Wait for the postman driving from Birch Hill
> With birthright by blackmail, the arrant page
> That unfolds a new destiny to fill. . . . (93)

While the passage pays homage to white colonists and pioneers, it also conveys the speaker's preference for the Indians they killed, thereby echoing the speakers of Frost's "Genealogical." For the speaker, the mystic wisdom of the Indian marks the limitations of his European forebears: the ghost of the "slain Iroquois" can guide the poet "farther than scalped Yankees knew to go." The genealogical fantasy—wherein Americans descended from Europeans are "naturalized" as Indians—enables the speaker to face up to his country's past and move beyond it into a new frontier of creative possibility. The speaker aims to transcend the limits imposed by his past through the figurative "transmemberment" of race.

Escaping blood lines that exact from him a "birthright by blackmail," the speaker steps out onto a terra incognita of the imagination. The poet's reference to a "sundered parentage" is clearly an allusion to his own parents, but in the context of the lines, the phrase also reflects the historic and geographical separation of non–Native Americans from their Old World ancestors. As Frost acknowledges in "The Gift Outright" and as Williams makes clear in so much of his prose, any birthright conferred from overseas nations on their American heirs comes at the price of a blackmail that demands allegiance to the foreign nation in exchange for cultural recognition. According to such terms, the inferiority of American culture could only be lived down by accepting its secondary status. The extremes of the "arrant page," which designate the speaker's destiny, allude to the impressive landscape of a vast new world of the imagination while they also write him into a constraining script, imposing upon him a role to which he must conform.

Just as he fused personal and communal histories (with his references to "sundered parentage" and "birthright by blackmail" in "Quaker Hill" and "Van Winkle") with his remembered lessons about colonial heroes, Crane portrays the hoboes in "The River" in such a way as to bring together his boyhood memories with a body of history and legend surrounding a whole nomadic culture. As Richard Wormser writes, "In America, wandering workers were fairly common by the eighteenth century. There were many complaints about 'strangers' suddenly appearing in towns or villages seeking work or public assistance. These strangers were part of a small but growing number of wandering poor" (2). Crane champions these wanderers, rewriting his nation's mythology of pioneer prowess by characterizing modern hoboes as queered belated versions of such famous forebears. "They are," Crane wrote to Kahn, "the leftovers of the pioneers in at least this respect—that their wanderings carry the reader through an experience parallel to that of Boone and others" (*O My Land* 348). He uses similar language in the poem, dubbing his hoboes "born pioneers in time's despite" who are "Grimed tributaries to an ancient flow—" (60). As Crane's lines perhaps suggest, hoboes were the inheritors of an unjust legacy of U.S. settlement, the figurative scions of vagrant forebears. "Many towns," Wormser observes,

> openly discriminated against "strangers," refusing to allow them to enter or even to settle nearby. Local law enforcement officials patrolled the towns at night looking for "night walkers," people who, the police believed, did not belong in the area and had no means of supporting themselves. Such persons were often whipped and banished from the town or sent to workhouses where they were forced to work for the community. (2–3)

As Wormser makes clear, one reason for the widespread existence of hoboes in Crane's day was the unresolved issue of colonial settlement. Crane's choice of "tributaries" as the word to characterize the hoboes puns handsomely on minor rivers and subject peoples, reflecting their status in his culture.[13]

While the hoboes succumb to the river of mortality like everyone else, they are also forced to pay tribute to a power that dominates and despises them. Like the Indians and the "floating niggers" in the river of American history, they too are a conquered population within a state that proudly defines itself as free. Like the tradition of Indian "removals" and "reservations," and like African American slavery and disenfranchisement, hobo history reflects a contradiction in American democracy. Crane writes of the hoboes that

> They win no frontier by their wayward plight,
> But drift in stillness, as from Jordan's brow. (60)

These lines recall the earlier ones in which "Hobo-trekkers . . . forever search / An empire wilderness of freight and rails." Crane concedes that his hoboes will win no ground of their own, but the very terms of his treatment of them suggests that their "failure" to stake out a new territory for themselves at the expense of others is far from being a cause for embarrassment or shame. Each of Crane's hoboes is, like the representative American tramp John Seelye analyzes, "the antithesis of the conventional American hero—the self-made man—for his success lies in what society terms failure" (553). The hoboes will "win no frontier" because none remains to be won. Instead, they explore an "empire" they do not own, a "wilderness" of boxcars and inanimate freight. The hoboes inhabit an industrial wasteland that constitutes the wealth of America's commercial overlords. As Giles suggests,

> the hobo-trekkers may be forever searching for the wilderness of freight and rails, but the business empire of freight and rails is similarly forever searching for them, because it knows that runaway hobo-trekkers can be easily exploited as cheap labour, and also that the hoboes pose less of a threat to the smooth running of the system once they have been integrated inside it. (*Crane* 52)

Crane's portrayal of hoboes evinces a fine irony: at the same time that the United States was consolidating its powers abroad, members of its own nation shared in a disenfranchisement similar to the kind that was visited upon the citizens of foreign countries brought beneath its imperial sway.

Although their drifting and their movement *away* from "Jordan's brow" may be interpreted as a condemnation of their behavior or their disenfranchisement, the fact that they "drift in stillness" may be read in more positive terms, as if to suggest that the hoboes possess an equanimity that makes them truly self-possessed. In addition, their drifting "as from Jordan's brow" is also ambiguous because it can imply that the hoboes have been baptized in this river and have crossed into a free and higher ground. Like "Atlantis," the territory bounded by Jordan is a metaphysical one and is therefore not coterminous with any particular territory. The animosity commonly expressed toward such nomads reflects the fact that their constant roving connotes a rival geography, another kind of freedom land, which violates the conventions of a political state that takes as its ideal the settled, property-owning citizen. The cultures of the Amerindians and the hoboes, which either do not recognize or do not respect the private ownership of land, suffer for their transgressions against property—even as the hoboes celebrate their alienation from it.

In the midst of the hoboes, Crane turns to an anonymous, omniscient "you." The apostrophe functions as both a personal address to the self and a public appeal to all members of his nation:

The River, spreading, flows—and spends your dream.
What are you, lost within this tideless spell?
You are your father's father, and the stream—
A liquid theme that floating niggers swell. (61)

In becoming one's "father's father," one gains a historical vantage on one's heritage and a personal advantage over paternal authority. This glimpse into national history allows the speaker to create himself through an oedipal displacement of the father.[14] In becoming his "father's father," he becomes his own progenitor. He may regard himself as independent because he conceives himself as constituting himself.

This moment of "The River" provides an explanatory context for the myth of the rugged individual that exercises such power over the American imagination. The scene dramatizes the genesis of this myth, revealing how the concept of the free individual is a historical construct that makes things possible but comes at the cost of a necessary forgetting. The poet portrays his speaker appropriating his parentage, figuring his birth as an autonomous act. In fact, of course, no one's birth is autonomous. Instead, it is the culmination of a series of histories and circumstances over which the individual exercises no control. This passage offers a heady vista of the past from the perspective of one's origin, even as it reveals the process of imagination whereby this self-generation becomes possible. Hence it both aggrandizes and dissolves, simultaneously celebrates and deconstructs, this process.

Near the end of "The River," Crane's train becomes a Mississippi riverboat, so that the poem covers as much geographical as metaphysical ground:

> Down two more turns the Mississippi pours
> (Anon tall ironsides up from salt lagoons)
>
> And flows within itself, heaps itself free.
> All fades but one thin skyline 'round . . . Ahead
> No embrace opens but the stinging sea;
> The River lifts itself from its long bed,
>
> Poised wholly on its dream, a mustard glow
> Tortured with history, its one will—flow!
> —The Passion spreads in wide tongues, choked and slow,
> Meeting the Gulf, hosannas silently below. (61)

The image of "wide tongues" repeats the earlier images of the flickering snakes' tongues in "Van Winkle" and the word Columbus pitches into the sea in "Ave Maria"; the "quarrying passion" of the river expresses itself as it "flows" into its delta, or mouth. The river's "Passion" paradoxically embodies both an idealized natural language and the oppression experienced by the dispossessed—in this case, murdered blacks. Like Emerson, Crane looks for tongues and tropes everywhere in his landscapes. But like his fellow modernists, Crane also questions the correspondence he would like to find between the world and the word. As in his lyric "A Name for All," Crane acknowledges that his language is a kind of imposition on his landscape. While this section fuses the poet's metaphors of language with the images of historical process, the pun on "Passion" also discloses the discontinuities between lived history and political ideal.

In fact, like the hoboes and black corpses of this section and like the Indians in the next ("The Dance"), the Mississippi River is itself "Tortured with history," for even in the midst of its flow, the memory of the past persists within its bed, giving rise to stratified sediments ("vascular with silted shale") that accumulate over time and exert an impeding pressure of their own. The river of time reflects the Joycean "nightmare of history," for, clotted with its offal, the river bears the bloated body of history as a resisting burden in the form of swollen black corpses and "De Soto's bones." Crane's language vividly symbolizes the unremitting force of the past in its actions upon the present, revealing the chaotic disarray of the world even in the midst of the poet's attempts to shape and transcend it. The legacies of colonization and slavery continue to scar the national landscape, showing the discrepancy between Crane's poetic ideal and the real flaws of his nation.

• In "The Dance," which follows "The River," Crane figures the seizure of land and displacement of Indians by white pioneers as the rape of a mythic woman. The ceremonial song of this section continues the metaphor likening the body of Pocahontas to the body of the continent. In the terms of this metaphor, Pocahontas becomes the symbolic mother of her dispossessed descendants rather than the benevolent grandmother of all modern Americans. Crane evokes her presence in his marginalia: "Then you shall see her truly— your blood remembering its first invasion of her secrecy, its first encounters with her kin, her chieftain lover . . . his shade that haunts the lakes and hills" (62). This passage bears out Kolodny's argument that "As soon as the land is experienced as feminine, no masculine activity in relation to it can be both satisfying and nonabusive" (142). The poet's apostrophe to his native goddess further supports this thesis: "There was a veil upon you, Pocahontas, bride— / O Princess whose brown lap was virgin May; / And bridal flanks and eyes hid tawny pride." The earth-colored skin of the goddess attracts the speaker, but his vision of her is frustrated by an obscuring veil he cannot lift. Like the "Mythical brows we saw retiring," Pocahontas retreats beyond the reach of her would-be partner (62).

The imagery of the snake and the eagle in this section may be interpreted in significantly different ways. Although the snake and the eagle are clearly associated with this section's Amerindian heroes, they are also political symbols associated with the United States. Because they turn out to be icons for the competing communities of Amerindians and immigrant Americans, or their descendants, the snake and the eagle figures are fraught with a political ambiguity that persists despite Crane's ritual fusion of the groups at the end of "The Dance" and "Atlantis." The snake, as Moore reminds her readers in "Virginia Britannia," appeared on the first flag of the United States. Appropriating a figure associated with ancient Rome, moreover, the United States came to adopt the eagle as its own national emblem. The powerful bird offers a compelling image of freedom, and it is an image Crane returns to when he describes the acrobatic "aeroplanes" of "Cape Hatteras." A political meaning of the eagle is also expressed in "Bacardi Spreads the Eagle's Wing." In this poem, the Eagle's wing extends beyond North America in a manner as imperial as the European colonization of the New World. "The Dance" reflects the cultural appropriation of native symbols for national ends, and *The Bridge* as a whole dramatizes how such symbols were systematically subsumed in the national myths of manifest destiny and imperial conquest. The eagle of an Indian headdress in "Cape Hatteras" becomes the image of the new imperial nation: "Now the eagle dominates our days" and "We know the strident rule / Of wings imperious" (78). As in "A Name for All," naming (or renaming) functions as an imposition and a usurpation. The symbol's change in meaning reflects the division between Native Americans and European Americans, indicating a colonial divide within the nation and thereby figuring its lack of unity.

In the speaker's dance with Maquokeeta, serpent and eagle intertwine in the boughs of a newly emerged tree—perhaps Crane's synthesis of the Tree of Liberty and the Tree of Life. Although Crane's ceremonial dance honors the Indian nations symbolized by Maquokeeta and Pocahontas, in the context of a poem about the United States, the meaning of the symbols shifts according to the political and social communities that give rise to them. This shift reflects the colonial appropriation of indigenous cultural symbols by the U.S. government. Whether it is read as an image of the predatory imperialist or as the majestic emblem of democracy, the eagle had come, by Crane's day, to be a familiar symbol of his country.

In its effort to heal the shattered nations of the people represented by Maquokeeta and Pocahontas, "The Dance" imitates the shamanism of Indian rituals and ceremonies. But the speaker of "The Dance" is an American of European descent striving to adopt an Amerindian rite, a fact that demands an interpretive strategy to account for the arrangement of the several perspectives at work in this section. The section integrates or domesticates the "savage" cultural practices of Amerindians in a distinctively English verse structure, for the shape and timbre of the quatrains into which Crane measures his music is "European" in significant ways. More important, however, the language here is the speech of a white American addressing red ones. The section invites an attention to the perspective and interaction produced by such an address. The poet seems to be writing in "redface," sympathetically adopting the method and interests of the Indians, but the section also reveals a discrepancy between the "white" perspective of the speaker and the "red" one he espouses.

The tale told by the pronouns in the first three quatrains demonstrates my point. The speaker introduces his heroic "winter king" in a blur of "swift red flesh." The linguistic marker "red" identifies the subject of the phrase according to his race. Although the speaker interrupts the propulsive meter of this introduction with the change in syntax of the second line (in which the interrogative pronoun of the question reverses the first foot from the standard iambic to the trochaic question "Who squired . . . ?"), he nonetheless maintains a European American frame of reference. The speaker refers to the Indians in the third-person singular: Pocahontas is "She" and Maquokeeta is "he." On the other hand, the speaker resorts to an easy "we" when referring to the affiliation of his own perspective ("Mythical brows we saw retiring . . ."). Just as in the work of Frost, Williams, and Moore, where the use of the third-person plural demonstrates their sense of participation in a national community, so Crane's use of "we" and "us" constitutes a coherent body of people easily identifiable as "the nation." This "we" signifies the white pioneers who both benefited from and dominated the Indians they encountered. The pronouns identifying Pocahontas and Maquokeeta seem to preclude the speaker's recognition of the political and social realities of their different affiliations.

Nevertheless, the wistful ellipsis at the end of the following quatrain represents more than a sentimental nostalgia:

> Mythical brows we saw retiring—loth,
> Disturbed and destined, into denser green.
> Greeting they sped us, on the arrow's oath:
> Now lie incorrigibly what years between . . . (62)

"The Dance" is an act of remembrance, an elegy to the Indians killed by the colonists in the series of wars between the two groups. In the emphatic present of its "Now," the last line of the stanza embodies the historical space "between" the speaker's present and the remembered past he elegizes, while the "retiring" marks of ellipsis represent the unspoken evil of that incorrigible lacuna. The ellipses mark the gap in historical accounts that pass over the violence suffered by the Indians.

It is significant that after this address to Pocahontas, one that identifies her explicitly for the first time in the main text of *The Bridge,* the speaker shifts from the communal "we"—a designation of the national—to the lyric "I." As the dance advances, the solidity of the national "we" breaks down into a lyric "I" of shared experience. The poem fuses its "white" speaker with a mythic Indian "other." As Paul writes, Crane "calls attention to his identification with the Indian ('I too was liege'), an act . . . of separation that permits him to double the intensity of the experience by observing it for us ('I heard . . . ,' 'I saw . . .') in the spirit of Whitman's 'I am the man, I suffer'd, I was there'" (220). The boundaries between the two figures break down under the analytic power of the poet's imagination, so that what formerly appeared to be a matter of fixed essence becomes one of fluid performance.

But this poetic ritual is not a simple one-step process in which the speaker marches out of one camp directly into another. Instead, it is a dialectic in which he systematically trades allegiances. First he identifies the "winter king" and "glacier woman" as "others" to be addressed, while the community to which he belongs is simply summoned as an "us." Then he surrenders to the "I" that tries to unite with those others through the sympathetic magic of a generous imagination. But he also swings back to the distinguishing "us" in the midst of his embracing "I"—before he merges with Maquokeeta at the end of the section. In this dialectic, the speaker surrenders his communal allegiance in order to become a more fluid, inclusive "I":

> I left the village for dogwood. By the canoe
> Tugging below the mill-race, I could see
> Your hair's keen crescent running, and the blue
> First moth of evening take wing stealthily.
>
> What laughing chains the water wove and threw!
> I learned to catch the trout's moon whisper; I
> Drifted how many hours I never knew,
> But, watching, saw that fleet young crescent die. (62)

As the verbs imply, the speaker's transformation into a roving Indian permits vision ("I could see") and stimulates understanding ("I learned"). Verbs from subsequent stanzas show how this self avoids placid stagnation through movement and decisive action: "I left the village"; "I /Drifted"; "I left my sleek boat nibbling"; "I sped"; "I could not stop." Other verbs signal advance: "I gained the ledge," "I took the portage climb." They also reveal the risk to the integrity of the self that undertakes it, for the white poet has forsaken his ties to the community of pioneer forebears in order to enjoy the perspective of the Indians. The speaker shifts his frame of reference by altering his allegiance. This shift nurtures the sympathy toward the Amerindian in the good faith with which he began his ritual surrender. At the height of his exultant mood, the speaker is attuned to the "padded foot / Within" himself.

The enrichment of the speaker's sympathetic insight leads him to acknowledge colonial injustice: "The long moan of a dance is in the sky. / Dance, Maquokeeta: Pocahontas grieves . . ." (63). It permits him to see and mourn the successive deaths of Indian cultures in the form of a waning moon: "watching," he saw "that fleet young crescent die." Two stanzas later, however, the speaker confesses his difference from Maquokeeta through the grammar of his address:

> Dance, Maquokeeta! snake that lives before,
> That casts his pelt, and lives beyond! Sprout, horn!
> Spark, tooth! Medicine-man, relent, restore—
> Lie to us,—dance us back the tribal morn! (64)

With these words, the speaker moves from ecstasy to a recognition of his allegiance to a community that is different from the Indian one he longs for and admires. His admiration sees in the Indian a source of spiritual vitality and redemption, which prompts his supplication that Maquokeeta "Lie to us" and "dance us back the tribal morn!" As this final line makes clear, the speaker's identification with the culture to which he belongs is an uneasy one; the readiness with which he had conceived himself as "we" has slid into a troubled "us." The white speaker lacks the kinship ties of the Indian's clan-based society. He seeks to regain the promising "morn" of a "tribal" unity through the primal offices of a native other. Lacking Emerson's confident access to "an original relation to the universe," the speaker turns to the cultures of the very peoples that his own had dispossessed (Emerson 7). That turn of course risks becoming another unjust appropriation: in this linguistic usurpation, the Indian becomes one American version of the modernist "primitive."

The urgency of the speaker's need drives his dialectic. By the end of the section, his choreographed ritual produces a new identity, a fusion of cultural influences that issues in a hybrid form, for the "We" at the end of the poem differs from the "we" at its beginning:

> We danced, O Brave, we danced beyond their farms,
> In cobalt desert closures made our vows . . .
> Now is the strong prayer folded in thine arms,
> The serpent with the eagle in the boughs. (65)

Crane's speaker goes native in the first line of this quatrain, but the pronouns register a transposition rather than a transcendence of identity. Keeping pace with the rhythms of the dance, the antecedents of "we" and "they" have reversed themselves, for the speaker refers to himself and Maquokeeta when he chants "we danced," and he distinguishes himself from white society when he contrasts the free movements of this dance with the staid fixity of "their farms." The speaker imagines his dance to be transcendentally "beyond" the geography of the agriculture of European pioneers and the state that protects them. (This "beyond" is analogous to the imagined land of freedom inhabited by the hoboes in "The River" and to the metaphysical regions of "Cathay" and "Atlantis.") By the end of the section, the speaker has united with the "Brave" and distanced himself from the whites who stole arable land for "their farms" and consigned its indigenous inhabitants to the "cobalt desert closures" in which the straining couple perform their portentous dance. Yet Crane acknowledges his vision's willful fictiveness in calling upon Maquokeeta to "Lie to us" (64). "The Dance" thus reflects the postcolonial disunity of the United States, for by attempting to synthesize the experience of red man and white, the poem reflects instead the discrepancies between them. While the U.S. government systematically subdued Native American groups, such efforts are called into question by the integrity of surviving Native American communities.

Like "The Dance," "Indiana" weaves together indigenous and European cultures, but this section also underscores the fact of Indian dispossession. "Indiana" reveals the way in which dispossession is masked by a fantasy current in Crane's day: the figurative appropriation of Indian ancestry by European Americans (Michaels 29–52; Gardner 25). The "squaw" whom the white mother sees in "Indiana" is "homeless," "bent westward, passing on a stumbling jade," presumably because she has been forced into exile by white usurpers (67). In mythic terms, the woman's westward emigration implies the death of a people; "the squaw" represents the many Indian peoples decimated by the advance of the Europeans (in this respect she becomes an avatar of Pocahontas). Like the hoboes in "The River" she has no home, but unlike them she finds herself persona non grata in a land stolen from her people. In its references to the greed of the gold rushes, the corruption of the gilded age that intervenes between the poet's era and the period described in this section, the exploitative travels of white generations (both the father and the son range away from home to seek their fortune in an imperial hinterland), and the homelessness and hybridity of the Indians, "Indiana" registers a host of social conflicts that work against the poet's synthesizing vision. These conflicts correspond to the contradictions between the alienated hoboes of "The River" and the ethic of success satirized in Crane's portrayal of the golfing businessmen of "Quaker Hill." In "Indiana" (as in "Cutty Sark"), differences between U.S. citizens correspond to the imperial differences between colonist and native "other."

"Cutty Sark" shares the constant movement that characterizes "Ave Maria," "The River," and "Indiana." It repeats this theme with its drunken, loquacious sailor as well as with the airplanes of "Cape Hatteras," the subway of "The Tunnel," and the "Tall-Vision-of-the-Voyage" in "Atlantis." These restless emigrations extend the ventures that originally spawned the nation, and they represent the global circulation of people and goods entailed by imperial trade. The economic forces that drove colonization in the past impel the commercial empire of the present:

> Migrations that must needs void memory,
> Inventions that cobblestone the heart,—
> Unspeakable Thou Bridge to Thee, O Love.
> Thy pardon for this history. (107)

A series of dislocations corresponds to the many emigrations of *The Bridge*. Images of homelessness abound: nomad hoboes appear in "The River," the "Homeless squaw" in "Indiana," and "homeless Eve" in "The Southern Cross." Through such representations, Crane shows that colonization is predicated upon dispossession, even though colonizers attempt to erase it in the process of consolidating their hegemony: "we must maim / Because we are usurpers" (119). The passage above from the closing hymn of *The Bridge* acknowledges this aspect of colonization by insisting that "Migrations must needs void memory." In this line, Crane acknowledges the willful oblivion that underlies his country's origins. The builders of a colonial nation "void memory" not only of their original homeland but of the sins they commit in order to establish a new one. Renan's claim that "the essence of a nation is" not only "that all individuals have many things in common" but also "that they have forgotten many things" is as germane to this passage as it is to the work of Robert Frost (11). Crane demonstrates the redemptive agenda of his mystical synthesis by remembering and imploring "pardon for this history," but in doing so he perhaps only temporarily refuses to forget such history.

As critics commonly observe, in "Cutty Sark" and "Cape Hatteras" Crane pays homage to Whitman and modernizes aspects of "Passage to India." The commerce and "rondure" that feature so grandly in Whitman's "Passage to India" come to fruition in various passages:

> Bright skysails ticketing the Line, wink round the Horn
> to Frisco, Melbourne . . .
>   Pennants, parabolas—
> clipper dreams indelible and ranging,
> baronial white on lucky blue! (73)

The "baronial white" of the ship's sails against the blue backdrop of the sea represents the commercial aristocracy that funds the ventures undertaken by Crane's drunken sailor and others like him. "Cutty Sark" provides an example of a man who participates in the large-scale movements of people that Whitman celebrated in "Passage to India." As Butterfield points out, moreover, "the title . . . refers to Crane's favourite brand of whisky, named after the clipper which established a speed record for the England–China (Cathay) trading route" (175). Like the real-world references to Taeping and to the other vessels involved in the tea trade, the name Cutty Sark echoes the allusions to Cathay in "Ave Maria" and Kahn's financial investments in China. The sailor's disjointed dialogue gives glimpses of a world whose unification is increasingly achieved through the labor of such men. His abrupt halts and shifts in syntax issue in a bewildering collage of mythic, literary, and commercial references that reflect the growing global intercourse foreseen by Whitman in "Passage to India."

In the end Crane's telegraphic patchwork of Eliot, Melville, and Poe may seem less effective than his portrayal of the sailor as a salesman and facilitator of trade. If the sailor's stint in the "Yucatan selling kitchenware" echoes Whitman's reference to his muse "install'd amid the kitchenware" from "Song of the Exposition," the sailor's report of his other jobs similarly reflects Whitman's celebrations of work and commerce. One of his occupations, for example, was in an area central to U.S. expansion: "I ran a donkey engine," he tells the speaker, "down there on the Canal / in Panama" (71). As Joseph Freeman and Scott Nearing point out, "The completion of the Panama Canal" in 1914 "gave the United States a strategic point for the struggle for commercial and political supremacy in the Pacific" (40). Crane's allusion to the canal recalls Whitman's reference to the Suez Canal in "Passage to India," and like this poem, "Cutty Sark" emphasizes the globalization of trade. Indeed, in his reference to the canal, Crane cites a landmark achievement in the evolution of U.S. military and economic power. As John Major explains, it performed a dual role as both a thoroughfare for maritime commerce and . . . a conduit for sea-power. But whereas the trade route was intended for the merchant shipping of the world, the strategic highway was designed with only one battle-fleet in mind: the U.S. Navy. In the judgment of General Tasker Bliss, "it double[d] the military resources of the United States for operations in the Orient." (155)

Crane's poem shows that "This turning rondure" is rendered "whole" through such new trade routes as the Panama Canal (48). *The Bridge* reflects the global reach of U.S. commercial and military intervention.[15]

In addition, Crane's portrayal of the drunk sailor in "Cutty Sark" extends his portrayal of marginal figures in the previous sections of the poem. Like the bums who rove around the train yards of "The River," the sailor of "Cutty Sark" occupies a precarious position in the social order. "Sold on an imperialist dream of grandeur," writes Yingling, Crane's sailor "goes to Panama only to encounter the beginnings of a displacement and wandering that will not end" (207). In the dyspeptic dawn of his ranting dissipation, the sailor barely escapes death:

> Outside a wharf truck nearly ran him down
> —he lunged up Bowery way while the dawn
> was putting the Statue of Liberty out—that
> torch of hers, you know— (72–73)

The light of liberty, in other words, dims for such stumbling bums. The sailor is a man, writes Yingling, "whose life is proof against the myth of freedom that drives American self-consciousness" (208). Nevertheless, through the irony of his satire, Crane's dozing homosexuals, loafing hoboes, drowned blacks, conquered Indians, and oceangoing sailors become the representative men and women of America.

Although "Cutty Sark" is far from a lesson in economics, it does suggest a mercantile link between the singing sailor and the well-to-do men his labor serves. The profit derived from the goods that the sailor transports benefits the rich businessmen Crane derides in "Quaker Hill." Like the hoboes whom Crane saw behind his father's factory, the sailor occupies a dubious social position. Perhaps more so than the odd jobs of the hoboes, however, his work produces the wealth of an elite that scorns him. Whereas the hoboes are failed pioneers, Crane's Melvillian sailor has successfully pioneered the sea. The narrator of "The River" assures us that the hoboes "win no frontier by their wayward plight," but in "Cutty Sark" the sailor's interlocutor recognizes him as a pioneer of the waves: "I saw the frontiers gleaming of his mind." The economy represented in "Cutty Sark" links the labor of the working class to the riches of leisured capitalists just as (in a figurative echo of Kahn's work with American entrepreneurs in China) it unites the commercial enterprise of the East ("Taeping") with the financial capital of the West (74). Crane wrote to Malcolm and Peggy Cowley that "all the clippers mentioned . . . had extensive histories in the Tea trade—and the last two mentioned were life-long rivals" (*O My Land* 266). Moreover, Crane's closing reference to "Ariel" alludes not only to a ship but to the mastered spirit of Shakespeare's *The Tempest,* a work inspired by European ventures in the New World. As Butterfield argues, in "Cutty Sark" Crane's "synthesis of America" may be found "only in the inebriated mind of the protagonist, where anyway it is founded on a 'lie'" (178). Like other sections of *The Bridge,* "Cutty Sark" portrays the power of an imperial economy to generate great wealth for some while impoverishing not only those whom it subdues abroad but those whom it subjugates at home. The section reveals the moral as well as the financial costs of empire.

In "Cape Hatteras," Crane adopts the voice of the world-traveler as a device for responding to Whitman's vision of global rondure in "Passage to India." At the beginning of the century of American empire, the reach of the national "we" grows more expansive and cosmopolitan:

> But we, who round the capes, the promontories
> Where strange tongues vary messages of surf
> Below grey citadels, repeating to the stars
> The ancient names—return home to our own
> Hearths, there to eat an apple and recall
> The songs that gypsies dealt us at Marseille
> Or how the priests walked—slowly through Bombay—
> Or to read you, Walt,—knowing us in thrall
>
> To that deep wonderment, our native clay
> Whose depth of red, eternal flesh of Pocahontas—
> Those continental folded aeons, surcharged
> With sweetness below derricks, chimneys, tunnels—
> Is veined by all that time has really pledged us. . . . (77)

As in other sections of *The Bridge,* Crane features speech here as an earthy emanation. "The strange tongues" that "vary messages of surf" recall Columbus's document-laden cask in "Ave Maria," the snakes' tongues in "Van Winkle," the "storied" City of New Orleans in "The River," and the singing pebbles of Colorado that bear God's "gleaming name" in "Indiana." Like pebbles in "Indiana," the watery tongues of "Cape Hatteras" tell a story of the natural source of language, reflecting the poet's desire for identity between signifier and signified without the caution he evinces elsewhere that the effort to unify word and thing entails a usurpation. The poet is the artist who, attendant to the "strange tongues" of nature, hears them "repeating . . . / The ancient names" and translates them for his readers.

What he hears, however, is that the restless interest of Americans may drive them to the exotic settings of Marseilles and Bombay, to a free trade and travel that makes them "at home abroad," yet that insures they will be most truly at home when they return to the private "Hearths" of their own country. As if to express the problems with the very idea of a natural language, Crane records the process whereby human greed prefers gold to the God whose speech it incarnates in "Indiana." Marseilles and Bombay can be so fully enjoyed because the well-traveled American may look forward to remembering his adventures from the comfort of his own hearth. Crane's choice of this old-fashioned word evokes the warmth and familiarity that defines "home." The hearth, the place where meals were made when the word was not old-fashioned, conjures all that grounds and secures the identity of its owner. The hearth is indeed the heart of the proprietary citizen, the place where he or she can recollect the spontaneous overflow of emotions in protected tranquillity or enjoy the ruminations of a fireside poet. In contrast to the homeless Indians and hoboes portrayed earlier in the poem, "Cape Hatteras" presents a picture of the citizen proper, the independent man of means who owns his home—an inviting house with a yard rather than a cramped and noisy tenement—and thereby affords a space congenial to an imperious imagination.

Turning from his rhapsodies over the realization of human flight, Crane introduces more somber considerations through references to a fallen Adam and a fallen nation:

> Adam and Adam's answer in the forest
> Left Hesperus mirrored in the lucid pool.
> Now the eagle dominates our days, is jurist
> Of the ambiguous cloud. We know the strident rule
> Of wings imperious . . . Space, instantaneous,
> Flickers a moment, consumes us in its smile:
> A flash over the horizon—shifting gears—
> And we have laughter, or more sudden tears. (78)

Like the golden bird in Yeats's "Sailing to Byzantium," Crane's eagle is artificial and metallic. It recalls the eagle and snake of "The Dance" section (an emblematic pair to which Crane also refers in "Atlantis"). As in "The Dance," the words Crane associates with the bird evoke the political connotations of the eagle as the emblem of America. The eagle, Crane insists, "dominates our days" and "is jurist / Of the ambiguous cloud." This domination refers to the hold exercised by the airplane over the popular imagination in the early days of its development, but it also recalls the European domination of Native Americans and blacks depicted in earlier sections of *The Bridge* (and it eerily foretells the imperial power of later U.S. warplanes). While the phrase "jurist / Of the ambiguous cloud" is itself ambiguous, the term "jurist" evokes the world of political and social affairs, especially by virtue of its proximity to "dominates" and "imperious." Crane's "ambiguous cloud" is potentially ominous, and the declaration that "the eagle dominates our days" may be interpreted as a darkening of the life of freedom both within the United States and the nations that fell prey to its imperial authority.

In contrast to the critical perspective of such language, Crane reflects his support for an imperial impulse in his address to Walt Whitman:

O Saunterer on free ways still ahead!
Not this our empire yet, but labyrinth
Wherein your eyes, like the Great Navigator's without ship,
Gleam from the great stones of each prison crypt
Of canyoned traffic. (78)

In acknowledging that "this" is not "yet" "our empire," Crane figures the spiritual "state" he seeks in imperial terms. In contrast to the order or glory of empire, he sees the life of his nation as imprisoning and deadly. But the passage also reveals the contradictions informing Crane's language, for he looks with as much yearning to the "free ways still ahead" as he does to the unachieved empire of his country. In fact, he appears to conflate "empire" with "free ways" and to project them into the unfulfilled future of his desire. Mariani supplies an anecdote along these lines that reveals a possible connection in Crane's thinking between a larger-than-life sexual desire and a potentially imperial militarism: "Once, standing in the middle of Brooklyn Bridge, he watched the U.S. Fleet sail up the East River as if it were streaming between his legs. Such was his fantasy" (*Broken Tower* 15). Crane's fantasy expresses sexuality in terms of extravagant military power. It symbolizes his poetic potency by fusing sex, the central emblem of his epic, and the busy military force of his nation. Like the sexual power he associates with the spectacle of the navy, the aerial aggression of "Cape Hatteras" suggests that Crane represents his poetic power in terms of violent military exchanges that establish American dominion.

The perspective of "Quaker Hill" is more critical and coherent than those induced by such fantasies of violence, for it shows that the Puritans' "city on a hill" has foundered. In its degeneration, the city dangerously quakes, and now the vision of a Promised Land is displaced by a circular ideology asserting that the "business" of the nation "is business":

This was the Promised Land, and still it is
To the persuasive suburban land agent
In bootleg roadhouses where the gin fizz
Bubbles in time to Hollywood's new love-nest pageant.
Fresh from the radio in the old Meeting House
(Now the New Avalon Hotel) volcanoes roar
A welcome to highsteppers that no mouse
Who saw the Friends there ever heard before. (93)

In "Quaker Hill," it turns out that the success and wealth the Puritans thought of as the reward for hard work is not distributed on the basis of merit and effort. The "Czars / Of golf" rule the nation, and the "Persuasive suburban land agent" advises and assists them, carving up the landscape into neatly defined properties. Crane's parody of the Promised Land and his satire against the acquisitiveness of the "land agent" comport with the cultural criticism of the

Young America critics. It suggests that despite the country's youthful vigor, the United States suffered from a serious spiritual decline. The haven sought out in the Mayflower pilgrimage becomes a commercial "Promised Land" where slick real estate men cut deals in the seamy darkness of a speakeasy.

In the following passage, the poet asks after his ancestors, as if to suggest that he and his contemporaries lack the purpose, commitment, and wisdom of their forebears.

> What cunning neighbors history has in fine!
> The woodlouse mortgages the ancient deal
> Table that Powitzky buys for only nine-
> Ty-five at Adams' auction,—eats the seal,
> The spinster polish of antiquity . . .
> Who holds the lease on time and on disgrace?
> What eats the pattern with ubiquity?
> Where are my kinsmen and the patriarch race? (93)

In the question of the final line, the speaker wonders about the communal forces that shape and nurture the self. With its echo of Villon's "Où sont les neiges d'antan?" the line commemorates the importance of the forefathers and the coherence they can give to the world, but its nostalgia also indicates the speaker's sense of his society's spiritual paralysis. Like Frost's "Genealogical," *The Bridge* draws on family history as a metaphor for national history. Crane's line conveys the speaker's sense of disorientation in a world where traditional values come under question and continuity with the past is severed. The speaker's question suggests that, since he does not know where his "kinsmen" are, he is as lost as the anonymous inhabitants of Frost's "Cabin in the Clearing."

The question may also satirize the speaker's "patriarch race," however, for the honorable fathers who founded the republic were no less preoccupied by mammon and power than their latter-day counterparts "in plaid plusfours" (93). Contemptible sons, it seems, have sprung from onerous fathers. While the leaders of the American Revolution inaugurated a new era of democracy, they still left many burdened by the unjust relations of the past. Rather than working to lift that burden, they preferred to preserve their interests by denying political rights to the enslaved and unpropertied. And for their fortunate heirs, the class of men who framed and benefited most from the Constitution became a burden in a different way, for by offering an ideal of freedom that they deliberately restricted, they left a legacy of inevitable conflict. Having cynically curtailed enfranchisement, the "factions of the dead" preside in complacent resignation, but the adventurous poet must "shoulder the curse of sundered parentage" and mark out a new course under the mysterious tutelage of his homeland's first natives.

• In "The Myth of American Imperialism," a speech delivered on December 30, 1924, to the League for Industrial Democracy, Crane's patron Kahn declared that "never, in the thirty years concerning which I can speak from personal observation, have I encountered Imperialism in this country" (160). In the same speech, he refers to Haiti, Nicaragua, Honduras, and Santo Domingo (the Dominican Republic) as the "back yard" of the United States (162). He also leaves his personal involvement in the financing of the Chinese projects (described earlier in this chapter) out of his consideration of U.S. imperialism. In an intensification of the principles first outlined in the Monroe Doctrine, Kahn's rhetoric figures the whole of the Western hemisphere as the "family property" of the United States.[16] While insisting, during the course of his career, that the United States has not engaged in imperialism, Kahn uses metaphors that betray his paternalism toward countries south of the U.S. border:

> When we look out of our national window, they are within our sight. They are situated athwart one of our main trade and strategic routes. It is within our duty as neighbors, within our natural rights and our legitimate self-interest, to see to it that they cease to be centers of perpetual disturbance, that the rudiments of decent, orderly and civilizing government be observed by, and for the benefit of, their people, that these fertile regions become adequately useful to the world and to their own inhabitants. (162)

Because of their proximity to the Panama Canal, Caribbean nations fall within the scope of the United States' "national interest." After advancing this view, Kahn seeks to identify issues common to "Radicals, Liberals and Conservatives," denying Lenin's claim that imperialism impinges on the lives of the dominating nation's working people: "I would frankly question . . . whether alleged Imperialism and such-like highly contentious matters do cut an appreciable and immediate figure in the life of the average worker and his family, for good or ill" (177). In another address, Kahn identifies art as a common ground for different factions in a democracy. Crane's vocabulary of transcendence and synthesis in relation to *The Bridge* suggests that Kahn might have read Crane's poem—or wished to have read it—as proof of his doctrine that art offers a common ground. If he did, he would have been forced to ignore the genuinely critical elements in *The Bridge,* the poem's ritual, or performative, rebellions against a variety of national dominions.

Despite Crane's avowed aesthetic aims, *The Bridge* reflects the social, political, and economic connections between the domestic and foreign policies of his country. Almost despite himself, "Crane manages . . . to remain critically outside his own myth of America" (Santos 88). As Thomas S. W. Lewis writes, the poet "was taken with the fact that the Brooklyn Bridge has corrupt wires woven into its cables, and yet it triumphs" ("O Thou" 26). Unlike the bridge designed and begun by Washington Roebling and finished by his son, Crane's poem does not overcome the fierce polarity of the contradictions it seeks to reconcile. Instead, at its moment of greatest clarity about the world and its language, Crane's work substantiates his claim in "A Name for All" that "we must maim / Because we are usurpers."

Chapter 5

FRAGMENTATION AND DIASPORA IN THE

WORK OF LANGSTON HUGHES

• Like other writers of his generation, Langston Hughes addresses American history in his poems, but his response to that history differs from, as well as corresponds to, that of the poets I have considered so far. These writers display an occasional awareness of the part played by African Americans in the development of American culture. In "Virginia Britannia" and "Enough," for example, Moore expresses the ironic disparity between the dream of democratic freedom and the reality of African slavery (which enriched many colonial forefathers), a disparity that clearly reflects the contradictions between republican and imperial democracy in the United States. Williams shows his enthusiasm for the culture of black Americans in a number of poems and in the "Advent of the Slaves" chapter of *American Grain*. Crane figures the dispossession of African Americans in "Black Tambourine" and *The Bridge*. Although these representations vary widely, they share a common interest in the role of blacks within the imagined community of their nation, an interest that helps define their conception of this community.

The focus here, however, is on a black perspective on this role, rather than on a white fascination with it. Most of this chapter is devoted to the writing of Langston Hughes, but it also analyzes Countee Cullen's portrayal of the Middle Passage in "Heritage." Because the heritage of slavery shapes these writers' sense of their nation in a way that is unique (although perhaps not universal) to African Americans, I argue that a conflict between "Africa" and "America" informs Hughes's thinking and writing about national matters. Africa and America rival each other throughout Hughes's work, both as historical places and as symbolic geographies, and it is from his dual vantage as a U.S. citizen and a member of the African diaspora that Hughes criticizes the failures of American democracy and challenges his country to live up to its founding dream of freedom. By the same token, his work registers the poet's sense of a double burden—a burden of, on the one hand, speaking for African Americans in a broadly representative way that often drove him toward abstraction[1] and, on the other, the need to respect the differences between various communities of African descent in the act of representing them. Like

Crane who also hoped to resolve social conflict through his poetic synthesis, Hughes memorably registers conflict more often than he resolves it through his discourse of utopian dreams, although, I argue, such discourse provides an effective cultural counterpoint to the political and social divisions among both African Americans and members of the African diaspora. Hughes's evocations of pan-African unity function as an ideal in a way that is analogous to Crane's utopia in "Atlantis," but Hughes's evocations seem to have had more measurable impact, at least in terms of the inspiration they provided for his African American readership and for the diasporic poets of the Negritude movement. Hughes's poetics of utopian hope had pragmatic effects in that they helped to unify both African American and pan-African cultural communities.[2]

For Hughes, the concept of America is multifaceted. America serves as one ground of his being, as a place from which he can argue that his people, the community of fellow African Americans, have been mistreated in ways that violate the social contract laid out in the nation's founding documents. In this respect, America's political self-definitions provide Hughes with the basis for challenging the status quo and demanding change from administrations that support it. As James Presley puts it, "for Hughes the American Dream . . . is the *raison d'être* of this nation" (380). When writing from this perspective, Hughes draws on the ideas behind the Declaration of Independence, the American Revolution, and the Bill of Rights in order to criticize racial injustice in both domestic and international arenas. Lloyd Brown makes this argument:

> the majority culture's dream of a progressive society based on individual fulfillment and social harmony . . . has created its own inevitable legacy—that is, the Black American Dream of realizing those dreams and ideals that have been written down for white folks . . . . In short, the majority culture's mythos of revolution has been ironically transformed into the Black American's legacy of revolutionary possibilities. (17)

Brown develops this argument in the context of his discussion of "Harlem" and other "Dream-poems" by Hughes, but it applies to other poems also, poems such as "Justice" (1923), "I, Too" (1925), "America" (1925), "Let America Be America Again" (1936), "August 19th" (1938), "America's Young Black Joe" (1940), "Freedom's Plow" (1943), "Words like Freedom" (1943), "Dear Mr. President" (1943), "Beaumont to Detroit: 1943" (1943), "Freedom [I]" (1943), and "American Heartbreak" (1951).

In a similar vein, Donald Gibson writes that "Hughes's commitment to the American ideal was deep . . . and abiding. He held on to it despite his acute awareness of the inequities of democracy" (*Poets* 45). As Anthony Dawahare argues, in "Let America Be America Again," "Hughes participates in the myth-making processes of a rather popular version of American nationalism: the true 'America' of the future will embody Jeffersonian political ideals: it will be a nation of, by, and for 'the people,' based on the notion of inalienable rights, and free from tyranny." In this poem, "'America' signifies the constitution of a free and democratic society" (34).

From the competing perspective that Hughes also sometimes adopts, however, the United States is a nation to be deeply criticized if not rejected altogether. While Hughes remains inspired by a republican ideal of democracy for all, he turns to a criticism of American imperialism in many of his poems. He expresses his ambivalent attitudes toward his country, for example, through the repeated motifs of historical memory, slavery and its aftermath, colonial and neocolonial economic relations, and his diasporic "pan-Africanism."

Throughout its development, Hughes's work reflects an ongoing conflict between Africa-centered and African American ideals. As Adam Lively points out, this conflict reflects the immediate context of the period in which Hughes began to write. "The 1920s," he observes, "saw the birth of the idea of blacks as the inside outsiders of modern life" (7). In line with this idea, Hughes's reflections on his country and its history are double-tongued, exemplifying the double consciousness W. E. B. Du Bois regarded as constitutive of African American experience. As Raymond Smith argues, Hughes "could affirm with equal assurance his two credos of identity: 'I am a Negro' and 'I, Too, Sing America.' But while affirming these polar commitments, Hughes was alienated from both of them. As a black man, he was aware that his race had never been granted full participation in the American dream" (270). The political inflections of Hughes's poetic personae, the communal "I" and "we" he articulates in various ways, reveal the injustice of American history. In Onwuchekwa Jemie's words, "Hughes's insistence on a distinct black art . . . [acknowledges] the fact that Afro-Americans are a distinct people within the American nation" (12). Moreover, Hughes's configurations of "I" and "we" sometimes refer to a diasporic black community, rather than to the imagined community of the United States, a fact that indicates the complex nature of his national consciousness. From Hughes's perspective as an African American, the United States is a deeply divided nation. In the performances of his poems, Hughes often criticizes the hypocrisy and failure of American democracy, articulating what Edmund Morgan called "the central paradox of American history": the discrepancy between the founding fathers' political ideals and their practice of slaveholding (4). In his poems, the American Dream of equality and freedom wavers between being a fantastic hallucination and a meaningful political ideal worth pursuing.

In *The Harlem Renaissance in Black and White*, George Hutchinson argues that American blacks as well as whites were inspired by the concept of cultural nationalism in the first three decades of the twentieth century (9–15). For him, "the Harlem Renaissance" was as "caught up in a struggle for the meaning and possession of America" as white cultural nationalists were (15). Indeed, Hutchinson argues that "the entire development" of American cultural nationalism "must be situated within an understanding of the international dominance of the concept of nationality" (9). The dominance accounts for Hughes's frequent figurations of the nation in his poems, but it also accounts for the conflicts of allegiance (to the African diaspora on the one hand and to the American nation on the other) that lie at the heart of his work.

Hughes expresses this tension throughout his writing, but as James Smethurst points out, he increasingly came to do so through oral performances of his poems. In the early 1930s, Smethurst writes,

> Hughes began his extensive tours of poetry readings in the South, appearing for the most part at African-American churches and educational institutions. As Arnold Rampersad notes, this audience preferred a poetry that was uplifting, sentimental, and formally conservative. However, using, to paraphrase Hans Robert Jauss, the horizon of this audience's expectations, Hughes drew on a variety of "high" and "popular" African-American discourses to create a poetry that strained at the boundaries of those conservative uplifting and sentimental discourses. (95)

Like Moore and Frost, in other words, Hughes defined himself as a national poet partly through his public readings. He delivered these readings at black colleges, churches, and clubs throughout the country.[3] In the second volume of his autobiography, *I Wonder as I Wander,* Hughes explains that he habitually ended his readings with his Whitmanesque poem "I, Too" (59–60), a practice that testifies to the importance of the national in his writing. Because of his racial identity, however, Hughes's effort to express his criticism of American history and culture to his audiences was more pronounced than either Moore's or Frost's. For his readings, Hughes selected many poems that were "documentary, journalistic and topical" (*I Wonder* 58). The poems he read gave a black perspective on events and issues of national significance, including miscegenation (as in "Cross," a poem he regularly read) and the wrongful imprisonment and trial of the Scottsboro boys. In Elizabeth Davey's view, "Hughes thought that a mass black audience for literature would be built through public readings, rather than private consumption of books" (224). Hughes's courting of this audience through public recitations and the sale of an inexpensive pamphlet entitled *The Negro Mother* indicates the centrality of performance to his poetics (Davey 224, 227–28).

Beyond the contexts delineated by Hutchinson and Smethurst, however, Paul Gilroy's emphasis in *The Black Atlantic* on the concept of double consciousness provides a more particular point of departure for my analysis of Hughes's poetry. Through his concept of a continuum of black culture on both sides of the Atlantic, Gilroy extends the idea of double consciousness to all of the African diaspora, arguing that modern blacks simultaneously live both inside and outside the West. For Gilroy, the promise of such duality lies in its dialectical potential, for along with the alienation caused by slavery, this participation in two worlds gives rise to a valuable new perspective:

What was initially felt to be a curse—the curse of homelessness or the curse of forced exile—gets repossessed. It becomes affirmed and is reconstructed as the basis of a privileged standpoint from which certain useful and critical perceptions about the modern world become more likely. It should be obvious that this unusual perspective has been forged out of the experiences of racial subordination. I want to suggest that it also represents a response to the successive displacements, migrations, and journeys (forced and otherwise) which have come to constitute the black cultures' special conditions of existence. (111)

Gilroy's theorization of black modernity offers a model of double consciousness that points at once in the different directions of Africa and America. In addition, while he persuasively argues on behalf of the African diaspora as a paradigm for black cultural analysis, Gilroy also acknowledges the fictionality of such a model, recognizing the conflicts within its widely dispersed communities. This model is useful for understanding Hughes, whose poetry both evokes the African diaspora as a cultural ideal and registers the discrepancies between that ideal and the reality of pan-African disunity. In fact, Hughes defines the category of the national through recourse to the ideas of Africa and a black diaspora, and his representations of them inform, even constitute, his conceptions of the United States and his place within it. Africa is a necessary term in Hughes's configurations of the nation, and conversely, the category of the nation mediates his portrayals of Africa. In what follows, I examine Hughes's figurations of Africa, the African diaspora, and America in order to show how important Africa remains to his understanding of African American experience and to tease out the conflicts that shape Hughes's allegiances and his efforts to represent related but distinct populations.

• In "Afro-American Fragment," Hughes portrays the predicament of the modern African American, and in doing so, he evokes portentous ambiguities made out of simple language that may be interpreted as a uniquely black embodiment of American modernism. The poem enunciates contradictory views of race and memory at the same time that it mourns an inconsolable loss:

> So long,
> So far away
> Is Africa.
> Not even memories alive
> Save those that history books create,
> Save those that songs
> Beat back into the blood—
> Beat out of blood with words sad-sung
> In strange un-Negro tongue—
> So long,
> So far away
> Is Africa.

Subdued and time-lost
Are the drums—and yet
Through some vast mist of race
There comes this song
I do not understand
This song of atavistic land,
Of bitter yearnings lost
Without a place—
So long,
So far away
Is Africa's
Dark face. (*Collected Poems* 129)[4]

The poem's several dashes mark the lacunae in the experience and heritage of the speaker. They also bridge the blank gaps that trouble him and provide the impetus for the meditation that drives the poem. They represent the terrible, taunting unknown, the fierce x that bars his transatlantic past and its culture from himself. They are the unspoken, unspeakable lapses between the speaker's present and his history.

Just as Crane refigured his poetic and national heritage as a hybrid of culture and biological descent in "The Dance," Hughes initially tropes his sense of African American identity as a phenomenon of the blood. Yet the poem differs in terms of the "yearning" and grievous loss that intervenes between the African American speaker and a primordial African past. As Gilroy comments, "The need to locate cultural or ethnic roots and then to use the idea of being in touch with them as a means to refigure the cartography of dispersal and exile is perhaps best understood as a simple and direct response to the varieties of racism which have denied the historical character of black experience and the integrity of black cultures" (112). Hughes demonstrates his awareness that "Afro-American Fragment" is a lament for a heritage, identity, and community that are as arbitrated by time and distance as they are by politics and commerce.

The poet also acknowledges the socially mediated nature of identity and genealogy. The syntax of the poem reflects the disjunctions the speaker feels between himself, his cultural origins, and his heritage. The pace of the first sentence for instance, broken as it is into three cropped lines, beats like the exhalation of a sigh. The parallel phrasing of the first two lines reinforces the elegiac tone that the repetition of the refrain itself conveys. The first sentence, with its full stop, belongs grammatically to the several lines that follow, for the first sentence enunciates the cause of the events that follow, while the remaining lines form a strict clause of result. An elliptical syntax characterizes this section (as much as the rest of the poem), for a subordinate clause such as "That there are"—which would render the connection between the actual clauses explicit—has been elided and the link between the two units of thought ("so long" and "so far away" on the one hand, and "Not even memories alive" on the other) is broken by the period. The oral quality of the poem, with its short lines and repeated phrases, emphasizes the violent transformation of African cultures, history, and peoples by the Middle Passage and slavery.

The anguish of the speaker lies in a realistic appraisal of his historical predicament. Slavery often deprived its victims of a living connection to their historical past, violating the religious sensibility of the many African cultures in which the spirits of the ancestors play so important a role. Hughes expresses the devastating effect of this loss by including the simple word "even": "Not even memories alive / Save those that history books create, / Save those that songs beat back into the blood." In these lines, the speaker expresses the fragility of memory and culture. He points out the constructedness of history, for the "history books create" memories. In other words, the books do not transparently report memories as fixed phenomena; instead, they bring them into being. The speaker experiences the history that is given back to him from books as alien, however, for it has become an abstraction, not a knowledge experienced in the body with the rhythms of the breath and blood.

At least not at first. The repetition of the phrase "Save those that" turns the speaker's despair against itself and wrests it into a new and hopeful rhythm. As Smethurst writes,

> The halting short lines sandwiching longer, heavily alliterated lines and the irregularly rhyming lines of the first stanza formally mirror the notion of a link between Africans and African-Americans that has been disrupted or transformed to the point that it can no longer be clearly defined and yet remains as an African deep structure in African-American expressive culture. (98)

The mood changes from despondency in the face of an alienated history to hope and mournful exultation at the thought of the communal music the speaker experiences viscerally. In this respect, as Smethurst suggests with his linguistic metaphor of an "African deep structure," Hughes seems to be making something constructive out of a "diminished thing."

The role of orality in both African and African American cultures remains intact here at the same time that its medium is literally negated. The sung and spoken words of the African American come back to him in an alienated form, as a compromised and "strange un-Negro tongue." If the experience of the song seemed physically immediate, the very tongue in the speaker's mouth belies such immediacy, for it does not belong to him. While Hughes's designation of the tongue as "un-Negro" is perhaps a way of aligning his African American speaker with the African ethos and identity he desires, it is nevertheless a curious expression. Instead of characterizing the tongue as un- or non-African, Hughes calls it "un-Negro," thereby suggesting an uneasiness on his part with the very language through which he comes to know himself and in which he must communicate. Here, moreover, "Negro" evidently distinguishes "African American" from "African."

Hughes's "un-Negro tongue" points to the linguistic effects of slavery. It is the poet's painful acknowledgment that the very substance of his art is the bequest of his ancestors' enslavers. In this regard, the "songs" and the atavistic "memories" of Africa were alike beaten out of the blood of slaves by usurping masters who wrenched even the words in their mouths from them and made them foreign to their children. "Songs, like history books," David Jarraway writes,

> endeavor "with words" to replicate the elusive black experience of Africa, "so long, / So far away." But though words seem capable of internalizing some of the reality that is "Africa"—the experience beaten "back into the blood"—part of Africa escapes. The phrase "beaten out of the blood" suggests not only that these songs come out of black suffering but also that something is always lost, "beaten out of [the] blood" of those who hear them. The closing of the poem reinforces this notion. (821)

Hughes's "strange un-Negro tongue" bears witness to one of the chief cultural losses suffered by the descendants of black slaves: access to the particular forms of thought and expression that, as modern linguistics suggests, any particular language entails. With the forced surrender of their language, slaves and their descendants suffered the loss of these cultural forms, although, of course, this loss was by no means complete.

The poem's refrain repeats the geographical and temporal facts that separate the speaker from Africa. The title does the same, for it points to the felt lack, the incompletion of the self engendered from the African and American "halves" of his being. "Fragment" testifies to the mutilation of African American history, for it emphasizes the fact that the poet's desire to recapture an authentic origin, or the foreclosed legacy of his unknown ancestors, is not possible because it has been decimated by intervening history, rendered fundamentally foreign by the erasures of such subjugating violence. The title figures the poem as a diminished part of the fuller text of an irretrievable African past. Not only is the speaker rendered incomplete by his sociohistorical position, but his very testimony to that fact is incomplete. According to this point of view, even the lament registered by the speaker is oppressively curtailed. The "vast mist of race" that impedes the speaker's ability to comprehend his heritage emerges as the social effect of an obscuring fragmentation wrought by slavery.

For Hughes, then, the African past can only be glimpsed "Through some vast mist of race." Despite the speaker's desire for a sense of connection, he understands that there is no simple way to recover the history lost to him. The language of the final stanza evinces a displacement, for, as the speaker asserts,

> There comes this song
> I do not understand
> This song of atavistic land,
> Of bitter yearnings lost
> Without a place—

This passage enacts what Bhabha calls an "unhomely moment," for it reveals the placelessness of a host of things, including "this song / I do not understand" (which can in one sense be read as a metonym for the poem itself), the "atavistic land" that "this song" is about, the "bitter yearnings" embodied by the land of Africa, and the speaker's self as it is constituted in the lament and longing of the poem. "Afro-American Fragment" gives a name to the intolerable condition of existing "Without a place," a name that is not only hybrid but fragmented. The drums that the speaker would hear and respond to through what he imagines to be the mist of race are "Subdued and time-lost." This last adjective, compounded as it is, profoundly testifies to the worried homelessness of the poem, for it weds time to space by figuring time in spatial terms. Yet those terms are ungrounded rather than concrete, for from the African American speaker's point of view, Africa is lost in an invisible abyss of time. As in Cullen's "Heritage," the tragic pathos of the poem lies in the fact that "Africa's / Dark face" remains indecipherable, "lost / Without a place." The yearning for origin and wholeness communicated by the speaker remains frustrated, even as it testifies to the value of that origin and wholeness.

In Hughes's poem, the African American experiences his Americanness as a split within the self—precisely the phenomenon Du Bois dubbed double consciousness. In the chapter entitled "Of Our Spiritual Strivings" in *The Souls of Black Folk,* Du Bois distinguishes the position of the African and the African American from that of other races on the stage of world history:

> After the Egyptian and Indian, the Greek and Roman, the Teuton and Mongolian, the Negro is a sort of seventh son, born with a veil, and gifted with second-sight in this American world, —a world which yields him no true self-consciousness, but only lets him see himself through the revelation of the other world. It is a peculiar sensation, this double-consciousness, this sense of always looking at one's self through the eyes of others, of measuring one's soul by the tape of a world that looks on in amused contempt and pity. One ever feels his twoness, —an American, a Negro; two souls, two thoughts, two unreconciled strivings; two warring ideals in one dark body, whose dogged strength alone keeps it from being torn asunder.
>
> The history of the American Negro is the history of this strife—this longing to attain self-conscious manhood, to merge his double self into a better and truer self. In this merging he wishes neither of the older selves to be lost. He would not Africanize America, for America has too much to teach the world and Africa. He would not bleach his Negro soul in a flood of white Americanism, for he knows that Negro blood has a message for the world. He simply wishes to make it possible for a man to be both a Negro and an American. (5)

Bhabha's concept of the rift between the two modes of national self-representation—the pedagogical and the performative—corresponds to the internal division Du Bois ascribes to the African American. "In the production of the nation as narration," Bhabha writes, "there is a split between the continuist, accumulative temporality of the pedagogical, and the repetitious, recursive strategy of the performative. It is through this process of splitting that the conceptual ambivalence of modern society becomes the site of *writing the nation*" (*Location* 145–46). Du Bois's double consciousness is one of the effects of the conflict between the performative and the pedagogical, and since the antagonism between these two forces gives rise to ideological narratives of nationhood, it makes sense to trace Du Bois's double consciousness back to its origins in this conflict. From this perspective, the African American population belongs to the two different but overlapping communities of nation and diaspora. The concepts of nation and diaspora reflect the social and historical qualities of black life in America.[5]

As a member of the diaspora, the speaker of "Afro-American Fragment" experiences his heritage as nearly mediated out of existence. The Middle Passage and slavery have alienated him from the land and culture of his origins. The legacy of the past, the vital connection to the spirits of the ancestors that so many African cultures revere, has been skewed by slavery. In this respect, the poem reflects the speaker's alienation from Africa. While this alienation must be read in conjunction with Hughes's willed celebrations of Africa in other lyrics, it also registers a painful truth about Hughes's personal encounter with Africa, one that had ramifications for his sense both of nation and diaspora.

Hughes traveled to Africa as a young seaman in 1923 and gained some sense of its colonial domination and of his status as an outsider there. His story of his encounter with mainland Africans reflects his awareness of Marcus Garvey and his effort to "unify the black world, and free and exalt Africa" (*Big Sea* 102). He experienced his first direct interaction with Africa, in other words, within the context of a pan-African consciousness. Hughes demonstrates the far from idyllic character of that interaction by dramatizing the discrepancy between Garvey's political vision, on the one hand, and the actual disunity among people of African descent, on the other:

> "Our problems in America are very much like yours," I told the Africans, "especially in the South. I am a Negro, too."
>
> But they only laughed at me and shook their heads and said: "You, white man! You, white man!"
>
> It was the only place in the world where I've ever been called a white man. They looked at my copper-brown skin and straight black hair—like my grandmother's Indian hair, except a little curly—and they said: "You—white man." (*Big Sea* 102–3)

The insistent appellation of the Africans ("You, white man!") is a peculiar form of hailing, or interpellation, for it both identifies and misidentifies its addressee in order to classify and exclude him from the recognizably African community. Hughes's seriocomic treatment of this misnaming calls attention both to its inaccuracy and its socially divisive power, for while he points out the inaccuracy of their claim by putting it in a global context (nowhere but in Africa is Hughes considered white), he also acknowledges the social reality of its alienating power. Hughes goes on to point out that one of the Africans, a Kru from Liberia "who had seen many American Negroes, of various shades and colors, and knew much of America," explained their response to him:

> "Here . . . on the West Coast, there are not many colored people—people of mixed blood—and those foreign colored men who are here come mostly as missionaries, to teach us something, since they think we know nothing. Or they come from the West Indies, as clerks and administrators in the colonial governments, to help carry out the white man's laws. So the Africans call them all *white* men."
>
> "But I am not white," I said.
>
> "You are not black either," the Kru man said simply. "There is a man of my color." And he pointed to George, the pantryman, who protested loudly.
>
> "Don't point at me," George said. "I'm from Lexington, Kentucky, U.S.A. And no African blood, nowhere."
>
> "You black," said the Kru man. (*Big Sea* 103)

As Rampersad hints, this and other stories of Hughes's experiences in Africa reflect the poet's concomitant desire for and alienation from his historic motherland as well as his difference from a fellow black American who disclaims his African descent. "That he would want to be considered black," Rampersad writes, "struck the Africans as perverse, perhaps even subtle mockery" (1: 78).

Hughes's account of these interactions plainly shows the lack of unity between Africans and colored peoples of African descent, but his poems often work against this lack by asserting the reality of a unified diaspora. This assertion reflects Hughes's attempt to project an imagined community that is at once American and not American. Such metaphorical dual citizenship (in both Africa and the United States) corresponds to Gilroy's redefinition of Du Bois's double consciousness as a uniquely black perspective on the nature of modernity (111). Although "Hughes did not go to Africa to find a new place to live," writes John Cullen Gruesser, he did travel there "to experience firsthand a land with special significance for people of the diaspora like himself" (79–80).

As Rampersad observes, the Africans' rejection of Hughes as a fellow black "only stirred [him] to assert the unity of blacks everywhere, as in his little poem 'Brothers,' : 'We are related—you and I. / You from the West Indies, / I from Kentucky.'" Rampersad characterizes the contradictions between Hughes's desire for Africa and his exclusion from it as "anxiety." I am arguing that this anxiety has both a psychological and a sociological dimension to it, and Hughes not only suffers from this anxiety but also sublimates and transfigures it in many of his poems. In "Brothers," for example, Hughes does this by imitating the voice of his fellow crewman George but altering his perspective to approximate the unifying one he himself expresses in the passage from the autobiography. According to Rampersad, moreover, Hughes's "anxiety over Africa also inspired" "My People," which was first entitled "Poem" (1: 78):

The night is beautiful
So the faces of my people.

The stars are beautiful,
So the eyes of my people.

Beautiful, also, is the sun.
Beautiful, also, are the souls of my people. (36)

Rampersad's characterization of Hughes's feelings about Africa as anxiety points to the political and cultural disunity of the African diaspora at the time such poems were composed. Hughes's relationship to the "we" articulated by this poem is vexed and contradictory, for it includes both yearning and alienation.[6] The repeated invocation of "my people" in the poem has two contrasting aspects. On one hand, the repetition attests to Rampersad's "anxiety," for the poem's insistence on the speaker's membership in the "family of Africa"—understated and gracious though it is—points to a lingering fear that the people of Africa are not really "his" at all. The poet's desire for Africa reflects his corresponding alienation from the United States, which fails to function for him as a definitive homeland. As Kenneth Warren puts it, "To be cognizant of oneself as a diasporan subject is always to be aware of oneself no matter where one is, as from elsewhere, in the process of making a not quite legitimate appeal to be considered as if one were from there" (400–401).

On the other hand, Hughes's articulation of "my people" and a sometimes national, sometimes international "we" in a range of poems (including not only "My People" but also "Our Land," "Afraid," "Poem to a Dead Soldier," "Fog," "Prelude to Our Age," "Children's Rhymes," and "A Ballad of Negro History") call into being an idealized community, performing it into existence by constituting the poet's audience as a common body. As a speech act, the poem imagines the African diaspora as a viable community, celebrating it as a realistic as well as desirable goal. The poem presents an alternatively imagined, cosmopolitan "nation" or political alliance that offers a sense of belonging, heritage, and pride to people of African descent throughout the world. In contrast, in "Afro-American Fragment," Hughes variously evokes communities of black Americans through the plural pronouns "we" and "us" and through his remarks to a generalized "you" in such poems as "Black Dancers," "How Thin a Blanket," "Vagabonds," and possibly "Youth," "Walkers with the Dawn," and "Being Old."

• Hughes's concerns with the African dimension of his national and personal identity were shared by many of his contemporaries, and some of these concerns are registered in the work of other Harlem Renaissance poets such as Claude McKay ("Outcast"), Gwendolyn Bennett ("Heritage"), and Countee Cullen. In his poem "Heritage," Cullen offers a meditation on his African ancestry and his problematic relationship to Africa in terms that correspond to Hughes's "Afro-American Fragment":

What is Africa to me:
Copper sun or scarlet sea,
Jungle star or jungle track,
Strong bronzed men, or regal black
Women from whose loins I sprang
When the birds of Eden sang?
One three centuries removed
From the scenes his fathers loved,
Spicy grove, cinnamon tree,
What is Africa to me? (36)

Cullen evokes Africa via the conventions of modernist primitivism, adopting the mythical approach of modernism in his association of Africa with primordial Eden. "Africa," Michael Lomax writes, "was a frequent symbol in New Negro poetry for a pristine black identity which had not been confused by the values, 'progress' and materialism of Western society. Ironically, this pastoral image bore little actual relation to contemporary colonial Africa or even to Africa three centuries before" (241). Although his mythic primitivism may appear decorous and genteel, it nonetheless mediates the speaker's meditation upon the land of his ancestors. Despite "Cullen's historical naivete," Lomax continues, "the essential personal problem still emerges, the conflict between a conscious and intellectualized Western self and a self which intuitively senses a bond with a lost past as well as elements of a degraded present" (242). To Nicholas Canaday, Cullen's handling of the myth of Africa is more deliberate and self-conscious than it seems for Lomax. "To Cullen Africa is a symbol," Canaday writes. "One must not expect the real Africa to be depicted here; Cullen knew no more about the real Africa than did Keats about Provencal. Cullen has translated a myth into poetry in order to embody concretely, not to deny, the power of that myth" (121). Cullen emphasizes the mythic character of the Africa he is describing in order to underscore the psychic distance his speaker feels from his heritage as a black man in America. In fact, Cullen's whole approach to his subject is encapsulated in the question of his refrain, "What is Africa to me?" With each repetition of this questioning lament, it becomes progressively more clear that the Africa of Cullen's "Heritage" and Hughes's "Fragment" are equally distant from their respective speakers. But in the intensely sensual imagery of "Heritage," Africa is further mediated through the tableaux of modernist primitivism. It is as if the speaker knows Africa only at second hand, through the artistic depictions of the avant-garde.

In this respect, Cullen's title takes on a subtle overtone, for the poem suggests that Cullen's heritage as an African American is every bit as mediated and double-edged as Hughes's. One envisions his portraits of the fauna of Africa to be rendered after the fashion of a wooden panel carved by Gauguin:

So I lie, who all day long
Want no sound except the song
Sung by wild barbaric birds
Goading massive jungle herds,
Juggernauts of flesh that pass
Trampling tall defiant grass. (Cullen 36)

If the poem seems to share the mesmerizing rhymes and rhythms of the poetry of Poe and the appetite for the barbaric of Whitman, Stevens, and Williams, its relationship to the Old World is far different from that of such poets. Whereas, in "The Gift Outright," Frost writes that the European emigrants to America were too focused on their homeland in the Old World, the speakers in the poems by Hughes and Cullen are alienated not only from the United States, but from their ancestral origins in Africa. However, as Gilroy suggests in his rereading of Du Bois's double consciousness, African Americans (like other members of the African diaspora) learned to use the unique insights of their double alienation against the degradations it entailed. Cullen figures this process in theatrical, painterly, and religious terms, whereas Hughes sublimates it, through his idealizations of Africa and his poetic invitations to black unity and consciousness.

As in "Afro-American Fragment," the consciousness of historic loss courses throughout "Heritage." Cullen expresses this loss by echoing Villon's "Où sont les neiges d'antan?" and then repeating his refrain:

What is last year's snow to me,
Last year's anything? The tree
Budding yearly must forget
How its past arose or set—
Bough and blossom, flower, fruit,
Even what shy bird with mute
Wonder at her travail there,
Meekly labored in its hair.
One three centuries removed
From the scenes his fathers loved,
Spicy grove, cinnamon tree,
What is Africa to me? (38)

If Cullen's question asserts Africa's distance from the speaker, his repetitions of the question indicate its lingering hold over the speaker's imagination. Despite the loss of an organic link to Africa (as symbolized in Cullen's image of the tree), the speaker still yearns for connection. The loss of the heritage symbolized by Africa is a wound the speaker survives but from which he constantly suffers: "The tree / Budding yearly must forget / How its past arose or set." Just as compulsive and involuntary, however, is the speaker's need to tell himself he must forget his African background. Despite his best efforts, he cannot accept the loss he mourns. The compulsive repetitions in the poem point to the psychic centrality of Africa and the loss it represents for the narrator of "Heritage."

Like Hughes's speaker, Cullen's knows Africa only at second hand, through the agency of print:

> Africa? A book one thumbs
> Listlessly, till slumber comes. (37)

Cullen's speaker thinks of Africa in terms of a dull book, one that interests its reader enough to make him try to read it but that baffles and torments him. As Houston Baker points out, however, "The vivid descriptions of its fierce flowers and pagan impulses show that Africa is much more than bedtime reading for the narrator" (68). Just as Hughes does in "Fragment," Cullen figures the history intervening between himself and a primordial Africa in terms of physical and mental space when he describes his speaker as "One three centuries removed." By transposing the temporal into the spatial, Cullen expresses the alienations of African American history through the trope of distance. The ships that removed slaves from Africa to America separated the descendants of slaves from their ancestral homeland both spatially and temporally. These twin distances inform the poem and account for its speaker's recourse to the playing of "a double part" and to the practice of a furtive worship that links him to pagan Africans:

> Lord, I fashion dark gods, too,
> Daring even to give You
> Dark despairing features where,
> Crowned with dark rebellious hair,
> Patience wavers just so much as
> Mortal grief compels, while touches
> Quick and hot, of anger, rise
> To smitten cheek and weary eyes.
> Lord, forgive me if my need
> Sometimes shapes a human creed. (Cullen 40)

Cullen's speaker looks at the "heathen gods" of Africa and sees them as "Quaint" and "outlandish," but in the same stanza he quietly laments that "My conversion came high-priced" (39). This and subsequent stanzas dramatize the speaker's alienation from both Africa and America, for although he confesses Christian belief, he characterizes that confession as a form of lip service when he says that "although I speak / With my mouth thus, in my heart / Do I play a double part" (39). This duplicity reveals the confession to be a self-dividing one, which is at once anguished and cunning in its double-tongued effort to survive the dispossessions of African American "heritage" and lay claim to its potential strengths.

The speaker's self-division persists in the final lines of the poem in the reference to "my heart or head." If this dichotomy is thoroughly conventional, the inability of either heart or head to comprehend the full meaning of its "civilized" state is not. Rather than being locked in contradiction with one another, the speaker's head and heart are united in their alienation from the "civilizing process" of slavery and its aftermath. Throughout the poem, Cullen plays with the trope of the primitive, flirting with an aesthetic of the neopagan that may seem rarefied in comparison with that of, say, Ezra Pound. He does so, however, not merely for the sake of an aesthetic pose and its attendant pleasures, for the poem's closing quandary calls into question the very category of the civilized by confusing it with the primitive, against which it defines itself and establishes its coherence. As Canaday writes, "The last stanza recapitulates but does not resolve the central tension of 'Heritage'" (124).

While Cullen's evocations of Africa and the anguish of its loss may sometimes seem as committed to the fiction of primitivism as they are doubtful about it, Hughes's autobiographical accounts of his reception in Africa and of his fellow seamen's economic deception of native Africans show that his poems praising Africa as the symbol of black unity were deliberate fictions (*Big Sea* 108–9). His response may be read as a psychological compensation for the alienation from Africans he must have felt but carefully avoids recording in his autobiography. At the same time, the poems that praise Africa or imagine links between America and Africa may be interpreted in political terms as the expression of a utopian hope for genuine diasporic unity (an interpretation supported by the fact that Negritude poets found inspiration for their movement in Hughes's poetry).

A crucial chapter from *The Big Sea* provides an important context for interpreting a series of poems that feature references to drumming as both psychic compensation and cultural symbol. In the chapter called "Burutu Moon," Hughes tells the story of an evening he spent on shore with "Tom Pey, one of the Kru men from [his] boat." The chapter opens with a lush, moonlit scene that represents Burutu as desirable, almost paradisal: "Sometimes life is a ripe fruit too delicious for the taste of man: the full moon hung low over Burutu and it was night on the Nigerian delta." Hughes links the inhabitants of the town with the beauty and remoteness of his emblematic moon: "Dark figures with naked shoulders, a single cloth about their bodies, and bare feet, passed us often, their footsteps making no sounds on the grassy road, their voices soft like the moon." He rounds out a paragraph full of such spare sentences with a renewal of his lunar imagery: "In the clearing, great mango trees cast purple shadows across the path. There was no wind. Only the moon" (117–18).

Pey breaks the spell of the moon when he informs Hughes that the villagers will shortly "make Ju-Ju." When Hughes's responds with enthusiastic interest, Pey politely replies that "'Christian man no bother with Ju-Ju. . . . Omali dance no good for Christian man.'" When Hughes presses his case, Pey flatly refuses: "White man never go see Ju-Ju. Him hurt you! Him too awful! White man never go!" (*Big Sea* 118). Hughes offsets his account of this second exclusion by the Africans with a story of the hospitality shown him by Nagary, an African Muslim trader. Nagary offers his only chair to Hughes and shows him an array of African riches, including "beaten brass," "statuettes that skilled hands had made," woven "fiber-cloth," skins, and ivory. Hughes explains that "Nagary did not ask me to buy any of these things. He seemed satisfied with my surprise and wonder. He told me of his trips up the river to Wari and down to Lagos. He gave me a great spray of feathers. When I left, he said, with outstretched hands: 'God be with you'" (118–19). The bittersweet mixture of reception and rebuff in this account provides an odd but striking analogue to Du Bois's notion of double consciousness. It functions as a kind of mirror image of that concept, for just as black Americans experience a divided self in the face of white prejudice, Hughes's mixed treatment at the hands of his African hosts suggests that African prejudice against his light skin induced a feeling of betrayal. The people of his beloved motherland repudiated him as its authentic descendant. In his narrative, Hughes artfully balances Nagary's hospitality against Pey's hostility, but he also lets the prejudice of Pey's opposition speak for itself.

Hughes complicates the meaning and emotional impact of the chapter in his autobiography by following up his account of the visit with Nagary with a portrait of some African prostitutes pointed out to him by Pey. Hughes describes a scene involving one of their customers: "In front of one hut three white sailors from a British ship were bargaining with an old woman. Behind her, frightened and ashamed, stood a small girl, said to be a virgin. The price was four pounds. The sailors argued for a cheaper rate. They hadn't that much money" (*Big Sea* 119). Hughes's report deftly conveys the personal tragedy it describes, but together with the later paragraphs in the chapter, it also comes to function as a painful allegory of the rape of Africa:

> We came to the docks where the great ships from the white man's land rested—
> an American boat, a Belgian tramp, an English steamer. Tall, black, sinister ships,
> high above the water.
>
> "Their men," say the natives, "their white strong men come to take our palm oil
> and ivory, our ebony and mahogany, to buy our women and bribe our chiefs . . . ."
>
> I climbed the rope ladder to the deck of the Malone. Far off, at the edge of the
> clearing, over against the forest, I heard the drums of Omali, the Ju-Ju. Above, the
> moon was like a gold ripe fruit in heaven, too sweet for the taste of man.
>
> For a long time I could not sleep. (120)

In this chapter Hughes provides a poignant testimony both to his own alienation from the Africans whose acceptance he sought and to the colonial rape of the continent. He brilliantly conveys the pain of his exclusion and the devastation wrought by Western imperialism—in his repeated references to the drumming he hears, his carefully understated report describing the forced prostitution of the frightened young girl, and his striking image of the ships, all of which come to a head with his simple closing statement announcing his inability to sleep. The passage articulates a consciousness that is profoundly troubled by the various divisions wrought by neocolonial conquest.

• It is out of such consciousness that Hughes came to compose not only his poetry about Africa, but the poems that reflect upon the situation of black people in America. "Hughes could not deny the double nature, the dual-consciousness" writes Smith, "of being an American as well as a black" (267). "Afro-American Fragment" laments the lost memories that might have served to unite its speaker with the Africa he desires, but in many other poems Hughes makes the drum his instrument for the recuperative work of memory. These poems include "Drums," "Danse Africaine," "Poem" ("All the tom-toms of the jungles beat in my blood"), "Negro Servant," "Prelude to Our Age: A Negro History Poem" ("the beaten drum / That carried instant history / Across the night"), and "The Jesus." In these poems, the talking drums of Africa and America speak in a voice that is richer and more complicated than the simple primitivism sometimes associated with modernism.[7]

"Drums" reconstitutes African American history not only by tracing its origins in Africa but also by alluding to the beginning of slavery in the New World, to the distinctive drumming and dancing of slaves in Congo Square in New Orleans, and to jazz. Such landmarks reflect Hughes's sense of an African America, a nation of distinct cultural traditions within the larger political community of the United States:

> I dream of the drums
> And remember
> Nights without stars in Africa.
>
> Remember, remember, remember!
>
> I dream of the drums
> And remember
> Slave ships, billowing sails,
> The Western Ocean,
> And the landing at Jamestown.
>
> Remember, remember, remember!
>
> I dream of drums
> And recall, like a picture,
> Congo Square in New Orleans—
> Sunday—the slaves' one day of "freedom"—
> The juba-dance in Congo Square.

I dream of the drums
And hear again
Jelly Roll's piano,
Buddy Bolden's trumpet,
Kid Ory's trombone,
St. Cyr's banjo,
They join the drums . . .
And I remember.

Jazz!

I dream of the drums
And remember.

Africa!
The ships!
New shore
And drums!

Remember!
I remember!
Remember! (543–44)

The first three lines of "Drums" echo the Burutu chapter of *The Big Sea*, but the poem's repetitions of the word "remember" function as a powerful antidote to the melancholic loss of history in "Afro-American Fragment." The repeated verbs of the fourth line can be interpreted as continuing the syntax of the initial sentence, "I remember," in a parallel repetition, but they can also be read as an imperative. The second option emphasizes the oral context presumed by Hughes's poetry, for in this reading the speaker is an orator or American griot who counsels his listeners to remember the histories spoken by the drums of which he dreams. References to those drums both open and close the poem, and they appear as well on the New World soil of Congo Square in New Orleans. In addition, the poem pointedly refers to the image of a ship, but in a way that transfigures the symbolic valence of the ships in the "Burutu" chapter of *The Big Sea*, where the ships rise menacingly "high above the water." In the poem, although the ships are indeed slavers, they are placed in a larger historical context that accurately links African Americans to the heritage mourned in "Afro-American Fragment." "Drums" commemorates the culture that enabled slaves and their descendants to cope with slavery and its legacy; the poem celebrates the exuberance and beauty of black Atlantic culture in order to overcome the division and anxiety of "Fragment."

Although Hughes's "American Heartbreak" (1951) is similar to "Drums" in that its subject is African American history, the poem conveys its speaker's complex relationship to the nation he writes about in a way that corresponds to the mixture of longing and lament in "Afro-American Fragment." The correspondence is by no means exact, however, for "American Heartbreak" combines the historical meditation of "Fragment" with critical satire. Whereas the speaker of "Fragment" looks to Africa for a sense of identity, the speaker of "American Heartbreak" recognizes his central, troubling position in American culture. "American Heartbreak" exemplifies the double consciousness that, according to Gilroy, characterizes not only black Americans but those of African descent on both sides of the Atlantic. In the language of the playfully ironic "Consider Me" (1952), blackness registers itself in the world as a divisive presence-through-absence:

> Forgive me
> What I lack,
> Black,
> Caught in a crack
> That splits the world in two
> From China
> By way of Arkansas
> To Lenox Avenue. (386)

According to the viewpoint expressed in this poem, the position of black Americans is such that they are simultaneously "in" American society yet not "of" it because of their distinctive cultural heritage. For this reason, Gilroy argues that the double perspective of black experience reveals certain contradictions in Western traditions and cultural practices.

From this point of view, "American Heartbreak" supplements the civil geography of Jamestown delineated by Moore in "Virginia Britannia" and "Enough: *Jamestown, 1607–1957*":

> I am the American heartbreak—
> Rock on which Freedom
> Stumps its toe—
> The great mistake
> That Jamestown
> Made long ago. (385)

Like "Afro-American Fragment" this poem is fragmentary, for it too is punctuated by Dickinsonian dashes that simultaneously divide and unite the constituent elements of its syntax. In fact, it reads like an ironic addendum to the already ironic picture of social and colonial conflict rendered by Moore in "Virginia Britannia" and "Enough." Hughes's short poem provides a terse but important footnote to Moore's reflections upon the Jamestown site, elaborating on the narrative of conflict and contradiction she unearths in her pair of poems. "American Heartbreak" transfigures the more northerly Plymouth "Rock"—and the prevailing American mythology of the Pilgrims' landing associated with it—from a comforting foundation into an obstacle on which freedom stubs, or "stumps," its toe. Hughes makes it clear that the rock of slavery is the dirty open secret of American democracy, for the poem never names the "mistake" to which it alludes. The absence of the word *slavery* in the text of the poem suggests that the speaker assumes—and knows he can assume—that his audience will supply his missing term, the presence of its absence. This aspect of the poem projects a particular audience, for it is in an American context that the meaning of "mistake" must emerge. Through its use of the signifiers "mistake" and "Jamestown," the poem constitutes its audience in a particular way, a way that is similar to the voice of the national "we" assumed by Moore, Williams, Frost, and Crane. Yet this "we" is also obviously and significantly different from the one projected by these other poets, for while Hughes addresses a broadly American audience, he does so from an explicitly black perspective. His "I am" enunciates a division in the national community by opposing its representative, collective "I" to the personified "Freedom" that embodies an idealized national community. "I am" testifies to the existence of a community overlooked by monolithic national narratives, but in doing so, it also disrupts the coherence of the ideal community represented by such narratives. To put it in the vocabulary of Bhabha's "DissemiNation," Hughes's poem "performs" the story of his nation in a revisionist way, and in the process of doing so, it reveals the divided nature of his country's citizenry.

In fact, Hughes often articulates a national voice in his poems, but this voice is explicitly black and more often expressed in the first person singular than in the plural. Hughes projects a national community through his use of the "I" as a composite prophetic persona, but his national community refers to a specific part of the nation rather than to a vague totality. In speaking for this subgroup, Hughes implicitly critiques the moral and social coherence of the "we" espoused by his white contemporaries in a range of poems. In his performances of a dissenting "I" in "American Heartbreak," "Negro" (1922), "I, Too" (1925), and "Lament for Dark Peoples" (1924), for example, Hughes demonstrates the pedagogical fiction of the more comprehensive "we" articulated by Moore, Williams, Frost, and Crane. The robust "I" that Hughes voices in such poems stubbornly questions the confident enunciation of a homogeneous national "we."

In "I, Too," for example, Hughes overtly alludes to Whitman's celebrations of the United States, but he treats the subject of the nation in an ironically different way. "I, Too" draws on Whitman's example in order to expand upon and modify the earlier poet's formulation of the country. As Hutchinson argues, "'I, Too, Sing America' can be read in part as a signifying riff on 'old Walt's' songs, forthrightly challenging American rituals of incorporation and exclusion while more subtly playing off . . . Whitman's 'I Hear America Singing' with a dark minor chord" ("Hughes" 22). Although Whitman refers to blacks in "Song of Myself" and attempts to include them in the sweep of his poem, Hughes seeks to use Whitman's poetic example in a way that suits his own perspective. If, as Eloise Johnson puts it, "Hughes's Americanism" is "as profound as Walt Whitman's," it is also of a different order than Whitman's (105):

I, too, sing America.

I am the darker brother.
They send me to eat in the kitchen
When company comes,
But I laugh,
And I eat well,
And grow strong.

Tomorrow,
I'll be at the table
When company comes.
Nobody'll dare
Say to me,
"Eat in the kitchen,"
Then.

Besides,
They'll see how beautiful I am
And be ashamed—

I, too, am America. (46)

In the speaker's restless articulation of "Tomorrow," the poem contrasts his democratic vision with the reality of the American past and present, simultaneously claiming membership in the national "family" and protesting his unjust exclusion from it. Marilyn Miller's commentary on the poem emphasizes its performative power as a speech act and its testimonial authority as a document: "The expressive action of *singing* America in the first line is developed into the *ontological* action of being America in the last; the poet's song is itself proof of his belonging" (339). The poem aims not only to widen the scope of U.S. citizenship for its audience, but also to proclaim the beauty of African Americans and their culture. In this latter respect, the poem continues Whitman's Romantic celebrations of the American self. As Hutchinson points out, "I, Too" was the epilogue to Hughes's first collection, and he often concluded his poetry readings with this piece, in which "Hughes registers his own distinctive poetic identity as both black and American" ("Hughes" 22). His doing so flies in the face of his exclusion as "white" by the African longshoremen described in *The Big Sea*, which suggests that, as in "Brothers," Hughes is exercising a Keatsian negative capability in adopting the perspective of a "darker brother." At the same time, the poem may be calling attention to racism among African Americans, since colored "brothers" of various hues (some "darker," some lighter) coexist within the hybrid communities of the United States.[8] Both in terms of its free-verse rhythms and its subject matter, "I, Too" embraces the Whitman tradition of national representation and pointedly expands it. This poem testifies to the conflicts between the imperial and republican heritages of the United States as well as to the potential divisions within its black community.

"Lament for Dark Peoples" (1924) similarly distinguishes between white and colored communities, although this poem concerns itself with the plight of red as well as black people. The poem adopts the unifying, collective "I" of many other poems by Hughes, ironically adapting the opposition between primitive and civilized through the metaphor of the circus:

> I was a red man one time,
> But the white men came.
> I was a black man, too,
> But the white men came.
>
> They drove me out of the forest.
> They took me away from the jungles.
> I lost my trees.
> I lost my silver moons.
>
> Now they've caged me
> In the circus of civilization.
> Now I herd with the many—
> Caged in the circus of civilization. (39)

"Lament" critiques American democracy by pointing to the dehumanizing effects of its colonial origins on the red people displaced by European colonization and the black people enslaved by plantation elites. In its satirical portrayal of American civilization as an imprisoning circus founded upon the conquest of native peoples, the poem underscores William Appleman Williams's claim that American democracy developed in an economy based on empire. The surreal irony of the circus metaphor discloses the falsity of racist notions that blacks and Indians are bestial or freakishly subhuman, for it is the theater of white "civilization" that constructs them as such for its barbarous pleasure and self-assurance.

While Hughes may seem to favor a communal "I" in many of his poems, he does speak in the voice of the first person plural in a few others. In virtually every case, however, this "we" names a specifically black constituency, not a comprehensive national one.[9] "Afraid" (1924) and "Our Land" (1926) are two examples. In "Afraid," Hughes expresses his sense of continuity with his African ancestry, which makes the poem an interesting companion to "Afro-American Fragment":

> We cry among the skyscrapers
> As our ancestors
> Cried among the palms in Africa
> Because we are alone,
> It is night,
> And we're afraid. (41)

"Afraid" asserts the existential connections between African Americans and Africans that the speaker of "Afro-American Fragment" desires but cannot affirm. However melancholic the link forged by this poem between Africa and America, the text of the poem materially testifies to the solace derived from the affirmation of such a link. In recognizing the continuities of tradition and experience throughout "the black Atlantic," "Afraid" produces a source of strength and sustenance for African Americans. This poem's expression of lament, like the blues that so inspired Hughes, helps its audience to endure despite racial injustices. On the other hand, the poem's confession of fear testifies to the anxiety and potential disunity among the displaced blacks it describes.

"Our Land," which Hughes subtitles "Poem for a Decorative Panel," revisits the subject of "Afro-American Fragment" in a manner similar to Countee Cullen's treatment of Africa in "Heritage":

> We should have a land of sun
> Of gorgeous sun,
> And a land of fragrant water
> Where the twilight
> Is a soft bandanna handkerchief
> Of rose and gold,
> And not this land where life is cold.
>
> We should have a land of trees,
> Of tall thick trees
> Bowed down with chattering parrots
> Brilliant as the day
> And not this land where birds are grey.
>
> Ah, we should have a land of joy,
> Of love and joy and wine and song,
> And not this land where joy is wrong.
>
> Oh, sweet away!
> Ah, my beloved one, away! (32–33)

The rhetoric and style of "Our Land" exoticizes Africa in a way that is consistent with the primitivism that was in vogue at the time Hughes wrote and published the first version of the poem in 1923, and it reverses the situation in Stevens's "Comedian as the Letter C," in which the exotic, or barbaric, is also the indigenous. The "beloved one" of the 1926 text may be a version of the "'deferred' subjectivity" Jarraway associates with Hughes's figurations of women in many of his poems about Harlem (827–28). In the fantasy enacted in the poem, the speaker steals away with a personified and intimate Africa he is free to make his own. Hughes's phrase may also be akin to Toni Morrison's use of biblical discourse to commemorate the experience of American slaves in *Beloved* ("I will call them my people, which were not my people; and her beloved, which was not beloved"). According to this reading, Hughes's "beloved one" evokes the African diaspora scattered in the wake of slavery. It is a beleaguered but beloved community striving together for a common purpose.

"Our Land" projects the utopian hope of an idealized African diaspora, which shows how Hughes's version of American citizenship is at odds with the versions of American nationalism I have analyzed in the work of his contemporaries. It takes the rebuff of Hughes's African friend Tom Pey as a point of departure for a powerful reimagining of the fragmented African American's relationship to Africa. The poem offers a new synthesis of its African heritage, one that allows for a place in the diaspora of members whose skin would not qualify them for African status under the criteria of Pey and his tribesmen. This synthesis may be equated with the repossession of the value of one's culture and identity that Gilroy describes in *The Black Atlantic:* "The need to locate cultural roots and then to use the idea of being in touch with them as a means to refigure the cartography of dispersal and exile is perhaps best understood as a simple and direct response to the varieties of racism which have denied the historical character of black experience and the integrity of black cultures" (112).

• In another set of poems, Hughes shows his concern with national and international matters in a manner quite different from the search for home and unity in "Our Land." In poems written during the economic and social upheaval of the depression, a period when many writers and activists conceived of literature as an instrument in the service of a particular cause, Hughes makes his political message central. In this phase of his career, Hughes conceives his poetry as a form of social realism in an attempt to voice the just claims of the colonized in a revolutionary register. In the poems he wrote during this period, he criticizes the economic disparity and racial injustice of American culture in caustic terms, often through the metaphor of shipping as a means of imperial expansion and control. According to Dawahare, one basis for Hughes's criticism of nationalism in general and American imperialism in particular was his increasingly international perspective. Dawahare argues that the meeting of the Sixth Congress of the Communist International (Comintern) held in 1928 was an important influence on Hughes: "At the Sixth Congress," he writes, "the Comintern . . . formulated the political line that would inform the CPUSA's handling of the 'Negro Question' during the 1930s and beyond. The Communists resolved that black Americans were an oppressed 'nation within a nation' in the South and a 'national minority' in the North." Hughes found the Communist Party's "anti-racist, internationalist perspective" particularly congenial to his way of thinking as it developed in the 1930s (28–29).

In "Columbia" (1933), Hughes satirizes the military and commercial hubris of the United States from the Marxist perspective Dawahare describes. Hughes's composition and publication of the poem while he was in the Soviet Union support Dawahare's claim that the poet's work became increasingly international in outlook during the early years of the depression. Like its place of composition and its subject matter, the initial publication of "Columbia" in *International Literature* ("published six times a year, in English,

French, German, and Russian") underscores the cosmopolitan context of Hughes's thinking and writing during his sojourn in the Soviet Union in 1932 and 1933 (Rampersad 1: 266). Addressing his nation through the title's reference to Columbus, the poet notes the global reach of American power and condemns its stubborn will to see itself as infallibly just. Although the poem makes no references to ships, it certainly refers to his nation's military and commercial ventures by way of its controlling metaphor. As a consequence, "Columbia" echoes the symbolism of the "Tall, black, sinister ships" mentioned in the "Burutu Moon" chapter of *The Big Sea:*

Columbia,
My dear girl,
You really haven't been a virgin for so long
It's ludicrous to keep up the pretext.
You're terribly involved in world assignations.
And everybody knows it.
You've slept with all the big powers
In military uniforms,
And you've taken the sweet life
Of all the little brown fellows
In loin cloths and cotton trousers.
When they've resisted,
You've yelled "rape,"
At the top of your voice
And called for the middies
To beat them up for not being gentlemen
And liking your crooked painted mouth.
(You must think the moons of Hawaii
Disguise your ugliness.)
Really,
You're getting a little too old,
Columbia,
To be so naïve, and so coy.
Being one of the world's big vampires,
Why don't you come on out and say so
Like Japan, and England, and France,
And all the other nymphomaniacs of power
Who've long since dropped their
Smoke-screens of innocence
To sit frankly on a bed of bombs?
O, sweet mouth of India,
And Africa,
Manchuria, and Haiti.

Columbia, You darling,
Don't shoot!
I'll kiss you! (168–69)

In this piece of agitprop, Hughes portrays the United States as a meretricious woman. Her hypocrisy about her promiscuity obviously signifies the double-tongued rhetoric of American politicians who portray their statecraft as innocent of the calculating machinations of Old World politics; America is decidedly not the great exception to the follies of Western history that it traditionally conceives itself to be. In the political allegory of Hughes's poem, Columbia's aggressive sexuality figures U.S. imperialism as the successive, repeated rape of other less fortunate nations in a way that corresponds to the Burutu chapter in *The Big Sea*. Hughes's use of the word "Columbia" portrays U.S. imperialism as an undertaking that parallels Columbus's voyage to the New World, suggesting that U.S. imperialism is part of an entrenched history of colonial exploitation and domination. The title of the poem alludes to the various New World place-names that commemorate the Old World "discoverer," in order to satirize not only Columbus but also the political traditions that adopt him as their potent symbol. Hughes's speaker writes about his country from a distance that indicates his alienation from the culture he condemns but to which he nonetheless belongs. In ironically adopting the position of one of Columbia's client states, coaxing her to accept his kisses to prevent her from shooting him, Hughes's speaker acknowledges the impossibility of his escaping her reach and influence. The speaker of "Columbia" is both a member of American society and adamantly opposed to its government's foreign policy.

"The English" (1930) may be read as an interesting companion to "Columbia." Whereas the latter criticizes American imperialism directly, "The English" offers a historical context for the aggressive American entry into world markets known as the Open Door policy, which began by about 1916 (Parrini 1). While American politicians and bankers sought to crack the English domination of overseas markets, American political and commercial traditions were themselves very much a product of English culture. Although the English preceded the Americans in their domination of foreign markets, their example also parallels that of their colonial and cultural descendants. In "The English," Hughes satirizes English imperialism and propriety by playing off a catalogue of English military and economic conquests against his repeated line describing the personal toilette of English officers. "In ships all over the world," Hughes writes,

> The English comb their hair for dinner,
> Stand watch on the bridge,
> Guide by strange stars,
> Take on passengers,
> Slip up hot rivers,
> Nose across lagoons,
> Bargain for trade,
> Buy, sell or rob,
> Load oil, load fruit,

Load cocoa beans, load gold
In ships all over the world,
Comb their hair for dinner. (129)

The poem is an indictment of English imperialism, which irrationally counte-
nances the contradiction between the principles of liberty and equality and
the facts of colonial exploitation. The poem's catalogue of activity empha-
sizes the scale ("all over the world") and energy of English maritime com-
merce, but verbs such as "Slip up," "Nose," and "rob," which appear in the
middle of the poem, characterize that activity as insidious, underhanded, and
exploitative. It is no accident, moreover, that the last item in Hughes's cata-
logue of commodities is gold. As the commodity par excellence, it embodies
the commercial nature of the English colonial mission.

The English are busy tradesmen, but they are punctilious with respect to
their mien and the impression they mean it to make. The neatly coifed offi-
cers maintain their power through a strict regimen of management. In the
terms presented in the poem, British administration of its provinces proceeds
by a disciplinary attention to detail, composing its brave face so as to lend its
rule an air of easy power, of complacent composure in front of the oppres-
sions perpetuated by its decorous routine. As Bhabha points out in his read-
ing of a scene from Conrad's *Heart of Darkness,* such attention to detail buoys
English self-confidence by offering a way to organize experience, to impose
order on the chaos posed by the colonist's encounter with the colonized
Other. In Conrad's novel, Marlow praises Towson's *Inquiry into some Points of
Seamanship* for its articulation of "an honest concern for the right way of go-
ing to work," a concern that for Marlow lends the book an almost religious
aura of significance, rendering it "luminous with another than a professional
light." Reading the book comforts Marlow, for it provides "the shelter of an
old and solid friendship." As Bhabha explains,

> Towson's manual provides Marlow with a singleness of intention. It is the book of
> work that turns delirium into the discourse of civil address. For the ethic of work,
> as Conrad was to exemplify in "Tradition" (1918), provides a sense of right con-
> duct and honour achievable only through the acceptance of those "customary"
> norms which are the signs of culturally cohesive "civil" communities. These aims
> of the civilizing mission, endorsed in the "idea" of British imperialism . . . , speak
> with a peculiarly English authority derived from the *customary practice* on which
> both English common law and the English national language rely for their effec-
> tivity and appeal. (106)

Like Marlow's manual of seamanship and Conrad's larger concern with
"the ethic of work" as a model of "right conduct," the uniform grooming
of Hughes's English sailors comforts them by infusing their daily routine
with order and meaning and by acting as a standard or sign of civilized be-
havior. In both cases, compliance with a prescribed norm defines behavior

as civilized and thereby differentiates it from the behavior of people who "fail" to comply with or recognize such norms. The trope of civilization as a circus in "Lament for Dark Peoples" mocks this line of thinking by inverting it and taking it to absurd extremes in order to condemn its oppressive social consequences.

In an important sense, the ritual preparation for dinner and the practice of formal table manners symbolically convey the commercial power and profit of the English. The dinner for which the officers prepare displays the bounty of imperial trade and formally bespeaks the prestige of that bounty. The seemingly benign combing of hair turns out to be part of a larger rite of conspicuous consumption that symbolizes the power and splendor of English dominion. The poem implies that, from the perspective of the English, the superiority of the officers' manners signifies the superiority of English civilization. Hughes's ironic repetition of the line "Comb their hair for dinner" both likens the domestic behavior of the officers to the economic domination in which they engage and marks the difference between the two forms of action. The poem dramatizes the manner in which social niceties both reinforce the economic and military power of the English and hide any anxieties they may feel about what they are doing. The men who "Comb their hair for dinner" are both grooming themselves and being groomed by an economic and political system in which they assume a place of power as its agents. The satiric thrust of Hughes's repetition lampoons the English claim to cultural and moral superiority. In the view of Hughes's speaker, their preparation for dinner ritually attests to their appetite for power. As Gilroy suggests, however, the global transits of "The English" and other Western powers had the unintended effect of bringing about new points of contact between blacks on both sides of the Atlantic, and Hughes's poem, which echoes his experience as a sailor on a merchant vessel to Africa, reflects this fact. The English and others may act upon the land, commodities, and bodies of Africans and people of African descent, but the published text of Hughes's poem counters English and American dominion by satirically denying its legitimacy.

In this regard, Hughes's incisive poem "Fog" offers an illuminating perspective on "The English." Both poems feature ships, but whereas "The English" focuses on the manners of white overlords, "Fog" presents a portrait of African labor from the perspective of an onlooker whose unhappy relationship to his own "modern," technological culture leads him to characterize it as blinded by a pervasive moral fog:

> Singing black boatmen
> An August morning
> In the thick white fog at Sekondi
> Coming out to take cargo
> From anchored alien ships,

You do not know the fog
We strange so-civilized ones
Sail in always. (63)

"Fog" evokes the trope of the primitive in a self-reflective and questioning way, for the speaker looks with compassionate solidarity at the bodies of African laborers, but he registers his difference from them in the final three lines of the poem. The division between the speaker and the African men whom he hails repeats the alienation Hughes himself must have felt when shunned by the Africans he had tried to embrace, but it also compounds and complicates that alienation by enunciating a "We" that aligns the speaker with a community with which he feels at odds. The position of the speaker in this lyric is determined by a number of contingencies over which he has no personal control, and this speaks to the difficulties Hughes and fellow minorities face in thinking about American nationhood. The speaker of "Fog" is doubly divided, first from the black African "boatmen" with whom he wishes to align himself, and second from the "civilization" he reviles but to which he nonetheless belongs. The poem evokes the speaker's frustration concerning his inability to alter his "civilization." He perceives the "ships" that both he and the Africans serve as at once "alien" and "anchored"—as both "other" and yet firmly established. Both the speaker and the "Singing black boatmen" he addresses are subordinated to an economic system that values their labor but not their humanity. Like "The English," "Fog" articulates the speaker's political protest as well as his personal frustration.

• In the powerful late poem "The Jesus" (1960), Hughes writes about a real slave ship named *The Jesus*. Hughes published the poem under a pseudonym, perhaps in an attempt to protect himself against further political harassment of the kind he had experienced at the hands of Senator McCarthy's committee, or perhaps to defend himself against the kind of controversy that poems like "Goodbye Christ" provoked. In his poem Hughes returns to the theme of Africa as a place of origins; "The Jesus" may be compared with "Afro-American Fragment" in significant ways. While both poems undertake an imagination of Africa and its meaning for African Americans, for example, "The Jesus" refers to Africa in order to link it to American shores by way of the Middle Passage. The journey of "The Jesus" records the African American history that the speaker of "Afro-American Fragment" yearns to discover, yet it does so in an ironic way.

In a note he appends to the poem, Hughes explains that *The Jesus* was a "ship lent to Sir John Hawkins by Queen Elizabeth as support to his business venture in the slave traffic off Cape Verde in the latter half of the sixteenth century." Hughes narrates the advent of the slaver in a muscular, alliterative verse:

Until the crumpets and the christians,
Altars of grass bled paths
From Congo to Cape, shifting sacrificially
Through river beds, shifting
From saberthroat to sand
Voodoo rain drummed juju
Away and spring came,
Came with Galilee
Upon its back to chop
The naked bone of mumbo
Dangling like a dice
Swung from a mirror,
Captain of the stumps of Sir John
Lumped cargoes for Cuba
Among feathered kings rolling
Their skins in flax, moulded
To shaftsteel and psalm.
Through helms of smoke
Balloon dreams of grabber kings
Mooned at groaning girls
Bred on black sheets of seahull.
Was the deacon of pits blessing
The mumble of crumbs or
Trying to suck at his knuckles?
In this tambourine of limbs
Where crisscross droves of blackbirds croak
The Jesus weptwashed and slumped
Toward the mines of sugar cane. (468–69)

"The Jesus" figures the origins of black slavery by focusing on an actual rather than an archetypal slaver. While the poem's portrait of the individual experience of slaves remains as anonymous as the institution of slavery systematically rendered it, the poem identifies a particular ship involved in the trade in order to specify the imperialist motives informing slavery. The poem squarely positions the practice of slavery in the midst of European culture by pointing up the contradictions in the Christianity it professes and the brutal commerce it practices. The Jesus of Hughes's ship is not the biblical healer and prophet, but a trope for European conquest. *The Jesus* is a vanguard ship in the army of imperial Christendom, not a vehicle of Christian compassion.

Hughes's reference to a mirror in "The Jesus" might suggest his sense of the poem as a mimetic reflection of reality in the modern West. In documenting slave history, the poem holds a mirror up to the imagined community of its national and diasporic readers. "The Jesus" charts the advent of the slaves in a way that echoes the chapter devoted to the same journey in William Carlos Williams's *American Grain.* By emphasizing the violence of enslavement, the poem forces its readers to confront an institution that formed one of the very bases of modern economic exchange in the West. It also reflects the discrepancy between the Enlightenment ideals of reason and freedom and the degraded social practice of slavery. In an important sense, the poem mirrors the flaws at the heart of the nation that defined itself as the model of democracy in the modern world.

"The Jesus" offers a harrowing recapitulation of slavery and the Middle Passage in a series of lines that are dense with internal echoes and rhymes. The alliteration and compound nouns ("saberthroat," "shaftsteel," "seahull") recall Anglo-Saxon verse, as if to suggest the hybridity of cultural forms and of the African American writer's position, even as the speaker of the poem seeks to indict the crime of English and American slaving. The African vocabulary ("juju," "mumbo," "voodoo") further accentuates the theme of hybridity, but it also makes the poem resonate with the sense of threat and terror associated with the fetishes and spirits or demons it signifies. In a way that echoes the speaker's articulation of religious torment in Cullen's "Heritage," Hughes contrasts the religious contexts of "juju," "mumbo," "voodoo," and the African "Altars of grass" upon which sacrifices are made, with the "Christian" mission of the European slaver, the "deacon of pits" who ambiguously wrings his hands or uses them to bless the "mumble of crumbs" below, and the "psalm" to which the newly captured slaves will be "moulded" over time. This contrast between African religions and Christianity portrays the looting of Africa as both commercial and cultural in nature, for Europeans attempted to cut off the cultural traditions of the Africans they enslaved. The opposing religious vocabularies emphasize the ways in which modern slavery wounded Africa in psychic as well as commercial terms.

The reference to "stumps" in the line "Captain of the stumps of Sir John," moreover, seems to reinforce the trope of slavery as a wounding, for the word apparently figures the lumber out of which the ship is made as dead wood, so that Sir John's ship itself becomes both a dead thing and a harbinger of death. The spirits of the trees from which the slaver has been made are as dead as the consciences of the sailors that control it. The poem represents Sir John's commercial enterprise as so many stumps—of timber torn from the earth and of human bodies torn violently from their environment. Not only is Sir John's moral insight stumped, or stunted, by his trading in slaves, but his enterprise also turns slaves into human stumps. The redemptive blood of the ship's namesake displaces the sacrificial blood that flows from the African altars, figuring slavery as a massive dismemberment of the body of Africa. Hughes's slave ship is a menacing saber at the throat of the African continent.

In other words, "stumps" refers to fragments, to literal dead ends. This reference to dismemberment recalls "Afro-American Fragment," but the same word also appears as a verb in "American Heartbreak." In the latter poem, Hughes uses the word "stumps" rather than "stubs" ("I am the American heartbreak— / Rock on which Freedom / Stumps its toe—"), as if to suggest both that "American Freedom" is "stumped" (or baffled) and fragmented (or rendered an incomplete stump). And along with these meanings, of course, the word functions as a virtual synonym for "stubs," so that the full stride of American Freedom is broken against the unyielding rock of slavery. "American Heartbreak" makes clear that the legacy of slavery poisons the freedom of the whole nation, not just that of blacks. It undercuts the upper-case pretension of the familiar ideology in which "Freedom" becomes a peculiarly "American" possession. Hughes's brief lyric insists that American Freedom is not fully coherent, nor has it ever been. Through its allusion to slavery, the poem underscores one of the major conflicts of American culture, the conflict between the rhetoric of freedom and the reality of racial oppression.

In "The Jesus," Hughes counters this discrepancy between rhetoric and reality with another image of an African drum. Echoing other poems by Hughes discussed here, "The Jesus" features ritual drumming as well as the image of a ship, expressing Hughes's effort to participate in the drumming he was prohibited from witnessing in Africa. In Hughes's account of this prohibition in *The Big Sea,* Tom Pey explicitly links the drumming Hughes hears later to the fetish or demon figure Ju-Ju; Hughes's reference to "juju" in "The Jesus" echoes that moment in the autobiography. Hughes's poetic drumming revisits the scene in *The Big Sea* and makes a place for himself at its ritualistic site. "The Jesus" links the African American to his African heritage by retelling the story of enslavement in the condensed form of the lyric. Hughes's poetic account of slavery upholds the oral tradition of the African griot, even though it does so in the form of a written text. Although "The Jesus" provides no simple antidote to the melancholic wound of "Afro-American Fragment," it does offer the image of a specific slave ship as an example of the history that both links and divides diasporic blacks from mainland Africans. In this regard, the ironic, "weptwashed" history of "The Jesus" answers to the sense of fragmentation expressed in the earlier poem without pretending to overcome it with some simplistic formula. It also testifies to the cosmopolitan and contradictory character of African American history and citizenship by orienting its readers in two directions at once—"back" to an Africa of origins and "ahead" to the heterogeneous societies of the modern world.

Like "The Jesus," Hughes's famous early poem "The Negro Speaks of Rivers" powerfully counteracts the alienation and disunity of "Afro-American Fragment," but it does so by imaginatively realizing an ideal diasporic unity (rather than an exclusively national one) through the emergence of its annunciatory "I." The poem is an example of Hughes's successful evocation, or "performance," of the African diaspora, for its Whitmanian speaker maps a global geography of rivers in the confident epistemology of its opening sentence. In this regard, "The Negro Speaks of Rivers," like "The Jesus," offers an important counterforce to the loss lamented in "Afro-American Fragment" and other poems:

I've known rivers:
I've known rivers ancient as the world and older than the
    flow of human blood in human veins.

My soul has grown deep like the rivers.

I bathed in the Euphrates when dawns were young.
I built my hut near the Congo and it lulled me to sleep.
I looked upon the Nile and raised the pyramids above it.
I heard the singing of the Mississippi when Abe Lincoln
    went down to New Orleans, and I've seen its muddy
    bosom turn all golden in the sunset.

I've know rivers.
Ancient, dusky rivers.

My soul has grown deep like the rivers. (23)

The poem insists on the historical reality of the African diaspora, for the memory it conveys is geological, "older than the flow of human blood in human veins." But as a speech act, the printed transcript of an oral chant, the poem calls into being a diasporic consciousness. "Through his naming of Africa's major rivers," writes Richard Barksdale, Hughes "establishes a link with the American black man's romantic motherland" (17). Like the performance of an African griot, which the poem's structure echoes, "The Negro Speaks of Rivers" testifies to a past fraught with meaning for its community of New World hearers. As Fahamisha Brown suggests, an implicit history underlies the poem's succession of rivers:

> Hughes enumerates rivers associated with African American heritage and history to evoke a mystical sense of the eternal presence of the speaking "I." From the beginnings of recorded history, "the Euphrates"; through the greatness of empire and civilization, "the Nile" and its "pyramids"; through slavery and freedom, "the Mississippi"—the voice proclaims its presence and knowledge. (68)

The poem evokes the African and African American past by a sort of imaginative fiat and challenges its projected listeners to conceive of themselves as a cohesive community despite their disparate geography. The speaker announces his knowledge for the benefit of his audience, telling the story of a common past in order to cultivate a united consciousness in the present. Like the Whitmanian speaker of "Sun Song" ("Dark ones of Africa, / I bring you my songs / To sing on the Georgia roads"), the "I" projected by the poem is both an exuberant individual and an embodiment of the community whom he addresses ("I contain multitudes"). Particularly in the context of Hughes's reading tours, this act of enunciation serves as the occasion for building diasporic unity. The poem attempts to transcend the boundaries of the national by imagining its audience as a global community.

• I close with a discussion of a short lyric that was, as Hughes's editors point out, "published posthumously in *Crisis* (June–July 1968) . . . to mark the anniversary of Hughes's death." "Flotsam," they note, "is the last of seven poems which Hughes submitted to the magazine before he died" (683):

> On the shoals of Nowhere,
> Cast up—my boat,
> Bow all broken,
> No longer afloat.
>
> On the shoals of Nowhere,
> Wasted—my song—
> Yet taken by the sea wind
> And blown along. (562)

Hughes's submission of this poem late in his life and its posthumous publication give it a special place in his career. Just as Whitman, in "Song of Myself," bequeaths his body "to the dirt to grow from the grass I love," Hughes bequeaths his poems to the wind. More important, perhaps, "Flotsam" expresses the same dispossession and placelessness that "Afro-American Fragment" expresses, but it does so in a potentially more hopeful way.

If, for example, the "sea wind" disseminates the song that the poet thought was "Wasted," it scatters the seeds of his words to the four corners of a global Africa, where they may take root and grow. It is true that the speaker feels he has gotten "Nowhere"; he is disoriented and at a loss, and his references to waste reaffirm his anguish. At the same time, however, he begins to build a new future out of humble materials. As Monika Kaup argues,

> in the very evocation of the "shoals of Nowhere," an unspecified place of displacement, we can detect the seeds of another resurgence of the utopian hope of inclusion . . . . Placeless and timeless like Hughes' "nowhere" of displacement, the idea of utopia, too, suggests an unspecified place, a no-where. It could very well be to the shoals of utopia that Hughes' boat could be blown next. Clearly, while very pessimistic, "Flotsam" does not put a final stop to the fluid dynamic of the Black Atlantic. (107)

In a way that confirms Kaup's etymological reading of "Nowhere" as utopia, the closing vision of the poem turns wreckage into redemption, transforming the flotsam of loss into the elements of a song that the wind takes up, embellishes, and conveys to the disparate lands of the diaspora. It deliberately echoes the sea and ship imagery in "The English," "Fog," and "The Jesus" but sharply contrasts with them in order to offer, like "Drums," a potentially redemptive insight into the power of Hughes's poetry to unite disparate diasporic groups. The mercurial changes of the sea wind make the song's dissemination a matter of chance, but they also suggest the possibility that the song may be borne by a wind imagined as a new Mercury, the messenger god bringing the living tones of the poet's songs to the shores of his distant kin.

Epilogue

"WE THE PEOPLE" IN AN IMPERIAL REPUBLIC

• The poetic inflections of an American "we the people" as celebratory, anxious, ironic, dialectical, and utopian reflect historical continuities and social conflicts in a manner that enriches our sense of U.S. culture as a whole and its poetic traditions in particular. Characterizing, qualifying, and comparing these categories can show how the concepts of republic and empire inform the national consciousness of American modernists in both complementary and conflicting ways. In my view, conflict ultimately undermines the complementarity of these terms. While various national unities emerge, the plurality of communities and their discourses remain in conflict with one another in American poetry as well as politics, since the benefits of empire rule out the advantages of democracy for many citizens within the republic as well as for various populations outside it. In fact, the conflict between the nation as a republic and the nation as an empire may be one of the key features of democratic poetics in the United States, and the complex representation of this conflict may be one of the chief values of such poetics. By emphasizing the historical continuity of these two terms and the ways they conflict with one another in American history, I have aimed to show that modernist poets laid claim to the complexities of representation for social and political as well as aesthetic reasons.

A poetic dialogue between Robert Frost and Robinson Jeffers may stand as an example of how republican and imperial traditions of the United States complement and contradict one another throughout modern American poetry. As Derek Walcott conceives of them, the two poets make a powerful pair. For him, they are

> two avuncular recluses, outdoor figures, both opposed to Dickinson's confines, or caves, of parlor and chapel, one on the Pacific coast and the other on the Atlantic coast, both proffering rocky, granite-featured profiles to "the elements," one the companion of seals and spray, the other of deer and birds. They are stone heads of reassuring integrity, until we look more closely and see how frightening the cracks are in their classic, petrified composure, how alarming and even treacherous are their ambiguities of crossing shadows. (109)

If Walcott ultimately prefers Frost, his stony tableaux nonetheless adumbrate the national status of each poet, the complexity of their national representations, and their relevance to one another. In fact, the poets' common concern about the state of their nation took the form of a specific poetic debate. As a reply to Jeffers's "Shine, Perishing Republic" (1925), Frost's "Our Doom to Bloom" (1950) shows that the interaction between the republican and imperial strains of U.S. democracy permeate its field of discourse. The rhetoric in both poems is ironic and open-ended, but only Frost's poem articulates a truly unified (although anxious) "we," for the speaker of Jeffers's poem imagines himself as standing apart from the problematic "mass" of his fellow citizens. Jeffers conceives of his nation as a faceless collective rather than a unified group of individuals bound together in a social contract. "Shine" revolves around an "I/They" relationship, whereas the speaker of "Our Doom" assumes national unity and presumes to speak for its many constituents. Both poems reflect a certain discrepancy between the representative (and hence republican) status they aim for and the political realities behind them.

In "Shine, Perishing Republic," Jeffers addresses himself directly to his country, using the apostrophe of his title to comment on the state of his nation and to enunciate a personal ethics in contrast to it:

> While this America settles in the mould of its vulgarity, heavily
> > thickening to empire,
> And protest, only a bubble in the molten mass, pops and sighs out,
> > and the mass hardens,
>
> I sadly smiling remember that the flower fades to make fruit, the
> > fruit rots to make earth.
> Out of the mother; and through the spring exultances, ripeness
> > and decadence; and home to the mother.
>
> You making haste haste on decay: not blameworthy; life is good,
> > be it stubbornly long or suddenly
> A mortal splendor: meteors are not needed less than mountains:
> > shine, perishing republic.
>
> But for my children, I would have them keep their distance from
> > the thickening center; corruption
> Never has been compulsory, when the cities lie at the monster's
> > feet there are left the mountains.
>
> And boys, be in nothing so moderate as in love of man, a clever
> > servant, insufferable master.
> There is the trap that catches noblest spirits, that caught—they
> > say—God, when he walked on earth. *(Collected Poetry 1: 15)*

Jeffers's poem emphasizes the political tension between the republican and imperial elements in his country by figuring the nation as a decadent empire and himself as a virtuous republican. Like Frost, Jeffers denies the thesis of American exceptionalism, for, as Jessica Hueter points out, "'This America' implies that there have been and/or will be other Americas" (97). One of the factors, moreover, that makes America like other countries is its proclivity to empire. Jeffers's optative mood ("I would have them") acts out one of the principal ways modern poets engage national discourse, as in Crane's fantasy of white and Indian union in "The Dance" section of *The Bridge* and Hughes's utopian figurations of African American as well as pan-African unity. Like Hughes's optative, Jeffers's "I would have them" criticizes the state of the nation by exposing the fact that imperial ambition turns the "clever" republican "servant" into an "insufferable" imperial "master"; yet it also does so in order to articulate a personal value that contrasts with the "insufferable" condition of imperial mastery. Jeffers's phrase expresses his wish that, despite the fatal course of America's imperial republic, some remnant of principled protesters might coalesce from the hardening "mass" of its citizenry.

Jeffers's diction modulates from the unnatural "monsters" that pollute natural mountains to the inhumane "masters" who corrupt republican politics through their imperial machinations. Even though Jeffers figures political corruption as organic and inevitable in the central metaphor of his poem (thereby including but also dwarfing politics within the scheme of his worldview), he clearly expresses his preference for republican virtue over imperial aggrandizement ("corruption / Never has been compulsory"). The poem's oratorical flourishes enhance Jeffers's ethos by emphasizing the contrast between his maverick stance and the repulsively thickening "vulgarity" of his contemptible fellow citizens. In the dying republic of the poem, most citizens constitute a mere unthinking mass that "hardens" its heart to the individual virtue championed by the poet. By contrast, Jeffers's closing command—addressed implicitly to his readers as well as his sons, since it hails them alike as listeners—enunciates a shrewd policy (shun corruption; love moderately) that works against such hardening. Together with his paternal "I would have them" (a remark plainly aimed at an audience other than his sons), Jeffers's imperative implicitly invites his readers, not just his sons, to join the speaker's resistance to imperial mastery. In its complex use of rhetoric, the poem mixes political protest with its praise of nature.

In "Our Doom to Bloom," Frost responds to Jeffers's poem, both in terms of the Roman classicism it draws upon and the metaphors of organic growth and decay that organize it. Frost parodies Jeffers's stance and tone as well as his organic metaphor by spoofing the classical trappings of his dialogue and poking fun at them through his Byronic rhymes:

> Cumaean Sibyl, charming Ogress,
> What are the simple facts of Progress
> That I may trade on with reliance
> In consultation with my clients?
> The Sibyl said, "Go back to Rome
> And tell your clientele at home
> That if it's not a mere illusion

All there is to it is diffusion—
Of coats, oats, votes, to all mankind.
In the Surviving Book we find
That liberal, or conservative,
The state's one function is to give.
The bud must bloom till blowsy blown
Its petals loosen and are strown;
And that's a fate it can't evade
Unless 'twould rather wilt than fade." (459–60)

Both poems portray America as a latter-day Roman republic, but both (like Jeffers's "Ave Caesar") also intimate the parallel danger of decaying like the Roman empire. A fatalism informs "Shine" and "Doom," for in each case the state rises and falls with cosmic inevitability. Frost lampoons Jeffers, however, by distinguishing between wilting and fading in order to indicate that the end of a state may occur prematurely, before acting out its full fate. All living beings must "fade" due to death, but only some of them die due to wilting. Frost's "blowsy blown" parodies the rot and corruption in Jeffers's poem by hinting that its prophetic rhetoric (rather than the state it satirizes) is overblown or flyblown. Against the latter's deadly rhetoric, Frost champions the dogged sustenance of his "Surviving Book," which Robert Brophy glosses as the U.S. Constitution (15).

In contrast to "Shine, Perishing Republic," which implies rather than specifies its political ideals in the interest of criticizing the nation's failures, "Our Doom to Bloom" explicitly defines the purpose of the government it depicts, though it does so by means of the Sibyl's equivocal wisdom ("*if* it's not as mere illusion / All there is to it is diffusion—"). The oracle's conditional premise that "The state's one function is to give" echoes John Locke's view that the role of the state is to protect the individual and his property through representative, or republican, democracy ("votes"). From this perspective, the line means that the purpose of the state is to grant political freedom, protection, and security to the individual. More immediately, of course, the line summarizes the "diffusion—/ Of coats, oats, votes, to all mankind" in the new world order of expanding U.S. democracy, power, and interests in the aftermath of World War II. As Kenneth Rosen points out, Frost overtly linked political and economic diffusion with Franklin Roosevelt in a 1949 letter to Edward Munce that included an earlier draft of "Doom." Just as the speaker of Frost's poem hopes to "trade on" the information he seeks from the Sibyl, the "diffusion" his poem describes has an economic as well as a political cast to it. Rosen's observation, moreover, that the phrase "trade on" replaces the draft version's "handle" further underscores the importance of the economic in Frost's vision of America as a benevolent empire in the modern world (370). "The state's one function is to give," however, also implies that the state's function is to yield or be flexible under various stresses as well as to "give in" or "give way" to the sovereignty of the individual, which it is designed to preserve. In contrast to the expansionist ramifications of "trade on," these readings of the line underscore the republican strain of American democracy, and Jeffers as well as Frost would probably appreciate these Jeffersonian interpretations of the line.

With respect to the national "we" that emerges in these poems, Jeffers's speaker remains stubbornly individual, disdainfully outside the mass: his title renders the speech of a single voice commanding an impersonal public.[1] His national community remains implicit and is only indirectly represented by the speaker. In contrast, Frost assumes a national unity—a stable "unum" from an expansive and divided "pluribus"—in the possessive pronoun of his title. Frost emphasizes this contrast by juxtaposing his title with Jeffers's in his epigraph. "Doom" mocks the evident pessimism of Jeffers's political views, but it also echoes the etymological roots of the word as "judgment" when it quotes the Sibyl. Whereas Jeffers's poem portrays the decay of American culture as so extreme as to divide the national community into a benighted, passive mass in favor of empire and a lone opposing voice of republican protest, Frost's poem offers a coherent community by glossing over the differences between liberals and conservatives. The rhetorical context of Frost's poem, however, requires its readers to consider his perspective in relation to Jeffers's, so that the expression of dissent in "Shine" persists even in the unifying outlook of "Doom." Frost's comedy of sibylline ambiguity, moreover, throws into question the authority of the oracle, for its riddling syntax compromises its unity. In my readings of the five poets covered by this study, I have emphasized the persistence of such conflict in order to show how the negotiation and settlement it requires is necessarily open-ended in a genuinely democratic nation.

The intertextual dialogue between Frost and Jeffers suggests that their common political context is structured by a fundamental dichotomy, for each of their poems investigates the opposition between republic and empire in American political life. Their conversation in verse also suggests a way of thinking about American poetics in relational terms, as a continuous dialogue between disparate voices. As Walcott implies, Frost and Jeffers assume a representative status in the imperial republic of modern American letters by reminding their readers that its national discourse is, to echo Bhabha, split from within. Like the poems covered in the primary chapters of this study, "Shine, Perishing Republic" and "Our Doom to Bloom" reveal that the constitutional self-division of the United States has provided creative inspiration for its modern poets.

$\mathcal{N}otes$

INTRODUCTION

1. Marx provides a postcolonial interpretation of Stevens ("The Comedian as Colonist"), while Kusch offers one of H. D.

2. As I explain later in the introduction, William Appleman Williams expresses the same view. So do Van Alstyne, Magdoff, Chomsky, Perkins, Stephanson, Nobles, Calloway, Weeks, Jennings, Buell ("Postcolonial Anxiety" 213), Rowe, and Onuf.

3. For fuller definitions of *republic* and *empire*, see Wilson 21–50.

4. "The history of American imperialism," writes Amy Kaplan, "strains the definition of the postcolonial, which implies a temporal development (from 'colonial' to 'post') that relies on the spatial coordinates of European empires, in their formal acquisition of territories and the subsequent history of decolonization and national independence" (15). For other discussions of the relationship between postcolonialism and American studies, see Buell ("Postcolonial Anxiety"), King, Frankenberg and Mani, Mackenthun ("Adding Empire"), McClintock, Powell, Sharpe, Shohut, Singh and Schmidt ("On the Borders"), Spivak, and Stratton.

5. I am indebted to an anonymous reader for the suggestion that I codify this typology of national discourse.

6. The many scholars who have addressed this topic include Abrahams, Alexander, Blake, Breslin, Chabot, Conrad, Gardner, Hegeman, Hutchinson *(Harlem Renaissance)*, Kadlec, Koch, Kusch, Kutzinski, Michaels, Noland, North, Richardson, Spencer, and Wertheim.

7. Of all the poets I consider, Frank's influence on Crane is the most direct and the most like Emerson's influence on Whitman. Frank edited and wrote a preface to the 1933 *Collected Poems of Hart Crane* (New York: Liveright).

8. Rosu sketches the longer history of this concern (244).

9. Thanks to Suzanne Matson for directing my attention to this passage.

10. "Postcolonial Anxiety" is a revised version of "American Literary Emergence as a Postcolonial Phenomenon," which appeared in *American Literary History* 4 (1992): 411–42.

11. See Rodríguez García for a discussion of Williams's chapter on Rasles.

1: MARIANNE MOORE'S GEOGRAPHY OF ORIGINS

1. Unless otherwise noted, all quotations from Moore's poetry are from *The Complete Poems of Marianne Moore.*

2. William Carlos Williams also criticized this state of affairs when he wrote in 1925 that "To-day it is a generation of gross know-nothingism" (*American Grain* 68).

3. Berger also reads Moore's poem in light of Stevens's jar (284).

4. Moore's five-year stint as a teacher at the Carlisle Indian School no doubt

affected her perspective on the relations between European and Native Americans. She reports, "I felt myself to be an impostor there, . . . I was soldiering; it really wasn't my work" (Cantwell 83). Because Richard Henry Pratt based Carlisle on a military model as a means of educating and assimilating Indians, Moore's reference to soldiering takes on a special resonance. David Adams points out that, as part of a system of "acculturating Indian youth to 'American' ways of thinking and living," Carlisle was a pedagogical site dedicated to transforming Indians into "standard" American citizens (ix). "Pratt liked Indians," Adams writes, "but he had little use for Indian cultures" (51). Although Moore shared Pratt's belief in self-improvement, she shows in "Virginia Britannia" that she took an open-minded interest in Native American culture and did not consider it inferior to European culture.

5. According to Mackenthun, in *General Historie of Virginia, New England, and the Summer Isles* (1624), Smith sought to "reinforce" his "own position toward the Virginia Company's policy by starring Powhatan as a man too intelligent to bite at the bait of [the colonists'] imperial show. A man of Powhatan's size, Smith implies, can be dealt with only by a man like Smith" (*Metaphors* 204). Mackenthun's analysis provides an interesting gloss on "pugnacious equal."

6. Thanks go to Peter Norberg for pointing out Moore's pun on "We-re-wo-co-mo-co" and "we were."

7. Berger offers a feminist analysis of Moore's revisionist poetics.

8. Slatin, Costello, and Molesworth prefer Moore's earlier versions of the poem, and Borroff sees a significant slackening in the final stanza of the revised version. Merrin both agrees and disagrees with these critics (160).

9. I am indebted to an anonymous reader for the insight that the shape of Moore's stanzas parallels the boxes her poem describes.

10. The quoted phrase in this passage is from Wolf.

11. See Waselkov for a discussion of two kinds of Indian maps and the colonists' response to them (206–7).

12. See Stamy regarding Moore's treatments of China and its culture in her poetry.

2: NATION AND ENUNCIATION IN THE WORK OF WILLIAM CARLOS WILLIAMS

1. All quotations of Williams's poetry are drawn from *The Collected Poems of William Carlos Williams* and subsequently will be cited by the abbreviation *CP*.

3: NATIONAL FORGETTING AND REMEMBERING IN THE POETRY OF ROBERT FROST

1. All quotations are from Frost's *Collected Poems, Prose, and Plays* unless otherwise noted. "Geneological" printed with permission of the Estate of Robert Lee Frost.

2. As Lakritz explains, the cottage is "a good example of the uncanny" because it literalizes Freud's German equivalent of the word (*Modernism* 92).

3. For a recent discussion of the relation between Frost's commitment to individualism and his political views, see Andy Moore.

4. In "Decadent Aesthetics," Paul Giles emphasizes the importance of Frost's play with plural meanings in relation to his representations of America.

5. For discussions of the trope of the vanishing or ghostly Indian in American culture, see Bellin, Bergland, Dippie, Huhndorf, Maddox, Pearce, Scheckel, and Cheryl Walker.

6. I am grateful to Guy Rotella for calling my attention to the etymology of the word *barbecue*.

7. Lakritz discerns a similar duality in his reading of "The Road Not Taken," which for him both evokes and undercuts the myth of American exceptionalism through its allegory of pioneering individualism ("Frost in Transition" 211).

8. Giles characterizes Frost's ascent to the status of representative American as the effect of a complex process of rhetorical legerdemain ("Decadent Aesthetics").

4: EMPIRE AND AMERICA IN THE POETRY OF HART CRANE

1. Crane responded to Waldo Frank's challenge to articulate American culture more directly than the other poets of this study. Crane and Frank were personal friends, and Frank's enthusiastic responses to sections from *The Bridge* encouraged the poet to complete it, even after others had disapproved of it. Crane expressed his sense of kinship with Frank through such exuberant salutations as "Camarado" and "Brother" (*O My Land* 252, 263, 275, 265), while Frank addressed the poet in equally warm terms (Steve Cook 64, 68, 162, 169). Perry describes the common literary goals of the two men, while Hegeman sees *The Bridge* "as both faithful to, and critical of the implications of the structures that Frank established in *Our America*" (118).

2. Hammer's notes refer to an earlier edition of Crane's letters, edited by Brom Weber, rather than the later version Hammer himself expanded and edited. In contrast, I quote Hammer's text.

3. All quotations from Crane's poetry are from the collection edited by Marc Simon.

4. All subsequent quotations from this edition will be cited in the text as *Family*.

5. In letters of February and November 1917, Grace Crane wrote to her son regarding political events on the island that were complicating or threatening her tenure of the property there. In the November letter, she alludes to "the sugar proposition," which Lewis describes as "reports in newspapers . . . of Cuban rebels destroying the sugar crop" (*Family* 44, 93). In December 1923 she wrote of a visit with T. J. Keenan, who owned "a large estate on the Isle of Pines and operated the Isle of Pines Steamship Company." He was "president of the island's American Association" and "had been instrumental in preventing the United States Senate from ratifying the Isle of Pines treaty of 1899" (*Family* 244). In a letter of August 1924, Crane asks his mother and grandmother for details "about the present conditions on the island" (*Family* 339; also 393, 395, 400).

6. An editorial from the January 27, 1925, issue of the *New York World* that Crane enclosed in a letter to his mother gives a good account of the history of U.S. activities on the island, and it confirms his awareness of the political and financial circumstances surrounding them (see *Family* 384–86).

7. As Kahn points out in his speech "Art and America," he heard a European man exclaim in reference to Harriman, "Why, that supposedly 'hard-boiled' man is a great poet; only, he rhymes in rails!'" (19).

8. Despite this contradiction between the meaning and "means" (or financing) of his poem, Crane was dutiful in apprising his benefactor of his progress with it (Ormsby 114). For example, in a letter of June 20, 1926, to Frank, Crane ironically notes his sense of indebtedness to Kahn: "A bridge will be written in some kind of style and form, at worst it will be something as good as advertising copy. After which I will have at least done my best to discharge my debt to Kahn's kindness" (*O My Land* 260).

9. Butterfield makes the same point (176).

10. Compare Berthoff (100).

11. See also Stout (190) and Unterecker ("Critics" 187).

12. John Baker and Unterecker (*Voyager* 505) discuss the biographical context for Crane's figurations of the Twentieth Century Limited.

13. For a more elaborate commentary on this pun, see Giles, *Crane* 53.

14. In Edelman's view, Crane competes with his poetic father Walt Whitman, and this competition comes to a head in "Cape Hatteras" (185–257).

15. For a brief description of the creation of Panama and the development of the canal, see Lens 198–203.

16. See Powell for a discussion of the Monroe Doctrine "as the foundational document of the self-cloaking mechanism of American colonialist discourse" (351).

5: FRAGMENTATION AND DIASPORA IN THE WORK
OF LANGSTON HUGHES

1. I am indebted to two anonymous readers for this insight. For discussions of the issue, see Rampersad, "Origins of Poetry," and Herman Beaver.

2. This aspect of Hughes's poetry embodies Jameson's view of "culture as the expression of a properly Utopian or collective impulse" (293). See Davey regarding the dissemination of Hughes's poetry among African American readers (229) and Chrisman, Cobb, Kaup, Ellen C. Kennedy, Martin-Ogunsola, Marilyn Miller, and White and White for discussions of Hughes's international influence as a poet.

3. For more information about these tours, see *The Big Sea* (285), *I Wonder as I Wander* (1, 6, 41–67), and Rampersad (*Life* 1: 214–15, 220–26, 229–40). Davey considers Hughes's tours a means of building a national black audience and of gaining artistic and financial control over his writing.

4. All quotations from Hughes's poetry are from *The Collected Poems of Langston Hughes*, edited by Arnold Rampersad and David Roessel.

5. For a discussion of pan-Africanism and W. E. B. Du Bois, see Sundquist 540–625.

6. Gruesser offers other examples of the conflict between Hughes's solidarity with Africa and his alienation from it. In such poems as "Call of Ethiopia," "Air Raid over Harlem," "White Men," and "Song for Ourselves" (*Collected Poems* 184, 185–88, 194, 207), Hughes criticizes Mussolini's annexation of Ethiopia and sympathizes with those whom the dictator conquered. In "Broadcast on Ethiopia" (192), however, he both criticizes the fascist invasion and "reveals the African American disillusionment with the racial aloofness of the Ethiopian ruling class" under Haile Selassie (Gruesser 101).

7. See Torgovnick, Carr (147–256), Marx ("Forgotten Jungle Songs"), Chinitz, Lemke (4), Lively (99–104), and Pavloska (xi–xxix).

8. This possibility was suggested to me by an anonymous reader.

9. "Prelude to Our Age: A Negro History Poem" (1951) provides one possible exception. If it is an exception, it is, as its subtitle suggests, an equivocal one (*Collected Poems* 380–81). A short passage in *I Wonder as I Wander* provides another possible exception; see Hughes's account of his trip to the Soviet Union (193). It should be noted, however, that this "we" emerges in a foreign context, in a memoir that was published during the McCarthyite 1950s (*I Wonder* xv–xvi).

EPILOGUE

1. A cohesive though ironic "we" does emerge, however, in Jeffers's "July Fourth by the Ocean," "Ave Caesar," "Shine, Empire," and "We Are Those People" (*Collected Poetry* 1: 393, 2: 486, 3: 17–18, 201). In "Ave Caesar," "we" Americans "are not aquiline Romans but soft mixed colonists," "are easy to manage," and "love our luxuries." Jeffers's contemporary Americans share the founding fathers' equal dedication to republican "freedom" and imperial "wealth." The rhetoric of freedom and luxury also informs "Shine, Republic," although in a more hopeful way (*Collected Poetry* 2: 417).

Works Cited

Abrahams, Edward. *The Lyrical Left: Randolph Bourne, Alfred Stieglitz, and the Origins of Cultural Radicalism in America.* Charlottesville: UP of Virginia, 1986.

Adams, David Wallace. *Education for Extinction: American Indians and the Boarding School Experience, 1875–1928.* Lawrence: UP of Kansas, 1995.

Ahearn, Barry. *William Carlos Williams and Alterity: The Early Poetry.* New York: Cambridge UP, 1994.

Alexander, Charles C. *Here the Country Lies: Nationalism and the Arts in Twentieth-Century America.* Bloomington: Indiana UP, 1980.

Althusser, Louis. "Ideology and Ideological State Apparatuses (Notes towards an Investigation)." *Lenin and Philosophy and Other Essays.* Trans. Ben Brewster. New York: Monthly Review, 1971. 127–86.

Altieri, Charles. "Whose America Is *Our America:* On Walter Benn Michaels's Characterizations of Modernity in America." *Modernism/Modernity* 3 (1996): 107–13.

Anderson, Benedict. *Imagined Communities.* Rev. ed. New York: Verso, 1991.

Anderson, David Ross. "The Woman in the Tricorn Hat: Political Theory and Biological Portraiture in Marianne Moore's Poetry." *Journal of Modern Literature* 22 (1998): 31–45.

"Angiosperms." *Encyclopedia Britannica: Macropedia.* 1993 ed.

Association for the Preservation of Virginia Antiquities. *APVA Jamestown Rediscovery.* 18 July 2000 <http://www.apva.org/>.

Baker, Houston. *Afro-American Poetics: Revisions of Harlem and the Black Aesthetic.* Madison: U of Wisconsin P, 1988.

Baker, John. "Commercial Sources for Hart Crane's *The River.*" *Wisconsin Studies in Contemporary Literature* 6 (1965): 45–55.

Barksdale, Richard K. *Langston Hughes: The Poet and His Critics.* Chicago: American Library Association, 1977.

Barron, Jonathan N. "A Tale of Two Cottages: Frost and Wordsworth." Wilcox and Barron 132–52.

Beaver, Harold. *The Great American Masquerade.* London: Vision; Totowa: Barnes and Noble, 1985.

Beaver, Herman. "Dead Rocks and Sleeping Men: Aurality in the Aesthetic of Langston Hughes." *Langston Hughes Review* 9 (1992): 1–5.

Bellin, Joshua. *The Demon of the Continent: Indians and the Shaping of American Literature.* Philadelphia: U of Pennsylvania P, 2001.

Berger, Charles. "Who Writes the History Book? Moore's Revisionary Poetics." *Western Humanities Review* 53 (1999): 274–86.

Bergland, Renée L. *The National Uncanny: Indian Ghosts and American Subjects.* Hanover: UP of New England, 2000.

Bernstein, Michael A. *The Tale of the Tribe: Ezra Pound and the Modern Verse Epic.* Princeton: Princeton UP, 1980.

Berthoff, Warner. *Hart Crane: A Re-Introduction*. Minneapolis: U of Minnesota P, 1989.

Bhabha, Homi K. *The Location of Culture*. New York: Routledge, 1994.

Blackmur, R. P. *Language as Gesture*. 1952. New York: Columbia UP, 1981.

Blake, Cary Nelson. *Beloved Community: The Cultural Criticism of Randolph Bourne, Van Wyck Brooks, Waldo Frank, and Lewis Mumford*. Chapel Hill: U of North Carolina P, 1990.

Bloom, Harold, ed. *Hart Crane: Modern Critical Views*. New York: Chelsea House, 1986.

Borroff, Marie. *Language and the Poet: Verbal Artistry in Frost, Stevens, and Moore*. Chicago: U of Chicago P, 1979.

Bosmajian, Hamida. "Robert Frost's 'The Gift Outright': Wish and Reality in History and Poetry." *American Quarterly* 22 (1970): 95–105.

Bourne, Randolph. *The Radical Will: Selected Writings, 1911–1918*. Ed. Olaf Hansen. New York: Urizen, 1977.

Bremen, Brian A. *William Carlos Williams and the Diagnostics of Culture*. New York: Oxford UP, 1993.

Breslin, James E. *William Carlos Williams: An American Artist*. New York: Oxford UP, 1970.

Bridges, Robert. *Poetical Works of Robert Bridges*. Oxford UP, 1913.

Brooks, Van Wyck. "The Literary Life." *Civilization in the United States*. Ed. Harold E. Stearns. 1922. Westport: Greenwood, 1971. 179–97.

Brophy, Robert. "A Frost Poem on Jeffers." *Jeffers Studies* 3.1 (1999): 14–15.

Brower, Reuben A. *The Poetry of Robert Frost: Constellations of Intention*. New York: Oxford UP, 1963.

Brown, Fahamisha. *Performing the Word: African American Poetry as Vernacular Culture*. New Brunswick: Rutgers UP, 1999.

Brown, Lloyd. "The American Dream and the Legacy of Revolution in the Poetry of Langston Hughes." *Studies in Black Literature* 7.2 (1976): 16–18.

Brunner, Edward. *Splendid Failure: Hart Crane and the Making of* The Bridge. Urbana: U of Illinois P, 1985.

Buell, Lawrence. "Are We Post-American Studies?" *Field Work: Sites in Literary and Cultural Studies*. Ed. Marjorie Garber, Paul B. Franklin, and Rebecca L. Walkowitz. New York: Routledge, 1996. 87–93.

———. "Melville and the Question of American Decolonization." *American Literature* 64 (1992): 215–57.

———. "Postcolonial Anxiety in Classic U.S. Literature." Singh and Schmidt 196–219.

Bush, Harold K., Jr. *American Declarations: Rebellion and Repentance in American Cultural History*. Urbana: U of Illinois P, 1999.

Butler, Judith. "Further Reflections on Conversations of Our Time." *Diacritics* 27.1 (1997): 13–15.

Butterfield, R. W. *The Broken Arc: A Study of Hart Crane*. Edinburgh: Oliver, 1969.

Cady, Edwin H., and Louis J. Budd, eds. *On Frost: The Best from* American Literature. Durham: Duke UP, 1991.

Calloway, Colin G. *The American Revolution in Indian Country: Crisis and Diversity in Native American Communities*. Cambridge: Cambridge UP, 1995.

Canaday, Nicholas, Jr. "Major Themes in the Poetry of Countee Cullen." *The Harlem Renaissance Remembered*. Ed. Arna Bontemps. New York: Dodd, Mead, 1972. 103–25.

Cantwell, Robert. "The Poet, the Bums, and the Legendary Red Men." *Sports Illustrated* 15 Feb. 1960: 74+.

Carr, Helen. *Inventing the American Primitive: Politics, Gender, and the Representation of Native American Literary Traditions, 1789–1936*. New York UP, 1996.

Carruth, Hayden. "The New England Tradition." *Regional Perspectives: An Examination of America's Literary Heritage.* Ed. John Gordon Burke. Chicago: ALA, 1973. 1–47.

Chabot, C. Barry. *Writers for the Nation: American Literary Modernism.* Tuscaloosa: U of Alabama P, 1997.

Cheyfitz, Eric. *The Poetics of Imperialism: Translation and Colonization from* The Tempest *to* Tarzan. Expanded ed. Philadelphia: U of Pennsylvania P, 1997.

Chinitz, David. "Rejuvenation through Joy: Langston Hughes, Primitivism, and Jazz." *American Literary History* 9 (1997): 60–78.

Chomsky, Noam. *Year 501: The Conquest Continues.* Boston: South End, 1993.

Chrisman, Robert. "Nicolás Guillén, Langston Hughes, and the Black American / Afro-Cuban Connection." *Michigan Quarterly Review* 33 (1994): 807–20.

Cirasa, Robert J. *The Lost Works of William Carlos Williams: The Volumes of Collected Poetry as Lyrical Sequences.* Teaneck: Fairleigh Dickinson UP; Cranbury, NJ: Associated UP, 1995.

Clark, David R., ed. *Critical Essays on Hart Crane.* Boston: G. K. Hall, 1982.

Clifford, James. *The Predicament of Culture: Twentieth-Century Ethnography, Literature, and Art.* Cambridge: Harvard UP, 1988.

Cobb, Martha. *Harlem, Haiti, and Havana: A Comparative Critical Study of Langston Hughes, Jacques Roumain, and Nicolás Guillén.* Washington: Three Continents, 1979.

Cohen, David Steven. *Folk Legacies Revisited.* New Brunswick: Rutgers UP, 1995.

———. *The Ramapo Mountain People.* New Brunswick: Rutgers UP, 1974.

Conrad, Bryce. *Refiguring America: A Study of William Carlos Williams'* In the American Grain. Urbana: U of Illinois P, 1990.

Cook, Reginald L. "Frost's Asides on His Poetry." Cady and Budd. 30–38.

Cook, Steve H., ed. *The Correspondence between Hart Crane and Waldo Frank.* Troy, NY: Whitston, 1998.

Corseuil, Anelise R. "Modernism and American History: William Carlos Williams's Rearticulation of American Culture." *Estudos Anglo-Americanos* 17–18 (1993/94): 42–58.

Costello, Bonnie. *Marianne Moore: Imaginary Possessions.* Cambridge: Harvard UP, 1987.

"Cowbird." *Webster's Tenth New Collegiate Dictionary.* 1999.

Cox, Sidney. *A Swinger of Birches: A Portrait of Robert Frost.* Washington Square: New York UP, 1957.

Cramer, Jeffrey S. *Robert Frost among His Poems: A Literary Companion to the Poet's Own Biographical Contexts and Associations.* Jefferson: McFarland, 1996.

Crane, Hart. *Complete Poems of Hart Crane.* Ed. Marc Simon. New York: Liveright, 1986.

———. *Letters of Hart Crane and His Family.* Ed. Thomas S. W. Lewis. New York: Columbia UP, 1974.

———. *O My Land, My Friends: The Selected Letters of Hart Crane.* Ed. Langdon Hammer and Brom Weber. New York: Four Walls, 1997.

Cronon, William. *Changes in the Land: Indians, Colonists, and the Ecology of New England.* New York: Hill, Straus, 1983.

Cullen, Countee. *Color.* New York: Harper, 1925.

Davey, Elizabeth. "Building a Black Audience in the 1930s: Langston Hughes, Poetry Readings, and the Golden Stair Press." *Print Culture in a Diverse America.* Ed. James P. Danky and Wayne A. Wiegand. Urbana: U of Illinois P, 1998. 223–43.

Dawahare, Anthony. "Langston Hughes's Radical Poetry and the 'End of Race.'" *MELUS* 23.3 (1998): 21–41.

Dean, Tim. "Hart Crane's Poetics of Privacy." *American Literary History* 8 (1996): 83–109.

218   *Works Cited*

Dembo, L. S. *Hart Crane's Sanskrit Charge: A Study of* The Bridge. Ithaca: Cornell UP, 1960.

Derrida, Jacques. *Dissemination.* Trans. Barbara Johnson. Chicago: U of Chicago P, 1981.

Dippie, Brian W. *The Vanishing American: White Attitudes and U.S. Indian Policy.* Middletown: Wesleyan UP, 1982.

Doeren, Suzanne Clark. "Theory of Culture, Brooklyn Bridge, and Hart Crane's Rhetoric of Memory." *Bulletin of the Midwest Modern Language Association* 15.1 (1982): 18–28.

Du Bois, W. E. B. *The Souls of Black Folk.* New York: Penguin, 1989.

Edelman, Lee. *Transmemberment of Song: Hart Crane's Anatomies of Rhetoric and Desire.* Stanford: Stanford UP, 1987.

Editorial. *The Seven Arts* 1 (November 1916): 52–56.

Ehrenpreis, Irvin, ed. *American Poetry.* Stratford-upon-Avon Studies 7. New York: St. Martin's, 1965.

Emerson, Ralph Waldo. *Essays and Lectures.* Ed. Joel Porte. New York: Library of America, 1983.

Engel, Bernard F. *Marianne Moore.* New York: Twayne, 1964.

Faery, Rebecca Blevins. *Cartographies of Desire: Captivity, Race, and Sex in the Shaping of an American Nation.* Norman: U of Oklahoma P, 1999.

Faggen, Robert. *Robert Frost and the Challenge of Darwinism.* Ann Arbor: U of Michigan P, 1997.

Fanon, Frantz. *The Wretched of the Earth.* Trans. Constance Farrington. New York: Grove, 1963.

Ferry, David. "The Diction of American Poetry." Ehrenpreis 134–54.

Fisher-Wirth, Ann W. *William Carlos Williams and Autobiography: The Woods of His Own Nature.* University Park: U of Pennsylvania P, 1989.

Frail, David. *The Early Politics and Poetics of William Carlos Williams.* Ann Arbor: UMI Research, 1987.

———. "'The Regular Fourth of July Stuff': William Carlos Williams' Colonial Figures as Poets." *William Carlos Williams Review* 6.2 (Fall 1980): 1–14.

Francis, Lesley Lee. "Frost and the Majesty of Stones upon Stones." *Journal of Modern Literature* 9 (1981/82): 3–26.

Frank, Waldo. *Our America.* New York: Boni, 1919.

Frankenberg, Ruth, and Lata Mani. "Crosscurrents, Crosstalk: Race, 'Postcoloniality,' and the Politics of Location." *Cultural Studies* 7 (1993): 292–310.

Freeman, Joseph, and Scott Nearing. *Dollar Diplomacy: A Study in American Imperialism.* 1925. New York: Monthly Review, 1966.

Frost, Robert. *The Poetry of Robert Frost.* Ed. Edward Connery Lathem. New York: Holt, 1969.

———. *Robert Frost: Collected Poems, Prose, and Plays.* Ed. Richard Poirier and Mark Richardson. New York: Library of America, 1995.

———. *Selected Letters of Robert Frost.* Ed. Lawrance Thompson. New York: Holt, 1964.

Fuchs, Miriam. "Poet and Patron: Hart Crane and Otto Kahn." *Book Forum* 6 (1982): 45–51.

"Gardenia." *Compact Edition of the Oxford English Dictionary.* 1989.

Gardner, Jared. "'Our Native Clay': Racial and Sexual Identity and the Making of Americans in *The Bridge.*" *American Quarterly* 44 (1992): 24–50.

Gerber, Philip L. *Robert Frost.* Rev. ed. Twayne U.S. Author Series 107. Boston: Twayne, 1982.

Gibson, Donald B. "The Good Black Poet and the Good Gray Poet: The Poetry of Hughes and Whitman." *Langston Hughes: Black Genius.* Ed. Thurman B. O'Daniel. New York: Morrow, 1971. 65–80. Rpt. in Gibson 43–56.

———, ed. *Modern Black Poets: A Collection of Critical Essays.* Englewood Cliffs: Prentice, 1973.

Giles, Paul. "From Decadent Aesthetics to Political Fetishism: The 'Oracle Effect' of Robert Frost's Poetry." *American Literary History* 12 (2000): 713–44.

———. *Hart Crane: The Contexts of "The Bridge."* New York: Cambridge UP, 1986.

Gilroy, Paul. *The Black Atlantic: Modernity and Double Consciousness.* Cambridge: Harvard UP, 1993.

Gould, Jean. *Robert Frost: The Aim Was Song.* New York: Dodd, 1964.

Gruesser, John Cullen. *Black on Black: Twentieth-Century African American Writing about Africa.* Lexington: UP of Kentucky, 2000.

Hadas, Pamela White. *Marianne Moore: Poet of Affection.* Syracuse: Syracuse UP, 1977.

Hall, Donald. *Marianne Moore: The Cage and the Animal.* New York: Pegasus, 1970.

Halter, Peter. *The Revolution in the Visual Arts and the Poetry of William Carlos Williams.* New York: Cambridge UP, 1994.

Hammer, Langdon. *Hart Crane and Allen Tate: Janus-Faced Modernism.* Princeton: Princeton UP, 1993.

Hegeman, Susan. *Patterns for America: Modernism and the Concept of Culture.* Princeton: Princeton UP, 1999.

Hueter, Jessica. "A Patriot's Lament." *Robinson Jeffers: Poetry and Response, a Centennial Tribute.* Los Angeles: Occidental College, 1987. 97.

Hughes, Langston. *The Big Sea: An Autobiography by Langston Hughes.* 1940. New York: Hill, 1964.

———. *The Collected Poems of Langston Hughes.* Ed. Arnold Rampersad and David Roessel. New York: Knopf, 1994.

———. *I Wonder as I Wander.* 1940. New York: Hill, 1963.

Huhndorf, Shari M. *Going Native: Indians in the American Cultural Imagination.* Ithaca: Cornell UP, 2001.

Hutchinson, George. *The Harlem Renaissance in Black and White.* Cambridge: Belknap, 1995.

———. "Hughes and the 'Other' Whitman." Martin, *Continuing Presence.* 16–27.

Irwin, John. "Back Home Again in Indiana: Hart Crane's *The Bridge.*" *Romantic Revolutions: Criticism and Theory.* Ed. Kenneth R. Johnston, Gilbert Chaitin, Karen Hanson, and Herbert Marks. Bloomington: Indiana UP, 1990. 269–96.

Jameson, Fredric. *The Political Unconscious: Narrative as a Socially Symbolic Act.* Ithaca: Cornell UP, 1981.

Jarraway, David R. "Montage of an Otherness Deferred: Dreaming Subjectivity in Langston Hughes." *American Literature* 68 (1996): 819–47.

Jeffers, Robinson. *The Collected Poetry of Robinson Jeffers.* Volume 1: 1920–28. Ed. Tim Hunt. Stanford: Stanford UP, 1988.

———. *The Collected Poetry of Robinson Jeffers.* Volume 2: 1928–38. Ed. Tim Hunt. Stanford: Stanford UP, 1989.

———. *The Collected Poetry of Robinson Jeffers.* Volume 3: 1938–62. Ed. Tim Hunt. Stanford: Stanford UP, 1991.

Jemie, Onwuchekwa. *Langston Hughes: An Introduction to the Poetry.* New York: Columbia UP, 1976.

Jennings, Francis. *The Creation of America: Through Revolution to Empire.* Cambridge: Cambridge UP, 2000.

Johnson, Eloise E. *Rediscovering the Harlem Renaissance*. New York: Garland, 1997.

Kadlec, David. "Marianne Moore, Immigration, and Eugenics." *Modernism/Modernity* 1.2 (1994): 21–49.

Kahn, Otto H. *Of Many Things, Being Reflections and Impressions on International Affairs, Domestic Topics, and the Arts*. New York: Boni, 1926.

Kaplan, Amy. "'Left Alone with America': The Absence of Empire in the Study of American Culture." Kaplan and Pease 3–21.

Kaplan, Amy, and Donald E. Pease, eds. *Cultures of United States Imperialism*. Durham: Duke UP, 1993.

Kaup, Monika. "'Our America' That Is Not One: Transnational Black Atlantic Disclosures in Nicolás Guillén and Langston Hughes." *Discourse* 22 (2000): 87–113.

Kennedy, Ellen Conroy. *The Negritude Poets*. New York: Viking, 1975.

Kennedy, John Fitzgerald. "Poetry and Power." *Atlantic Monthly* Feb. 1964: 53–54.

Kilcup, Karen L. *Robert Frost and Feminine Literary Tradition*. Ann Arbor: U of Michigan P, 1998.

King, C. Richard. "Introduction: Dislocating Postcoloniality, Relocating American Empire." King 1–17.

———, ed. *Postcolonial America*. Urbana: U of Illinois P, 2000.

Knapp, James F. *Literary Modernism and the Transformation of Work*. Evanston: Northwestern UP, 1988.

Kobler, John. *Otto the Magnificent: The Life of Otto Kahn*. New York: Scribner's, 1988.

Koch, Vivienne. *William Carlos Williams*. Norfolk: New Directions, 1950.

Kolodny, Annette. *The Lay of the Land: Metaphor as Experience and History in American Life and Letters*. Chapel Hill: U of North Carolina P, 1975.

Kramer, Victor A., and Robert A. Russ, eds. *The Harlem Renaissance Re-Examined*. Troy: Whitston, 1997.

Kupperman, Karen Ordahl. *Settling with the Indians: The Meeting of Indian Cultures in America, 1580–1640*. Totowa: Rowman, 1980.

Kusch, Celena E. "How the West Was One: American Modernism's Song of Itself." *American Literature* 74.3 (2002): 517–38.

Kutzinski, Vera M. *Against the American Grain: Myth and History in William Carlos Williams, Jay Wright, and Nicolás Guillén*. Baltimore: Johns Hopkins UP, 1987.

Lakritz, Andrew M. "Frost in Transition." Wilcox and Barron 198–216.

———. *Modernism and the Other in Stevens, Frost, and Moore*. Gainesville: UP of Florida, 1996.

Lawrence, D. H. *Studies in Classic American Literature*. New York: Penguin, 1964.

Lemke, Sieglinde. *Primitivist Modernism: Black Culture and the Origins of Transatlantic Modernism*. New York: Oxford UP, 1998.

Lens, Sidney. *The Forging of the American Empire*. New York: Crowell, 1971.

Leone, Mark P., and Neil Asher Silberman, eds. *Invisible America: Unearthing Our Hidden History*. New York: Holt, 1995.

Lewis, R. W. B. *The Poetry of Hart Crane: A Critical Study*. Princeton: Princeton UP, 1967.

Lewis, Thomas S. W., ed. *Letters of Hart Crane and His Family*. New York: Columbia UP, 1974.

———. "'O Thou steeled Cognizance': The Brooklyn Bridge, Lewis Mumford, and Hart Crane." *Hart Crane Newsletter* 1.2 (1977): 17–26.

Lively, Adam. *Masks: Blackness, Race, and the Imagination*. Oxford: Oxford UP, 2000.

Lomax, Michael L. "Countee Cullen: A Key to the Puzzle." Kramer and Russ 239–47.

Lowney, John. *The American Avant-Garde Tradition: William Carlos Williams, Postmodern Poetry, and the Politics of Cultural Memory*. Lewisburg: Bucknell UP; London: Associated UP, 1997.

"Lyric." *Princeton Encyclopedia of Poetry and Poetics*. Ed. Alex Preminger, Frank J. Warnke, and O. B. Hardison Jr. Enlarged ed. Princeton: Princeton UP, 1974.

Mackenthun, Gesa. "Adding Empire to the Study of American Culture." *Journal of American Studies* 30 (1996): 263–69.

———. *Metaphors of Dispossession: American Beginnings and the Translation of Empire, 1492–1637*. Norman: U of Oklahoma P, 1997.

Maddox, Lucy. *Removals: Nineteenth-Century American Literature and the Politics of Indian Affairs*. New York: Oxford UP, 1991.

Magdoff, Harry. *The Age of Imperialism: The Economics of U.S. Foreign Policy*. New York: Monthly Review, 1969.

Major, John. *Prize Possession: The United States and the Panama Canal, 1902–1979*. New York: Cambridge UP, 1993.

Mariani, Paul. *The Broken Tower: A Life of Hart Crane*. New York: Norton, 1999.

———. *William Carlos Williams: A New World Naked*. New York: McGraw-Hill, 1981.

Martin, Robert K., ed. *The Continuing Presence of Walt Whitman: The Life after the Life*. Iowa City: U of Iowa P, 1992.

Martin-Ogunsola, Dellita L. "Langston Hughes and the Musico-Poetry of the African Diaspora." *Langston Hughes Review* 5 (1986): 1–17.

Marx, Edward. "The Comedian as Colonist." *Wallace Stevens Journal* 18 (1994): 175–96.

———. "Forgotten Jungle Songs: Primitivist Strategies of the Harlem Renaissance." *Langston Hughes Review* 14.1–2 (1996): 79–83.

Matthews, Kathleen D. "Competitive Giants: Satiric Bedrock in Book One of William Carlos Williams' *Paterson*." *Journal of Modern Literature* 12 (1985): 237–60.

McClintock, Anne. "The Angel of Progress: Pitfalls of the Term 'Post-Colonialism.'" *Social Text* 31–32 (1992): 84–98.

Merrin, Jeredith. *An Enabling Humility: Marianne Moore, Elizabeth Bishop, and the Uses of Tradition*. New Brunswick, N.J.: Rutgers UP, 1990.

Mertins, Louis. *Robert Frost: Life and Talks-Walking*. Norman: U of Oklahoma P, 1965.

Meyer, Kinereth. "Possessing America: William Carlos Williams's *Paterson* and the Poetics of Appropriation." *Mapping American Culture*. Ed. Wayne Franklin and Michael Steiner. Iowa City: Iowa UP, 1992. 152–67.

Meyers, Jeffrey. *Robert Frost: A Biography*. Boston: Houghton Mifflin, 1996.

Michaels, Walter Benn. *Our America: Nativism, Modernism, and Pluralism*. Durham: Duke UP, 1992.

Miller, Cristanne. *Marianne Moore: Questions of Authority*. Cambridge: Harvard UP, 1995.

———. "Marianne Moore's Black Maternal Hero: A Study in Categorization." *American Literary History* 1 (1989): 786–815.

Miller, Marilyn. "(Gypsy) Rhythm and (Cuban) Blues: The Neo-American Dream in Guillén and Hughes." *Comparative Literature* 51 (1999): 324–44.

Molesworth, Charles. *Marianne Moore: A Literary Life*. New York: Atheneum, 1990; Boston: Northeastern UP, 1991.

Monroe, Melissa. "Comparison and Synthesis: Marianne Moore's Natural and Unnatural Taxonomies." *The Text and Beyond: Essays in Literary Linguistics*. Ed. Cynthia Goldin Bernstein. Tuscaloosa: U of Alabama P, 1994. 56–83.

Moore, Andy J. "The Politics of Robert Frost." *The Journal of American and Canadian Studies* 15 (1997): 1–15.

Moore, Marianne. *The Complete Poems of Marianne Moore.* 1967. New York: Viking, 1981.

———. *The Complete Prose of Marianne Moore.* Ed. Patricia C. Willis. New York: Sifton, 1986.

———. *A Marianne Moore Reader.* New York: Viking, 1961.

———. *The Pangolin and Other Verse.* London: Brendin, 1936.

———. "Virginia Britannia." *Life and Letters Today* 13 (December 1935): 66–70.

Morgan, Edmund S. *American Slavery, American Freedom: The Ordeal of Colonial Virginia.* New York: Norton, 1975.

"Mull." *Webster's Tenth New Collegiate Dictionary.* 1999.

Mulvey, Laura. *Visual and Other Pleasures.* Bloomington: U of Indiana P, 1989.

Nobles, Gregory H. *American Frontiers: Cultural Encounters and Continental Conquest.* New York: Hill, 1997.

Noland, Richard W. "A Failure of Contact: William Carlos Williams on America." *Emory University Quarterly* 20 (1964): 248–60.

North, Michael. *The Dialect of Modernism: Race, Language, and Twentieth-Century Literature.* New York: Oxford UP, 1994.

Onuf, Peter S. *Jefferson's Empire: The Language of American Nationhood.* Charlottesville: UP of Virginia, 2000.

Ormsby, Eric. "Hart and Fangs." *Parnassus: Poetry in Review* 24.1: 96–130.

Parrini, Carl P. *Heir to Empire: United States Economic Diplomacy, 1916–1923.* Pittsburgh: U of Pittsburgh P, 1969.

Paul, Sherman. *Hart's Bridge.* Urbana: U of Illinois P, 1972.

Paulin, Tom. *Minotaur: Poetry and the Nation State.* Cambridge: Harvard UP, 1992.

Pavloska, Susanna. *Modern Primitives: Race and Language in Gertrude Stein, Ernest Hemingway, and Zora Neale Hurston.* New York: Garland, 2000.

Pearce, Roy Harvey. *Savagism and Civilization: A Study of the Indian and the American Mind.* 1953. Rev. ed. Berkeley: U of California P, 1988.

Perkins, Bradford. *The Cambridge History of American Foreign Relations: The Creation of a Republican Empire.* Volume 1. Cambridge: Cambridge UP, 1993.

Perry, Robert L. *The Shared Vision of Waldo Frank and Hart Crane.* University of Nebraska Studies New Ser. 33. Lincoln: U of Nebraska, 1966.

Phillips, Elizabeth. *Marianne Moore.* New York: Ungar, 1982.

Piñero Gil, Eulalia C. "Moore's Undermining Authority: The Poet as Marginal Historian." *Cuadernos de Literatura Inglesa y Norteamericana* 1 (1996): 51–61.

Poirier, Richard. *Robert Frost: The Work of Knowing.* New York: Oxford UP, 1977.

"Pomegranate." *Webster's Tenth New Collegiate Dictionary.* 1999.

Pound, Ezra. *Personae: The Shorter Poems of Ezra Pound.* Ed. Lea Baechler and A. Walton Litz. Rev. ed. New York: New Directions, 1990.

———. *Selected Prose, 1909–1965.* Ed. William Cookson. New York: New Directions, 1973.

Powell, Timothy. "Postcolonial Theory in an American Context: A Reading of Martin Delany's *Blake.*" Seshadri-Crooks and Afzal-Khan 347–65.

Presley, James. "The American Dream of Langston Hughes." *Southwest Review* 48 (1963): 380–86.

Rampersad, Arnold. *The Life of Langston Hughes.* Volume 1: 1902–41. New York: Oxford UP, 1986.

———. "The Origins of Poetry in Langston Hughes." *Southern Review* 21 (1985): 695–705.

Renan, Ernest. "What Is a Nation?" *Nation and Narration.* Ed. Homi Bhabha. New York: Routledge, 1990. 8–22.

Richardson, Mark. *The Ordeal of Robert Frost: The Poet and His Poetics.* Urbana: U of Illinois P, 1997.

Riddel, Joseph N. "Hart Crane's Poetics of Failure." *ELH* 33 (1966): 474–96. Rpt. in Bloom 91–110.

———. *The Turning Word: American Literary Modernism and Continental Theory.* Ed. Mark Bauerlein. Philadelphia: U of Pennsylvania P, 1996.

Robbins, J. Albert. "America and the Poet: Whitman, Hart Crane, and Frost." Ehrenpreis 45–67.

Rodríguez García, José María. "The Culture of Conversation and the Voice of the Indian in William Carlos Williams's 'Père Sebastian Rasles.'" *Neophilologus* 86 (2002): 477–92.

Rosen, Kenneth. "Visions and Revisions: An Early Version of Robert Frost's 'Our Doom to Bloom.'" *Frost: Centennial Essays.* Jackson: UP of Mississippi, n.d. 369–72.

Rosu, Anca. "Noble Imagery: Wallace Stevens and Mesoamerican Mythology." *Connotations* 5 (1995/96): 240–58.

Rotella, Guy. "Economies of Frost: 'Synonymous with Kept.'" *The Cambridge Companion to Robert Frost.* Ed. Robert Faggen. New York: Cambridge UP, 2001. 241–60.

Rowe, John Carlos. *Literary Culture and U.S. Imperialism from the Revolution to World War II.* Oxford: Oxford UP, 2000.

———. "The 'Super-Historical' Sense of Hart Crane's *The Bridge.*" *Genre* 11 (1970): 597–625.

Sale, Kirkpatrick. *The Conquest of Paradise: Christopher Columbus and the Columbian Legacy.* New York: Plume, 1991.

Sankey, Benjamin. *A Companion to William Carlos Williams's* Paterson. Berkeley: U of California P, 1971.

Santos, Maria Irena Ramalho de Sousa. "An Imperialism of Poets: The Modernism of Fernando Pessoa and Hart Crane." *Luso-Brazilian Review* 29.1 (1992): 83–95.

Scheckel, Susan. *The Insistence of the Indian: Race and Nationalism in Nineteenth-Century American Culture.* Princeton: Princeton UP, 1998.

Seelye, John D. "The American Tramp: A Version of the Picaresque." *American Quarterly* 15 (1963): 535–53.

Seshadri-Crooks, Kalpana, and Fawzia Afzal-Khan, eds. *The Pre-Occupation of Postcolonial Studies.* Durham: Duke UP, 2000.

Sharpe, Jenny. "Is the United States Postcolonial?" King 103–21.

Shohut, Ella. "Notes on the 'Post-Colonial.'" *Social Text* 31/32 (1992): 99–113. Rpt. in Seshadri-Crooks and Afzal-Khan 126–39.

Singh, Amritjit, and Peter Schmidt, eds. "On the Borders between U.S. Studies and Postcolonial Theory." Singh and Schmidt 3–69.

———. *Postcolonial Theory and the United States: Race, Ethnicity, and Literature.* Jackson: UP of Mississippi, 2000.

Sklar, Martin J. *The United States as a Developing Country: Studies in U.S. History in the Progressive Era and the 1920s.* Cambridge: Campbridge UP, 1992.

Slatin, John M. *The Savage's Romance: The Poetry of Marianne Moore.* University Park: Pennsylvania State UP, 1986.

Slote, Bernice. "Views of *The Bridge.*" *Start with the Sun: Studies in Cosmic Poetry.* Ed. James E. Miller, Karl Shapiro, and Bernice Slote. Lincoln: U of Nebraska P, 1960. 135–65.

Smethurst, James Edward. *The New Red Negro: The Literary Left and African American Poetry, 1930–1946*. New York: Oxford UP, 1999.

Smith, Raymond. "Langston Hughes: Evolution of the Poetic Persona." Kramer and Russ 259–73.

Sollors, Werner. *Beyond Ethnicity: Consent and Descent in American Culture*. New York: Oxford UP, 1986.

Spencer, Benjamin T. *Patterns of Nationality: Twentieth-Century Literary Versions of America*. New York: Burt Franklin, 1981.

Spivak, Gayatri Chakravorty. "Teaching for the Times." *Journal of the Midwest Modern Language Association* 25.1 (1992): 3–22.

Stamy, Cynthia. *Marianne Moore and China: Orientalism and a Writing of America*. Oxford: Oxford UP, 1999.

Stapleton, Laurence. *Marianne Moore: The Poet's Advance*. Princeton: Princeton UP, 1978.

Stephanson, Andars. *Manifest Destiny: American Expansion and the Empire of Right*. New York: Hill, 1995.

Stevens, Wallace. *Collected Poetry and Prose*. New York: Library of America, 1997.

Stout, Janis P. *The Journey Narrative in American Literature: Patterns and Departures*. Westport: Greenwood, 1983.

Stratton, Jon. "The Beast of the Apocalypse: The Postcolonial Experience of the United States." King 21–64.

Sundquist, Eric J. *To Wake the Nations: Race in the Making of American Literature*. Cambridge: Belknap, 1993.

Tapscott, Stephen. *American Beauty: William Carlos Williams and the Modernist Whitman*. New York: Columbia UP, 1984.

Thoreau, Henry David. *A Week on the Concord and Merrimack Rivers; Walden; or, Life in the Woods. The Maine Woods. Cape Cod*. New York: Library of America, 1985.

Thompson, Lawrance, and R. H. Winnick. *Robert Frost: The Later Years, 1938–1963*. New York: Holt, 1976.

Torgovnick, Marianna. *Gone Primitive: Savage Intellects, Modern Lives*. Chicago: U of Chicago P, 1990.

Townley, Rod. *The Early Poetry of William Carlos Williams*. Ithaca: Cornell UP, 1975.

Trachtenberg, Alan. "Cultural Revisions in the Twenties: Brooklyn Bridge as 'Usable Past.'" *The American Self: Myth, Ideology, and Popular Culture*. Ed. Sam B. Girgus. Albuquerque: U of New Mexico P, 1981. 58–75.

Trilling, Lionel. "A Speech on Robert Frost: A Cultural Episode." *Partisan Review* 26 (Summer 1959): 445–52.

Unterecker, John. "The Critics and Hart Crane's *The Bridge:* An Interview with John Unterecker." *Hart Crane Newsletter* 2.1 (1978): 22–33. Rpt. in Clark 184–91.

———. *Voyager: A Life of Hart Crane*. New York: Farrar, 1969.

Van Alstyne, R. W. *The Rising American Empire*. New York: Oxford UP, 1960.

Vogler, Thomas A. "A New View of Hart Crane's *Bridge*." *Sewanee Review* 72 (1965): 381–408. Rpt. in Bloom 69–90.

Walcott, Derek. "The Road Taken." *Homage to Robert Frost*. Joseph Brodsky, Seamus Heaney, and Derek Walcott. New York: Farrar, 1996. 93–117.

Walker, Cheryl. *Indian Nation: Native American Literature and Nineteenth-Century Nationalisms*. Durham: Duke UP, 1997.

Walker, Jeffrey. *Bardic Ethos and the American Epic Poem: Whitman, Pound, Crane, Williams, Olson*. Baton Rouge: Louisiana UP, 1989.

Warren, Kenneth W. "Appeals for (Mis)recognition: Theorizing the Diaspora." Kaplan and Pease 392–406.

Waselkov, Gregory A. "Indian Maps of the Colonial Southeast: Archaeological Implications and Prospects." *Cartographic Encounters: Perspectives on Native American Mapmaking and Map Use.* Ed. G. Malcolm Lewis. Chicago: U of Chicago P, 1998. 205–21.

Weeks, William E. *Building the Constitutional Empire: American Expansion from the Revolution to the Civil War.* Chicago: Ivan R. Dee, 1996.

Wertheim, Arthur Frank. *The New York Little Renaissance: Iconoclasm, Modernism, and Nationalism in American Culture, 1908–1917.* New York: New York UP, 1976.

White, Jeannette S., and Clement A. White. "Two Nations, One Vision. America's Langston Hughes and Cuba's Nicolás Guillén: Poetry of Affirmation: A Revision." *Langston Hughes Review* 12 (1993): 42–50.

Whitman, Walt. *Complete Poetry and Collected Prose.* New York: Library of America, 1982.

Wilcox, Earl J., and Jonathan N. Barron, eds. *Roads Not Taken: Rereading Robert Frost.* Columbia: U of Missouri P, 2000.

Williams, William Appleman. *The Contours of American History.* New York: Norton, 1988.

Williams, William Carlos. *The Autobiography of William Carlos Williams.* New York: Random House, 1951.

———. *The Collected Poems of William Carlos Williams.* Volume 1: 1909–39. Ed. A. Walton Litz and Christopher MacGowan. New York: New Directions, 1986.

———. *The Collected Poems of William Carlos Williams.* Volume 2: 1939–62. Ed. Christopher MacGowan. New York: New Directions, 1988.

———. *In the American Grain.* New York: New Directions, 1925.

———. *Paterson.* Ed. Christopher MacGowan. Rev. ed. New York: New Directions, 1992.

———. *The Selected Essays of William Carlos Williams.* New York: New Directions, 1969.

———. *A Voyage to Pagany.* 1928. New York: New Directions, 1970.

Wilson, James G. *The Imperial Republic: A Structural History of American Constitutionalism from the Colonial Era to the Beginning of the Twentieth Century.* Burlington, VT: Ashgate, 2002.

Wolf, Eric R. *Europe and the People without History.* Berkeley: U of California P, 1982.

Wormser, Richard. *Hoboes: Wandering in America, 1870–1940.* New York: Walker, 1994.

Yingling, Thomas E. *Hart Crane and the Homosexual Text: New Thresholds, New Anatomies.* Chicago: U of Chicago P, 1990.

Zeck, Gregory R. "'The Chan's Great Continent': Otto Kahn and *The Bridge.*" *Markham Review* 7 (1978): 61–65.

Zinn, Howard. *A People's History of the United States.* New York: Harper, 1980.

Index